GÖPPINGER ARBEITEN ZUR GERMANISTIK

herausgegeben von

Ulrich Müller, Franz Hundsnurscher und Cornelius Sommer

Nr. 159

# NARRATIVE ART IN WOLFRAM'S 'WILLEHALM'

by

**Marion E. Gibbs**

VERLAG ALFRED KÜMMERLE

Göppingen 1976

In der Reihe „GÖPPINGER ARBEITEN ZUR GERMANISTIK" erscheinen
ab Band 160 ausschließlich Bände zur Älteren Literaturwissenschaft und zur
Sprachwissenschaft. Veröffentlichungen zur Neueren Literaturwissenschaft
erscheinen unter dem Titel „STUTTGARTER ARBEITEN ZUR GERMA-
NISITIK" im Verlag H.D. Heinz, Stuttgart.

PT 16 82
W 8 G 5

Verlag Alfred Kümmerle, Göppingen 1976
Druck: Sprint-Druck GmbH, Stuttgart-30
ISBN 3-87452-283-0
Printed in Germany

# Acknowledgements

This book represents almost entirely the text of my thesis for the degree of PhD of the University of London, with some minor alterations and additions, and I wish to record my appreciation to my supervisor, Professor A T Hatto, for his advice and guidance.

I am grateful to Professor Ralph Tymms for the interest which he has always shown in the project and for the encouragement which he has given me at all stages of its development. I should like also to thank Mrs U E Burks for her skill and patience in producing the typescript.

M E G

Royal Holloway College
University of London

CONTENTS

## Preface

Joachim Bumke's study <u>Wolframs Willehalm, Studien zur
Epenstruktur und zum Heiligkeitsbegriff der ausgehenden Blüte-
zeit</u>[1] represented in 1959 an important step in <u>Willehalm</u>
research, a major interpretation of a work which had for long
remained almost entirely neglected by scholars deeply im-
mersed in <u>Parzival</u>. Indeed, for other major interpretations
of <u>Willehalm</u>, one had, at that time, to go back over two
decades, to the long article by Ludwig Wolff[2] and the study
by Bodo Mergell[3]. By the time Bumke came to compile his
survey of Wolfram research since 1945[4], the situation was
already changing, with the promise of the critical edition
in preparation in Marburg, and the work already published by
Werner Schröder and Heinz Schanze[5]. The second volume of
<u>Wolfram-Studien</u>[6] provides in itself ample evidence of the
growing concern of scholars for Wolfram's second great epic,
while two substantial and entirely complementary studies of
the Rennewart action which appeared within a few months of
one another[7] demonstrate the wealth of interest in this
profound and complex work. The Bibliography, though it cannot claim to be complete, lists major contributions on <u>Wille-
halm</u> in particular and on Wolfram in so far as they may be
considered relevant to the present theme, and it shows, too,
this intensification of interest in <u>Willehalm</u> in the course

of the last decade.

This study will, it is hoped, find a place in Wolfram research, complementing to some extent, in its examination of the way in which Wolfram tells his tale, the work which has already been done. To such work, and above all to the scholarship of Wolff, Mergell and Bumke, I am inevitably indebted, and to acknowledge this debt on all occasions would be impossible. Yet though they precede me in the study of Willehalm and though in many ways their work has pointed the way to an understanding of Wolfram's poem, my intention differs from theirs. Mergell, in his study of the relationship between Wolfram's work and his source, and Wolff and Bumke in their own individual interpretations of the poem, inevitably touch on facets of Wolfram's narrative technique, though this is not their principal concern. I, for my part, have become increasingly aware that the examination of the narrative means may not be divorced from questions of interpretation, and that, indeed, the treatment by Wolfram of his source is an important aspect of his narrative art. In other respects, however, in what is strictly speaking the subject of this study, I have found myself very little guided by previous research.

The field of narrative art, in relation to any work, is a large one, and inevitably, when one is examining the art of a narrator in presenting his tale, one becomes involved in issues which, each in its own right, might form the substance of a separate investigation. In pursuing the study of the narrative art in Willehalm I have set out from the acknowledgement of a fine tale brilliantly told and have endeavoured to isolate some of the means by which Wolfram achieves the impact of his narrative.

The aim of any narrator, and no doubt in particular of the narrator whose work is transmitted orally, must be to capture and retain the attention of his audience. That Wolfram succeeded in doing so is evident from the large number of manuscripts of Willehalm, which bears witness to its popularity in the Middle Ages. He had a responsibility, however,

not only to his audience, but to the source which he acknowledges early in the work and which was known to the patron
who provided it, as well as to many of his hearers (3,8-11;
4,30-5,15). Beyond this, Wolfram was an individual, creative
poet, who had his own conception of the material of his
source and was capable of endowing the familiar story with
his characteristic stamp. All three factors must surely
govern his telling of his tale.

The question arises of the extent to which one may assume
a conscious artistry in Wolfram, the poet who, with a responsibility to his audience and to his source, nevertheless
wished to narrate his story in his own way. The answer does
not readily present itself, for, while one can say for certain that he accepts or rejects or adapts features of his
source, and even suggest a reason for his doing so, one cannot be sure that in other respects he is guided by anything
more conscious at all than the instinct of any great artist
in handling his material. Thus when, in the following study,
I speak of Wolfram's 'technique', I do so without, for the
most part, venturing an opinion regarding the degree of consciousness involved. Rather do I assume that any artist, if
challenged, would find it impossible in many cases to say
whether a conscious decision had led to a particular effect,
or whether it were not, in the last resort, due to an in-
stinctive sense of the whole. Comparison with Parzival is
of little help in this matter, for though it is clear, from
the wilfully obscure opening passages, for example, that
Wolfram was capable of a conscious and mischievous retort to
his critics, the remainder of the work furnishes no firm
proof in the direction of conscious or of unconscious art.
Comparison with Wolfram's greatest contemporary, Gottfried
von Straßburg, leaves one with the impression that Gottfried
was very much a conscious artist, moulding his material and
using his language with extreme care and deliberation: yet,
again, the comparison establishes nothing about Wolfram's art,
save that it is as different as can be imagined from that of
Gottfried.

What one can say about Wolfram, however, is that,
particularly in Willehalm, he is very sure of the direction
of his narrative and that he has a firm sense, whether conscious or intuitive, of what is most fitting to his telling
of the whole story. The result is a work in which one is
aware first and foremost of the impact of the story and only
then, on close scrutiny, of the subtlety of the narrative
art.

In this study I have attempted this close scrutiny, in
order to show qualities of Willehalm which have not always
emerged in previous research. My concern is with the work
as a whole, and I have found it possible to see the narrative art in five broad areas, each containing a number of subordinate sections. Because we are dealing with a work of art,
it is inevitable that there are no rigid dividing lines; there
are overlapping features and the sections themselves are in
no way firm ones, their very headings no more than an attempt
to describe certain features of Wolfram's narrative.

After a discussion of the total impact of the work, in
which some of its general quality emerges, the narrative art
is treated under the following headings:

1. The harmony of the work.

Willehalm is a remarkably consistent work, in which
Wolfram achieves an overall unity of thought. This, it emerges,
may be attributed to a number of factors, both structural and
thematic. The two battles of Alischanz constitute an integrating framework, while three of the principal characters -
Gyburc, Willehalm and Vivianz - are important integrating
factors. In addition there is the unity of the spiritual
thought of the work, made possible above all through Gyburc
and so significant a feature in the impression of harmony of
the whole work.

2. The compression of the narrative.

The harmony of thought and theme is supported by a
number of important aspects of Wolfram's technique. By a

variety of distinct, though related, means, he achieves a
compression within the narrative which both furthers the
sense of direction of the whole and ensures its powerful
impact.  There is an immediacy in his narrative and a relationship among events which give it its characteristic
force.

3.  The texture of Wolfram's narrative in 'Willehalm'.

Narrative 'texture' is the term which I apply, not,
as in 2, to structural elements - the order of the account
and the relationship among the incidents - but to details
of his narrative means within the structural framework.
What emerges most clearly is the variety of these means,
the many distinct strands which contribute to an exciting
and effective weave.

4.  The significance of the setting.

The action of Willehalm is set against a vivid background which contributes to the sense of reality of the
whole work.  This section is devoted to an examination of
Wolfram's means in creating his settings in time and place,
and of his use of movement between distinct places.  Two
further aspects of his use of detail in his narrative -
his evocation of sounds and the occurrence of colours within
his description - contribute also to the vividness of his
settings.

5.  The emergence of individuals.

The central characters of the work have been seen to
bear its spiritual message and so to perform a distinctive
role.  It is in his treatment of minor characters that Wolfram shows again the interest in individuals so apparent in
Parzival.  Particularly in the battles, individual characters
emerge from the mass and dominate the action before resuming
their place in it.  In the other important sequence of events,
at the court at Munleun, Wolfram allows the minor characters

to come forward for brief periods. He thus emphasizes the
significance of the individual within the mass which dominates so much of the action but, equally, in allowing minor
characters to return to their place in the wider context, he
preserves the proportions of the whole and ensures that the
full focus of attention remains where it belongs in his conception of the material, with the central figures and the
abstract message of the work.

6.  The narrative art of Wolfram in 'Willehalm' and the end
    of the work.

The study of the narrative art in Willehalm draws attention to factors which can contribute to the much discussed
question of the ending of the work. Although many scholars
have held that the work is a fragment, others have felt that
it was, in fact, completed, though perhaps not in the way
that Wolfram had intended when he embarked on a work which
had a known source.

The study of the narrative art has shown Wolfram moving
steadily towards a conclusion which is totally consistent
with the thought and the mood of the work. The story of
Rennewart remains unfinished: of this there can be no doubt,
yet the examination of Wolfram's characters has shown that
he frequently isolates a character for close attention and
then allows him to fall back into the mass, to assume his
place in the integrated whole. Rennewart, too, it is held,
despite the vividness of his personality and the time which
Wolfram has expended on his story, may not, in the end,
distort the proportions of the whole work, nor detract from
the significance of the main characters, and particularly in
the end of Willehalm, to whom is entrusted the expression in
tangible terms of the abstract message which the work contains.

Aesthetically, this thesis holds, Willehalm is a completed work of art, a totally harmonious whole and the
product of a wonderfully original mind.

## Introduction

To look in <u>Willehalm</u> for the author of <u>Parzival</u> is to
invite a certain disappointment. He is there to be found,
but changed, not beyond recognition yet nevertheless considerably changed, in accordance with the change in material
and with the differences in so many respects between the two
poems. Where, in <u>Parzival</u>, one is conscious of the ideal-
istic, almost fairy-tale, quality of the background and the
events, <u>Willehalm</u> is deeply rooted in reality.[1] The story
of the young hero growing towards a spiritual goal within
the world is different in tone and stature from the account
of the struggle of a man and his wife faced with the tragic
dilemma contingent upon the conflict of faiths. These are
basic differences, borne out in the difference of detail in
Wolfram's attitude to the two works and consequently and inevitably of his narrative technique.

In his work <u>Der Gral in Wolframs Parzival</u>[2] Mergell
includes a table relating to the two works, and though some
of his comparisons are over-elaborate and somewhat strained,
he draws attention to the essential and considerable differences in tone of the two poems with such contrasts as
<u>harmonisierendes Weltbild</u> (in <u>Parzival</u>)/<u>tragische Entgegen-</u>
<u>setzung</u> (in <u>Willehalm</u>), <u>Ewiges im Zeitlichen spiegelnd/</u>

Überwindung tragischer Scheidung im Aufblick zu Gott,
Gott in der Welt/Welt unter Gott, Versöhntheit im Irdischen/
Irdisches hinter sich lassend. More succinctly, Bumke speaks
of the difference in Wolfram's attitude to his material, suggesting that it is this rather than a difference in the material itself which is relevant: "Wichtiger ist die verschiedene
Perspektive, aus der erzählt wird. Im Parzival vom Helden
aus; das dargestellte Geschehen konzentriert sich in seinem
Innern, und die äußere Welt ist nur eine Emanation der inneren. Im Willehalm vom Geschehen selbst aus, dessen vorder-
gründige Richtigkeit und Glaubwürdigkeit dadurch ein ganz
anderes Gewicht erhält; vom großen Zusammenprall zwischen
Christen und Heiden, der sich in den Hauptfiguren zurück-
spiegelt."[3] In the course of this study attention will be
paid to the important function of action in Willehalm, and to
its effect on the work as a whole. Bumke arrives at a conclusion which, though it may not find unanimous agreement,
reflects the impact of the later work: "der Willehalm ist
durchaus die reifere, die geformtere und auch die gewaltigere
Dichtung". Ludwig Wolff declares rather similarly: "Auch im
Willehalm steckt Wolfram mit seiner ganzen Kraft",[4] and his
final remark speaks of the essential unity of the work: "Diese
Einheit macht ihn zu einem Kunstwerk, das sich hoch über die
meisten Werke seiner Zeit erhebt".[5] That Wolff is fully aware
that qualities other than this unity contribute to the sur-
passing greatness of the work is clear from the whole article,
while his brief Nachtrag, written 30 years later, bears witness to his continued contemplation of a work so profound and
so complex that it must exercise repeatedly the mind of the
serious and devoted reader. Mergell sums up his understanding
of the depth and scope of Willehalm when he says: "Wolfram
verkündet ein Ethos von einer solchen Höhe und Reinheit, wie
es nur den größten seiner Zeit faßbar war und das, ganz im
Mittelalter wurzelnd, zu überzeitlicher Bedeutung emporwächst",[6]
while Fritz Martini characterizes the poem as 'ein Epos der
Menschlichkeit',[7] a lofty assessment which expresses in simple
terms the profound nature of the theme and the approach of

its author.

Both Wolff and Mergell see the unique quality of the
work and its power to transcend its own age, but it is another aspect which is emphasized by M. O'C. Walshe in an
assessment which seems to express the direct appeal of Wolfram's poem: "Whatever problems it poses and fails to solve,
Wolfram's Willehalm as sheer narrative succeeds as a tour de
force of incomparable genius".[8] Once more, the unique quality of the work is acknowledged, but, more than that, this
simple statement contains the essential clue to its impact:
above all, Willehalm is a tale brilliantly told. It is an
exciting story, full of activity and force, yet it is pervaded also by gentler qualities, the awareness of human emotions and the recognition of the value of human relationships.
It moves with speed and decision, yet side-by-side with such
movement are periods of rest and contemplation. Such contrasts contribute to the depth of a work which, even on a
superficial level, would succeed as an impelling tale of
mediæval chivalry. Such a work, indeed, was the Old French
chanson de geste on which Wolfram's work is based,[9] and a
considerable part of his achievement as a narrator is in
seeing the potential of this source and in giving to the prim-
itive strength of Aliscans a new subtlety.

There are a number of important works which are concerned principally, or to a considerable extent, with the
relationship between Aliscans and Willehalm, and with the
treatment by Wolfram of his source,[10] and it is certainly
not appropriate here to repeat the many observations already
made. However, it is appropriate to draw attention to the
essential differences between the two works, and above all
to note the outstanding differences in Wolfram's attitude to
his material which will clearly affect his narrative art.
S. M. Johnson observes: "Wolfram has retained the essential
outline of Aliscans as far as his work goes, but in his adap-
tation and remoulding of the elements of Aliscans he has
created a new work of art",[11] and this remoulding process
is dependent precisely upon his new conception of the old

material. Bumke points out that it is Wolfram himself who
has most aptly characterized his own work: "Wolfram hat das
Wesen seiner Dichtung am treffendsten umschrieben, als er
sie eine süeze rede, ein religiöses Epos nannte".[12] Willehalm is above all a religious work, using the material of
the Old French chanson and giving to it a concern for spiritual values which is completely original. Where Aliscans
presents the heathens as a mass, making little attempt to in-
dividualize them, still less to suggest an individual point
of view, Wolfram is careful to portray both sides in terms
of individual men, brave and noble, and fighting equally for
a cause to which they are committed. Though there is no
doubt of Wolfram's own standpoint, firmly established in the
opening prayer which extols the power and wisdom of God, and
reiterated throughout, his compassion for all men is evident
at all times and finds expression in the speeches of Gyburc
which contain the spiritual message of the whole poem. No
such message exists in Aliscans, where the Saracens are
represented as evil beings, in total opposition to the Christians and consequently to be slaughtered with the utmost ex-
peditiousness by those whose glory lies in the annihilation
of this terrible enemy. The idea that a heathen might share
qualities of chivalry with the Christian knight is alien to
the approach of Aliscans, while for Wolfram the common source
as the creatures of a great and benevolent God ensures the
validity of all human life, its claim to praise where praise
is due and to protection by the laws of humanity.[13]

The subtlety of Wolfram's approach is reflected in the
way in which the material of the source has been re-arranged
to form a new and thoroughly integrated whole. There is about
Aliscans the directness and simplicity of a good tale, told
to delight and entertain an unsophisticated audience. Events
are related swiftly with little preparation and without connection among them.[14] Wolfram's work, in complete contrast,
is very complex, with close attention to detail and the inter-
weaving of events and motifs: yet, for all that, it retains
as an essential quality a single-strandedness which means

that subsidiary events and matters are made to contribute
towards the main theme, ensuring an outstanding sense of
direction for the whole work.[15] Wolfram omits some events
of the source; others he changes or uses in a different way
or in a different place, in accordance with his conception
of the whole work, which, in consequence, becomes a carefully constructed, consciously integrated poem. In particular the two battles are constructed by Wolfram with a syste-
matic development lacking in the narrative of Aliscans.[16]

Wolfram's additions, too, are of the utmost importance,
for in these lies perhaps the firmest indication of his purpose. The speeches of Gyburc are focal points of the work,
containing the concentration of religious thought and pro-
nouncements. The tender love scenes are used by Wolfram to
bring into relief the harshness of battle and the urgency
which dominates the work. Details are added, too, and contribute significantly to the work as a whole and the integrity of his conception of it. Above all those passages of
the work which contribute to its great and original theme -
the Prologue, the religious debates of Gyburc and Terramer,
the prayer to Gyburc and the Matribleiz-scene - have no correspondence in the source, while the whole notion of minne
as a motivating force is Wolfram's own.

It is significant that Willehalm diverges increasingly
from the source in the course of the poem, but most of all
during the last three Books: this, surely, is Wolfram, the
great and original artist, the mediæval author with a firm
sense of responsibility to his source,[17] fulfilling the
potential of that source and transcending it, to the extent
that, in the last resort, his poem is a totally different
work from the French original. Wolff observes: "Einen frem-
den Stoff, der in seiner Vorlage in einer ihm völlig wider-
sprechenden Art behandelt war, hat er ergriffen und mit un-
erhörter Freiheit im Geistigen zum Gefäß seiner eigenen
Anschauungen und Gedanken geformt. Der Gehalt ist völlig
neu geworden, und die Form in gleicher Weise".[18]

With a mind which was at the same time clear and probing,

yet capable of apprehending the inexplicable workings of
human emotions, Wolfram had dealt in <u>Parzival</u> with the dilemma of the man who, in spite of himself, falls into guilt but
emerges from it as a finer being, through the Grace of God
and his own striving. Such a mind lies behind <u>Willehalm</u>, but
added to it is the experience which tells him that the ways
of God are mysterious, and that man does not always emerge
into worldly bliss. If in <u>Parzival</u> he had known that human
fortunes fluctuate - "hiute vreude, morgen leit" - then in
<u>Willehalm</u> he expresses this more emphatically, not only in
words, but in the rise and fall of battle and the finality
of undiscriminating death.

It is not surprising that, for this later work, he
turned to one of the great issues of the day, not to put
forward a solution, but to demonstrate the complexity of the
argument and its tragic insolubility. The story of Parzival
had risen above the personal and become a story of universal
significance, but in <u>Willehalm</u> he begins with a theme which
is wider in its immediate implications: here he is concerned,
not with the fate of one man, even if that man can be taken
to stand for any man, or every man, but with the fate of
whole races and the future of the human race itself. It is
indeed a vast theme, and in <u>Willehalm</u> it is expressed in a
work of immense scope and depth. This initial impression,
of a work of very great proportions, makes an appropriate
starting-point for an examination of Wolfram's narrative art.
Yet an awareness of the dimensions leads to the desire to
probe the artistic handling of such a wealth of material.
One becomes aware of the mass of detail on which the whole
structure rests, just as, within the story, Wolfram builds
the conflict of two great forces on the relationship of two
individuals.

## 1. The Harmony of the Work

The harmony which is an essential feature of <u>Willehalm</u> exists on many levels and, as will be seen, it is furthered by many aspects of his narrative. This work which expresses, as its ultimate theme, the hope in the unity of mankind through love, has a structural unity which overrides conflicting elements and draws its components into a coherent whole.

In his study of <u>Willehalm</u> Joachim Bumke has drawn attention to the careful structure of the work, which depends upon a parallelism of place and time.[1] The action begins and ends on the battlefield. The first battle of Alischanz is balanced by the second; Willehalm's flight to Gyburc in Orange and their united decision that he should seek aid is balanced by his return to her with this aid; he leaves the battlefield and rides to Orange, and from Orange he rides again to the battlefield. Between his two reunions with his wife lies his ride to Munleun and back, on each journey passing through Orleans and coming to the monastery; here, too, is perfect symmetry, with the second, unmolested passage through Orleans bringing with it the reminder of how he was stopped there for his toll on the first occasion, and the sight of the burnt monastery recalling how Willehalm found refuge there before. Centrally placed, from the point of view of action, is the

episode at the Court of Loys, which looks both back to the
first battle of Alischanz and forward to the second. A work
which is built on a framework like this has an innate unity
and this Wolfram uses and furthers by numerous means.

First, then, in this study of the narrative art of Wolfram in Willehalm, this unity is considered. It emerges that
this quality of the work which is so vital to its total impact may be attributed first and foremost to the harmony of
the thought and that this, in turn, rests with Wolfram's
depiction of the two central characters, Gyburc and Willehalm,
and his conception of their roles in the poem. Vivianz, too,
so closely related both to these two characters and to the
spiritual thought of the whole, is a significant integrating
factor, uniting the two battles and pervading the whole work
with his memory. The battles themselves, with the theme of
the second as a revenge for the first, and the recurrence of
names and motifs, constitute a further unifying element in
the structure of the work.

a) Gyburc as an integrating factor

The most powerful unifying force is Gyburc who, more than
anyone else, dominates the work with her spirit if not with
her physical presence. In fact she makes few physical appearances, and although these are important in themselves, their
greater significance is in the influence which they radiate
through the work. Gyburc's principal role in relation to the
whole work is to express its ultimate message of compassion
to all God's creatures, and her fitness to do so is firmly
established during the first half of the work, in order that
in the second half she may assume her more dominant role.

Like Vivianz, Gyburc both contributes to the structural
unity and is one of the most significant means by which Wolfram gives to the work the coherence of substance which is so
essential a part of it. The two things are again closely
related. On each occasion Gyburc appears at Orange: Orange
is identified with her, her essential place of action, representing as it does her home with Willehalm and the centre of

their Christian marriage. The symmetry is evident: Willehalm
rides to Gyburc in Orange after his terrible defeat in the
first battle, and he is with her before he departs for his
victory in the second one. She is the goal of his first ride,
the one solace which remains to him now, and, with Vivianz,
she is the reason for the second battle. She is related,
then, physically with Orange and abstractly with Alischanz.
In addition, the memory of her dominates the rides of Willehalm, and his sojourn at the French Court; Wolfram himself
calls her vividly to mind in the prayer which opens Book VIII,
and it is in token of his love for her that Willehalm performs
the gesture towards Matribleiz in the closing scenes. Wolfram's art is complex and varied, but he ensures that Gyburc
is present throughout the work and that she is able therefore
to unite its separate parts into a completely harmonious
whole, which accords with her advocacy of universal love.

The first mention of Gyburc is long before her first
appearance:

> Arabeln Willalm erwarp,
> dar umbe unschuldic volc erstarp.
> diu minne im leiste und ê gehiez,
> Gyburc si sich toufen liez. (7,27-30)[2]

Much is contained in these four lines: the two names of the
woman, her love for Willehalm and her marriage with him, her
baptism and the deaths of innocent people in consequence. So
already at this first reference the personal issue is set
side-by-side with the wider one which grows from it, and Wolfram speaks of the tragedy of innocent people in juxtaposition
to the love which is seen as its source. Thus at this first
mention of Gyburc, Wolfram supplies all the themes which are
to accompany his depiction of her and make her the core of
the work.

Before her first appearance, the name of Gyburc is kept
very much in the work and her position, though not developed
beyond what Wolfram has said at his first mention of her, is
reiterated in various ways. That she is the cause of the conflict is emphasized on a number of occasions during the first
battle. At the beginning of it, her role in the suffering

is given in two unambiguous lines:

> Gyburge süeze wart in sûr,
> Den heiden und der kristenheit.
>
> (12,30-13,1)

A little later, Wolfram lets out the brief lament:

> eyâ Gyburc, süeze wîp,
> mit schaden erarnet wart dîn lîp. (14,29-30)

That the suffering is the price of the love of Gyburc and
Willehalm is stated by Wolfram:

> Ey Heimrîch von Narbôn,
> dîns sunes dienst jâmers lôn
> durh Gyburge minne enpfienc.
> swaz si genâde an im begienc,
> diu wart vergolten tiure,
> alsô daz diu gehiure
> ouch wîplîcher sorgen pflac,          (14,1-7)

but more poignantly expressed by Willehalm himself in his cry:

> ey Gyburc, süeze âmîe,
> wie tiwer ich dich vergolten hân! (39,12-13)

It is again Wolfram himself who speaks of the particular position of Gyburc and so prepares the way for her own later ex-
position of her tragic dilemma.  He addresses her by her two
names, deliberately stressing the duality of her circumstances:

> Arabele Gyburc, ein wîp
> zwir genant, minne und dîn lîp
> sich nu mit jâmer flihtet:
> du hâst zem schaden gepflihtet.
> dîn minne den touf versnîdet:
> des toufes wer ouch niht mîdet,
> sine snîd von den du bist erborn.
> der wirt ouch drumbe vil verlorn,
> ez enwend der in diu herze siht.
> mîn herze dir ungünste giht.          (30,21-30)

Yet Wolfram immediately takes himself up on this condemnation
of Gyburc in his assertion of her innocence:

> War umbe? ich solte ê sprechen
> waz ich wolde rechen:
> oder war tuon ich mînen sin?
> unschuldic was diu künegin,
> diu eteswenne Arabel hiez
> und den namen im toufe liez
> durh den der von dem worte wart.      (31,1-7)

His words anticipate Gyburc's great speech (306,1-310,29).  He
acknowledges her personal grief in the double claim on her
loyalty and in her awareness that she is the cause of the con-

flict. Yet although he may momentarily blame her in recognition of her responsibility, he can still assert her innocence,
which rests on her motivation. She, on the other hand, echoes
his words in her acceptance of her guilt: this guilt, though
she may grieve for the widespread suffering, is one that she
is proud to bear, because it has been given to her by the
Grace of God and also through the love of Willehalm:

> ich trag al ein die schulde,
> durh des hœhsten gotes hulde
> ein teil ouch durh den markîs.  (310,17-19)

Thus, at the height of Gyburc's action, these early words of
Wolfram's will be given a new and positive significance by
Gyburc herself: her 'guilt' brings suffering on herself and
those about her, but it gives her the key to the role which
Wolfram intends for her. Because she stands uniquely between
two races, because she is the cause of the suffering on both
sides and because she must endure hatred from Christians and
heathens alike, she can also advocate love, the one to the
other, and hope that, by the God for whose sake she gladly
bears this burden, hatred will be replaced by love.

Much lies, however, between the early assertion by Wolfram of Gyburc's innocence and her own pursuit of the question
of her guilt. The other references to Gyburc before her first
appearance at Orange are less lengthy than this one, and less
individually significant. There are references to her baptism
and the grief which it has brought on her kinsmen (9,8-16),
and the shame of her son on account of his mother's rejection
of their gods (75,18-20). There is a further reference to the
wealth which she gave up for the sake of Willehalm (86,7-12),
and, although this may be taken as a passing comment, it also
has its echo in Gyburc's later assertion that she desires
poverty (216,1-3).[3)]

There remain, before the appearance of Gyburc, a great
many seemingly passing references to her, but these are far
from random. By far the greatest number links her with
Vivianz. It was she who brought up Vivianz (23,6-9; 41,10-12)
and loved him deeply (63,20-21; 66,13-17); yet there is irony
in what Wolfram tells us, for it was Gyburc who equipped

Vivianz so finely for combat (24,13-15). In her love for
him, she has equipped him for the battle which will bring
him death, and the irony is heightened in the more specific
statement:

> Gyburc diu wîse,
> diu mit kostlîchem prîse
> sande den jungen Vivîanz
> ûf daz velt Alischanz. (60,9-12)

The irony goes further, for Wolfram means to tell both how
Gyburc sent off into battle her young kinsman in his splendid
attire and how, in a broader sense, she was the reason for
the death in battle of Vivianz, the representative of all the
Christian soldiers. The love of Gyburc for Vivianz, and the
double impact of the grief which she will know at his death
and in the awareness of her own responsibility are anticipated by Willehalm (62,23-63,1).

In the first battle, Gyburc is linked also with both
Ehmereiz and Arofel. The identification of Ehmereiz as der
werden Gyburge suon (72,21) is only on one level to be seen
as mere convention, for it brings with it also the reminder
of the abandonment by Gyburc of her heathen family. It epitomizes briefly the tragedy of the conflict, with Willehalm
forced into opposition with his own step-son, but also the
breadth of the tragic situation of human beings engaging in
battle where there still remain the bonds of blood, or even,
as Gyburc will see, the ties of humanity. Later in the encounter, Ehmereiz is referred to as Gyburge barn (75,21),
stressing the reason that Willehalm spares this man, alone
among so many. Already, when Willehalm has refused to enter
into combat with Ehmereiz, Wolfram has commented:

> dem enwolt er dâ niht tuon.
> daz enliez er durch in selben niht:
> Gyburg diz mære des frides giht,
> in der geleite er dannen reit. (74,28-75,1)

Long before the great plea for mercy by Gyburc is this incident which shows Willehalm prepared to spare an enemy for her
sake, but this is not the case with Arofel, whom Wolfram describes as Gyburge veter (76,15). Towards him Willehalm com-
mits the brutal crime of slaughter, though he pleads for mercy,

and <u>rêroup</u>, that much despised act of divesting a corpse of
its armour; and Gyburc's part in this action which she could
not have condoned is implicit. When Willehalm has fended off
the attacks of Arofel and Tenebruns, Wolfram inserts a remark
which is only seemingly irrelevant:

> er wolde et ze Oransche hin,
> dâ Gyburc diu künegin
> sîn herze nâhen bî ir truoc.     (77,9-11)

It is the thought of his wife and his need to escape to reach
her that forces him on, and the insertion of this remark leads
one to believe that the intention is already there, to gain
heathen armour which will bring him to safety. However, it
is not of Gyburc that he thinks as Arofel pleads for mercy:
the premeditated intention of gaining the armour of his
opponent in order to escape to Orange is blurred by another
motive, revenge for Vivianz (79,28-80,1). Gyburc's role in
this action remains implicit, with the explicit motive given
as revenge for Vivianz; but there is another poignant reminder of the relationship of Arofel and Gyburc, when Wolfram
praises the <u>milte</u> of Arofel and says that Gyburc's generosity
was inherited from him (78,19-20). Yet Arofel's relationship
with Gyburc does not save him, for at this stage there can be
no place for sentiment in the face of grim expedience and the
grief-stricken desire for revenge.[4]

The final mention of Gyburc before she appears in person
is when Wolfram refers to Willehalm as <u>Gyburge bote</u> (88,15),
and again the reference has more than one significance, for
Willehalm is indeed the messenger, bringing his news to Gyburc,
but he is her messenger in a wider sense, forced into battle
because of her and fighting for her sake. By the time Wolfram
comes to the first physical appearance of Gyburc, her position has been established, and the first scene in Orange shows
her linked with both battles of Alischanz. In Wolfram's brief
account of the losses sustained and the power of the heathen
army (93,26-94,4) and in Gyburc's lamentation at the side of
her sleeping husband (100,28-102,20), the scene looks back
to the first battle, but it looks forward to the second, as
Wolfram describes the preparations being made by the heathen

armies and the beleaguering of Orange (96,6-99,8), as well
as Willehalm's own preparations for a second battle in the
decision which he makes, with Gyburc, to ride for aid from
the King and his own kinsmen. Gyburc is at the centre,
physically encircled by the enemy, and her role from the
beginning of this scene is one of defence. It is in this
state that Willehalm finds her, when she refuses to unbolt
the door to one of whose identity she is unsure, and it is
in the same state of defence that he leaves her, when she
silently lets him out by the door. When she learns that
Terramer himself has invaded the land, she fears for their
lives, but her manner is again the characteristic one of
fortitude, and Wolfram comments:

> manlîche sprach daz wîp,
> als ob si manlîchen lîp
> und mannes herze trüege.                    (95,3-5)

Already he is anticipating the later scene when Gyburc actively
defends Orange, but here too the readiness to suffer physically is matched by its gentler partner, the love of Gyburc
and Willehalm which at all times Wolfram shows as the basis
of the suffering. Thus, in the midst of the preparations for
the siege, Wolfram includes a love scene, during which Gyburc
both tends Willehalm's physical wounds and, by her love,
relieves his pain. Wolfram comments:

> ich wæn dô ninder swære
> den marcrâven schuz noch slac.     (100,18-19)

Expressed for the first time here is an essential theme of
the work: that, though the love of Willehalm and Gyburc pro-
duces suffering, it has itself the power to alleviate it. It
is her love for him which prompts her to urge him to remember
that love and remain true to her while they are apart, and
Willehalm, in his oath, widens the interpretation and links
love and suffering further when he vows to remain in sorrow
until he has released her.

This vow accompanies Willehalm's actions and is one of
the constant reminders of Gyburc during their separation.
Wolfram expresses the perfection of their love through the
motif of the exchange of hearts (109,6-10), but Willehalm

himself expresses his allegiance to Gyburc by his interpretation of his oath. He has promised to remain in grief and to eat only bread and water: this he does. On the first occasion, no mention is made of Gyburc or of the oath, but there is an exact verbal echo which brings the oath vividly to mind:

> niht wan wazzer unde brôt
> im selbem er ze spîse nam.     (112,18-19)

Later he refers to the oath in explanation of his abstinence (134,2-135,7), and again at the Court he recalls it (176,10-177,7). On another occasion he calls for a less comfortable seat (132,16-23) and later he declines the fine clothes which are offered to him (174,27-29). More frequently, extending his abstinence still further, Willehalm refuses to exchange kisses. On the first occasion when he declines he offers the explanation:

> den rehten kus ich liez in nôt
> an Gyburge ûf Oransche nuo.
> die wîle ir gêt sölh angest zuo,
> sô lâz ich mir niht werden kunt
> daz mannes oder wîbes munt
> an den mînen rüere     (119,6-11)

and he echoes his own words when he tells his father:

> mîn kus ûf Oransch ist belibn:
> dâ hât mich Tybalt von getribn.
> den rehten kus ze Oransche ich liez.
> (149,5-7)

When he takes Alyze's face in his hands, he regrets that he cannot kiss her:

> mîn kus dir schiere wære bekant,
> wan daz ich kuss enterbet pin     (156,22-23)

and at the feast Wolfram repeats:

> swer im küssen bôt,
> sô dâht er an des kusses nôt,
> der im ze Oransche was beliben,
> und wie er von dem was vertriben. (177,7-10)

It is interesting that, though the name of Gyburc occurs very often during this period, it does not occur in the last three examples. It is as though, in a sense, Gyburc has become more than an individual person, rather an abstraction, love itself, epitomized in the kiss left behind in Orange, and

Wolfram can afford to employ this abstract impression because, in other respects, Gyburc as a person is so very much present in the work.

The memory of Gyburc, then, is constantly with Willehalm, and the oath which he gave her forms a bridge between their parting and their reunion, when he has fulfilled his promise to bring her aid and so has earned release from the formal manifestation of sorrow which he has taken upon himself. More than conventional greeting is contained, therefore, in the kisses which Gyburc and Willehalm exchange when they meet again, and this is emphasized by the way in which Wolfram himself combines in this reunion a reference backward to their parting:

> sine het ouch niht sô liehten schîn,
> als dô er von ir schiet,
> als im ir süezer munt geriet,
> der dâ vil geküsset wart. (229,20-23)

Here at last is the formal seal on their reunion.

There are, in addition, many isolated references to Gyburc during the period of Willehalm's separation from her which stress that, initially, the need is to amass a force which will release her. Willehalm meets with people who are anxious for news of Gyburc and ready to aid her (120,3; 121,4-7; 121,10-14). Always at the back of his attempts to obtain aid is the memory of her (123,2; 139,7-8; 162,16-20; 178,14-17; 183,16-21) and Wolfram repeatedly reminds us that Gyburc will benefit from the aid given (170,21-22; 172,20-23; 184,30; 185,28-30). These references are factual ones and are not of any particular significance, except in that they uphold the sense of Willehalm's purpose. There are two others, however, which are rather more subtle.

When Alyze is pleading with Willehalm for forgiveness for her mother, she says that she asks for the sake of her grandmother, his own mother, and also for her lady Gyburc. She recalls how Gyburc held her in her arms when she was a child, and she concludes with the wistful statement:

> diust mir leider nu ze verre komn. (157,30)

The appeal to Willehalm's emotions is well-timed, and it has

the desired effect of softening his attitude towards his
sister. The power of Gyburc over Willehalm, as Alyze knows,
is great, and even at this distance she can calm his rage.
After the reconciliation of Willehalm and the Queen, and when
Loys has agreed to give aid, Wolfram links Willehalm's sister
and his wife once more, this time more closely. The Queen
tends his wounds,

die Gyburc hete verbunden       (186,28)

and with that line comes the memory of the tender love scene,
with Gyburc binding the wounds of her husband and giving him
also the love which acted as a healing force. Thus Wolfram's
next two lines deepen in meaning, in their relationship to
the earlier scene:

er wart dâ sîner wunden heil<br>
und durch des küneges helfe geil.<br>
(186,29-30)

There is both the physical healing of his wounds and the
healing of his grief through the King's offer of help which
will bring him again to Gyburc. It is the power of Wolfram's
art in his depiction of the two brief scenes in Orange which
allows them to dominate the whole of the next part of the
work, and in particular keeps the memory of Gyburc alive, so
that the slightest echo is capable of producing an important
effect like this one.

Because Gyburc dominates the action in this way while
she is not physically present, she is able to assume a role
of importance when she enters it again, with Wolfram's return
to her before the arrival of Willehalm and his forces in
Orange. What she has endured in the meantime is not specifically described at this stage, though it is epitomized in
the comment that she has often had to bear weapons (215,7),
a remark which recalls her staunch determination to defend
Orange. The trials which she has suffered are passed over and
only implied by the relief which causes her to swoon when she
recognizes Willehalm's voice, and Wolfram says:

von sîner kunft was in benomn<br>
vil angest der si phlâgen ê.     (228,24-25)

Gyburc's defence of Orange is not described at length but

conveyed in a few vivid pictures: Gyburc armed for battle
defending her faith against the attacks of her father (215,10-
221,26); the fire at night and Gyburc left alone with a very
small army in the castle to defend the inner part of the city
(223,7-21); Gyburc hurling great stones at the enemy (230,4),
or setting up the dead men on the battlements (111,17-27).
Perhaps the most powerful picture is the static one which
greets Willehalm as he looks up at his castle:

> nu stuont vrou Gyburc ze wer
> mit ûf geworfeme swerte
> als op si strîtes gerte.          (227,12-14)

In this Wolfram conveys the essence of Gyburc, her readiness
to fight with her sword if the need arises. It is the culmination, too, of his depiction of her during the first half
of the work, when he establishes her right to the role which
she performs increasingly in the second half. This depiction,
as has been seen, is a very consistent one, a gradual building-
up, in which echo and anticipation play a part, and in which
physical presence combines with abstract influence to create
a character commensurate with the role which she is to perform.
It has already been seen, too, that Gyburc unites events and
themes of the work, but her most powerful unifying function
remains to be examined, in the relationship between this woman
and the spiritual thought of the work.

b) __Gyburc and the unity of the spiritual thought__

Wolfram's __süeze rede__ contains, not isolated passages of
religious matter, but the total expression of a profoundly
religious theme. At the centre of the spiritual content is
Gyburc who, in this respect too, unites the work and assures
the harmony of the whole.

Although Gyburc is, as has been seen, capable of action,
this is not what Wolfram stresses in her, for her role is to
convey his message of love, and this she does with words. Her
activity centres on her speeches and culminates in her great
plea for mercy towards the heathen. The speech with which
she sends the Christian army into the second battle of Ali-

schanz is in no way an isolated manifestation of her eloquence
or the depth of her emotion. It grows out of the speech which
opens Book V: the second group of scenes in Orange is framed
by these two speeches by Gyburc. Moreover, the first of them
(215,10-221,26), which is contained within a conversation
between Gyburc and Terramer, may be seen as the continuation
of a conversation begun much earlier. When Willehalm has
parted from Gyburc, Wolfram does not turn at once to his progress but remains in Orange, where Gyburc is being besieged
by her father's army and threatened by Terramer himself. Although Gyburc does not say much during the course of this
conversation, she is forced to listen to his attack on her
faith and his description of the choice of deaths he is offering her if she refuses to give up her baptism. Her refusal
to be intimidated ends the conversation for the time being,
but Wolfram observes that it was subsequently continued
(110,10). Meanwhile he turns to Willehalm and for a long
period concentrates on his exploits, though with Gyburc constantly in his thoughts. The conversation between Gyburc and
Terramer is, however, taken up later, when, at the beginning
of Book V, Wolfram recalls how often Gyburc has been threatened
by her father. The echo of the former occasion bridges the
time interval, so that Gyburc's speech can be seen as the
reply to Terramer's attack on Christianity.

Terramer is shown, like Willehalm, as a man who is personally afflicted. As he speaks, in the early speech, of the
revenge which he has initiated for the sake of his gods, he
reveals himself as a father who is prepared to sacrifice his
daughter and who seems to be suppressing his ordinary human
feelings in his determination to bring dishonour upon her
God through her:

> ich wil und hân mir des erdâht,
> daz ich manege unkunde nôt
> Arabeln gebe und smæhen tôt,
> des Jêsus gunêret sî:
> der wille ist mîme herzen bî.     (108,18-22)

In his contemptuous, bald, analysis of the Christian faith,
he betrays his lack of understanding of the religion which
his daughter has adopted:

> ûf mînen goten ich dô swuor,
> daz ich den goten ir êre
> so geræch daz nimmer mêre
> dehein mîn kint des zæme
> daz ez den touf genæme
> Durch Jêsum, der selbe truoc
> ein kriuze dâ man in an sluoc
> mit drîn nageln durch sîn verch.
> mîn geloube stüend entwerch,
> ob ich geloubte daz der starp
> und in dem tôde leben erwarp
> und doch sîn eines wæren drî.
> ist mir mîn alt geloube bî,
> sô wæn ich daz sîn Trinitât
> an mir deheine volge hât.      (107,26-108,10)

What Terramer isolates in the Christian faith is the drama of
the Crucifixion and the seeming paradox of the Resurrection
and the Trinity. He misses completely, presumably because he
does not know of them, the features which will dominate in
Gyburc's later great confession of her faith: he overlooks
the forces of love and compassion which she will emphasize
and stresses instead the miraculous elements, for which, though
he may mock at them, he nonetheless has a deep-rooted fear
and a reluctant respect, when he sees them manifested, as he
believes, in the military power of his opponents:

> ich mac der kristenheite gote
> alêrst nu grôzes wunders jehen:
> selh wunder ist an mir geschehen,
> daz ein hant vol rîter mich
> hât nâch entworht durch den gerich,
> daz ich den ungelouben rach ...    (107,18-22)[5]

The speech prepares the way for the dreadful choice which he
places before his daughter concerning the manner of her death
(109,22-29) and his subsequent siege of Orange (111,1-14).
More important, however, is the way in which it anticipates
the speeches by Gyburc which contain the central spiritual
thought of the work. It anticipates them by means of contrast. Where Terramer, the opponent of Christianity, has
reduced it to its baldest terms, Gyburc will stand as the
great exponent of Christianity, radiating its foremost message of universal love and forgiveness. Where Terramer
speaks of her as a traitor to her own gods and deserving of
the death of a traitor, she will express the positive aspect

of her conversion, with its source in the human love which
has led to divine love, and she will show herself prepared,
happy even, to accept the suffering which is not the punish-
ment of a treacherous criminal, but the inevitable accom-
paniment of a greater spiritual stature.

In responding, after the time interval, to the attacks
by her father, Gyburc begins with a statement of her motivation in accepting baptism: she has sought Christianity for
the sake of Him who created all things and who created also
the elements, but she unites with God the Margrave who serves
her and desires her love. As so often, God and Willehalm are
united in her mind, and they remain united as she goes on to
speak of the poverty which she has assumed in her marriage
with Willehalm:

> Durch den hân ich mich bewegen
> daz ich wil armüete pflegen,
> und durch den der der hœhste ist. (216,1-3)

Baptism she calls der sêle rîcheit, for the sake of which she
is prepared to endure des lîbes armuot (216,28-29), but poverty is, for Gyburc, a positive concept, so that this speech in
which she affirms her allegiance to Christianity can culminate
in the appeal:

> und lâz mich mit armuot lebn. (221,26)

This speech is essentially a personal statement of faith, beginning with her reasons for accepting baptism - ich hân den
touf genomn... - (215,10), and ending with her plea that she
be allowed to continue in this state of relative physical
privation which represents spiritual wealth. But her acceptance of poverty for the sake of Christ goes further, to embrace the suffering which is now being imposed upon her because
of her belief: this theme will be taken up in her other great
speech but it is intimated already in her readiness to accept
any burden which is placed upon her for the sake of the God
who has power over all things.

The speech is, therefore, both the response to the accusations and threats of her father, and a statement which has
a wider relevance to the work as a whole. In its latter function it is perfectly timed, at a central point of the work and

between the two battles, and its structural position coincides, of course, with its relationship to the content of the work. Gyburc's words obliterate any possible suspicion that the sacrifice of so many in the first battle was a vain one, and they give new force and meaning to the preparations for the second battle and to the battle itself. Wolfram has never cast doubt on the validity of the motivation for the conflict, but the intervention at this point of Gyburc, who is the very personification of the motivating force, is brilliantly effective and gives a new vigour to the work.

The significance of the speech is reflected in its complex structure: Gyburc covers a range of related subjects, as she passes from her baptism and her marriage, with her consequent sacrifice of her material wealth, to a statement of the nature of her God. She contrasts the wisdom of the Christian God with that of the heathen god whom she has rejected:

> wâ fund ouch Tervigant den list
> den êrst ervant Altissimus?       (216,4-5)

The words recall Terramer's mocking accusation of her treachery in betraying the heathen gods, but Gyburc is not attempting to reply to the unconsidered words of her father. Rather does she rise above them in her description of the God who is all-powerful.

It is her description of the nature of the God whom she worships which unites Gyburc with the Prologue of the work and so gives her her place in the wider context. The Prologue had been addressed to a Creator whose power is limitless:

> dîner hœhe und dîner breite,
> dîner tiefen antreite
> Wart nie gezilt anz ende.
> ouch louft in dîner hende
> der siben sterne gâhen,
> daz sin himel wider vâhen.
> luft wazzer fiur und erde
> wont gar in dînem werde.
> ze dîme gebot ez allez stêt,
> dâ wilt unt zam unt umbe gêt.
> ouch hât dîn götlîchiu maht
> den liehten tac, die trüeben naht
> gezilt und underscheiden
> mit der sunnen louften beiden.       (1,29-2,12)

The correspondence is evident between this early passage and
the statement now by Gyburc as she links her own conversion
with the power of God over the universe:

> der pôlus antarticus
> unt den ander sternen gab ir louft,
> durch den hân ich mich getouft;
> derz firmamentum an liez
> unt die siben plânêten hiez
> gein des himels snelheit kriegen.
> sîn wâge kan niht triegen,
> diu al daz werc sô ebene wac,
> daz ez immer stæte heizen mac
> unt immer unzerganclîch.
> sint iwer gote dem gelîch,
> der den luft wol wider væhet
> unt al sîn dinc sô spæhet,
> mit fluzze ursprinc der brunnen,
> und der drî art der sunnen
> gap, die hitze, und ouch den schîn:
> si muoz ouch ûf der verte sîn:
> daz nimt und bringet uns daz lieht.
>
> (216,6-23)

In both cases the emphasis is on the divine ordering of the
universe, and the supreme control over elemental forces. The
God in whom Gyburc believes is the God to whom the work is
dedicated, but, more than that, it is the God to whom, as the
work closes, Willehalm commends his opponent, Matribleiz.
Willehalm's description of the nature of his God is brief:

> ich bevilh iuch, künec Matribleiz,
> dem der der sterne zal weiz
> Unt der uns gap des mânen schîn
>
> (466,29-467,1)

but the same idea is there: knowledge of the infinite and
power over the elemental. It is this idea which links the
end with the beginning, but they are linked the more forcefully by the centrally placed speech by Gyburc. This is not
only a further factor in the structural harmony of the work,
but it contributes also to a deepening of the spiritual theme.
Gyburc asserts her personal faith in her God, but her position
allows her also to stand as the representative of the Christian
faith. In the midst of the action Gyburc alone expresses the
motivating force of that action, and when the Christians are
fighting to defend their faith, it is Gyburc who proclaims
the nature of this faith. In taking up Wolfram's theme in the

Prologue, she ensures that her religion will extend beyond
the personal and take on new proportions as the guiding force
behind all the action until, in its ultimate form of love, it
echoes in Willehalm's gesture towards the heathen at the end
of the work. The harmony of the thought is thus complete.

The first great speech by Gyburc is emphatically related
to the activity about her. Book IV had ended with Willehalm's
despair at the sight of the fire at night, and of the conversation Wolfram says that it took place in a lull in the battle
(221,27). Gyburc emerges from the conflict to assert her
allegiance to her faith and to acknowledge her awareness that
she is the source of the conflict. This relationship is
maintained in her speech to the assembled princes before the
second battle: in fact, the speech is preceded by one of
Wolfram's most specific statements of her responsibility:

Durh Gyburge al diu nôt geschach.

(306,1)

The speech is in some measure an extension of the earlier one
to Terramer. Her loyalty to her faith has been acknowledged
and need not be restated: instead she can pass on to a wider
issue, which rests on her personal decision, it is true, yet
goes beyond it. She is concerned now, not so much with her
own relationship with God, as with that of the fighting Christians, and their attitude in turn to their heathen opponents.
She bases her plea for mercy on the unity of mankind as the
creation of the God who Himself forgave those who killed Him
(309,1-6). Yet this, one of the greatest expressions of love
in the whole work, begins with a statement of the awareness
of hatred (306,12ff). Gyburc can accept that the hatred of
both Christians and heathen is directed towards her because
of her love for God and for Willehalm, and she can acknowledge
her responsibility for the hatred between two races: yet to
this hatred of herself she can respond with love, and hope to
turn their mutual hatred into something closer to its opposite, in her plea that the Christians should look with mercy
upon their opponents in reverence of their common source as
the creatures of a loving God. That love can give rise to
hatred she acknowledges again in her words later in this speech:

des trag ich mîner mâge haz;
und der getouften umbe daz:
durh menneschlîcher minne gît
si wænent daz ich fuogte disen strît.

(310,5-8)

Wolfram sees love and hate as the motivating forces of the
battle, then, and though he knows that they are ultimately
incompatible emotions, he knows also, as Gyburc does, that
the one can give rise to the other. He allows the full force
of both to be concentrated in Gyburc, who is at the same time
the foremost exponent of love in the work and the single being
who must endure the greatest impact of hatred. It is in this
speech that he shows her most clearly in the full irony of her
position and puts into her mouth the actual expression of
this irony, drawing together those aspects of her role which
he has shown elsewhere, into a last view of her which is at
the same time both tragic and hopeful. Her speech ends with
her grief, as she weeps for the loss of so many noble Christians. Their deaths she sees as the bitterness of her love of
Willehalm:

ey Willalm, rehter punjûr,
daz dir mîn minne ie wart sô sûr!

(310,21-22)

and her words echo Willehalm's own grief-stricken cry during
the first battle:

ey Gyburc, süeze âmîe,
wie tiwer ich dich vergolten hân!

(39,12-13)

Yet one remembers also their antithesis, when Wolfram had
given the assurance that the love of Gyburc was full compensation to Willehalm for his losses:

Gyburc mit kiuscher güete
sô nâhe an sîne brust sich want,
daz im nu gelten wart bekant:
allez daz er ie verlôs,
dâ für er si ze gelte kôs.          (280,2-6)

Again, the tragic duality of the situation is shown clearly.

The impact of her speech is expressed in the reaction of
her brother-in-law, Gybert, who jumps up and embraces her,
but the truest response to her words is not this personal expression of sympathy and affection for a sorrowing human being,

but a wider, impersonal action which nevertheless has its
source in the personal. Though Gyburc is now seen for the
last time,[6] it is her influence which pervades the closing
scene of the work, with Willehalm's gesture towards the
heathens. She has shown herself willing and able to give love
in exchange for hatred, and Willehalm, too, substitutes love
for the hate and lust for revenge which filled him after the
first battle. Between the death of Vivianz and the loss of
Rennewart lies a softening in Willehalm, brought about, Wolfram makes clear, by Gyburc and her capacity for love.[7]

The men go into battle with the words of Gyburc in their
ears and this is one of the means, and there are many of them,
by which Wolfram ensures that the memory of Gyburc and all
she stands for will pervade the remainder of the work, during
which she appears not at all. Gyburc kisses the men as they
depart for battle:

> si wolten fürbaz
> kêren, strîts si luste.
> Gyburc si weinde kuste          (312,28-30)

and the lines contrast the passive grief of the woman with the
desire for activity of the men. The same contrast is maintained as, immediately afterwards, Wolfram shows Gyburc watching at the window, while the army assembles on the field below
(313,6-11). The burden of responsibility rests on Gyburc, and
it is expressed in her physical presence as the men prepare to
fight, but the poet places in God the ultimate power to direct
the action:

> got waldes, sît ers alles phligt.
> der weiz nu wol wer dâ gesigt.   (313,29-30)

Book VI ends, then, with this commendation of events to God,
and the bringing together of Gyburc and her God at this point
sets the tone for the battle in which there is no reason for
further explicit reference to its motivation.

Wolfram approaches the end of Book VIII and the slaughter
which it brings with it with a threefold lament: alas, he says,
that Terramer must come to bring the Christians into such
distress:

> ôwê daz er nu komen sol,
> durch den diu sorclîchiu dol

> und daz angestlîche lîden
> die getouften niht wil mîden!     (399,7-10)

He grieves that the love of ladies and the greater gift of
eternal peace are inflicted on the Christians with thrusts
and blows:

> Owê kristen liute,
> guoter wîbe getriute,
> und ir gruoz unde ir minne,
> und die hœhern gewinne
> (ich mein die ruowe âne ende),
> wirt nu von maneger hende
> ûf iuch gestochen und geslagen!     (400,1-7)

His final cry

> ôwê nu des mordes .....     (401,30)

heralds a general lamentation at the murder on both sides
and is, as Mergell has said, directed towards the events of
Book IX,[8] though it is surely to be seen also as the cry
which accompanies the sight of so much carnage on the arrival
of Terramer and his great force.

The ascending urgency of these three ejaculations is the
prelude, surely, to Wolfram's brief but impressive appeal to
Gyburc at the beginning of Book IX. When human grief can
hardly find expression, he substitutes for his cry of woe an
appeal to the woman who has been seen throughout as the source
of the suffering and to whom he nevertheless gives now the
designation of saint. The relationship between this suffering
and the sanctity he gives to her is thus made clear. The
appeal to Gyburc is perfectly timed, coming as it does half-
way through the battle, when the fortunes of the Christians
are at the turning-point. The appeal is not, however, for
the Christians but to them (403,7ff): this is Wolfram appealing for his own salvation to Gyburc and to those who fought
for her in this battle and thereby gained their own eternal
salvation. These events are in the past, yet the integrity
of the sense of this work is so complete that the relationship
of the brief prayer to its context is clear. Wolfram is
appealing for guidance, just after he has expressed his readiness to allow another to continue his story which must tell
of appalling suffering in battle. The offer is surely not to
be taken seriously, for Wolfram is at the height of his powers

in telling of this great battle, but he knows that he is
approaching a new and more terrible stage of it, and his
appeal to 'Saint' Gyburc is both the generalized plea for
the salvation of his soul and the specific one for aid in
his immediate task.[9]

More important, however, is not the nature of the prayer
at all, but the very fact that, at this vital point, he brings
Gyburc back into the work, not in person, but in a new and
significant form, elevated by that same suffering which is
the substance of his narrative. From his privileged position, then, he sees beyond the time which is the setting of
his work to another time beyond the events of which he is
speaking, when the fulfilment not achieved within the framework of his work is attained in the person of Gyburc and expressed in the sanctity which he now gives to her. The address,
then, is a culmination of the physical appearances of Gyburc.
He has shown her filled with a love which can endure hatred
and even respond to it with love, and he has shown her accepting that love for her husband and for God is accompanied by
suffering, both personally endured and inflicted through her
on countless people. Wolfram's personal elevation of her to
the status of saint needs no further explanation: what makes
her a saint in his eyes is her ability to love and to suffer.[10]

Wolfram has just announced the murder which is to ensue
on the field of Alischanz (401,30ff) and the name of Gyburc
is evoked most appropriately, to bring with it the memory of
Gyburc herself, urging the assembly of Willehalm's troops to
take their revenge for the death of Vivianz, but in doing so
to spare the creatures of God, to be merciful in victory to
those whose only crime is the ignorance of God. Her powerful
speech at that time needs no reiteration now, as the Christians enter the stage of the battle which will bring them to
victory. Gyburc's presence is felt throughout Book IX, because
she is the cause of the fighting, but her spirit pervades it,
in the recollection of her plea for compassion. Wolfram ensures that her presence is felt not, as he did in the first
battle, by his constant references to her, but by means of

this single brilliant reference to her at the beginning of
Book IX. Nor is it just her responsibility which he thus
implies - this alone would not justify the designation
heilic vrouwe - nor his sense of her presence throughout the
battle, but his awareness that, if the end has anything of
optimism about it, then it is due to her. The beginning of
the final Book and the end of it are most perfectly linked,
in the sense of the spiritual presence of the wife and the
physical action of the husband. In his prayer Wolfram speaks
of those who fought for Gyburc and so saved their souls from
the claims of the devil, and one recalls how Gyburc urged
them to preserve themselves for eternal bliss by sparing the
heathen (306,25-28). It is Willehalm who, by sparing Matribleiz, shows deference to her words and points to the reality
of Wolfram's prayer.

c) **Willehalm as an integrating factor**

Willehalm, then, has his role to fulfil in reiterating
the message of Gyburc, not as she has done in words, but in
the final magnanimous gesture towards Matribleiz. Wolfram's
technique is quite different in these two central characters,
and this is inevitably the case. Though Gyburc shows herself
prepared to act and capable of doing so if the need arises,
her role is first and foremost one of supplying, by the assurance of her love and support, the inspiration to the activity
of her husband. Willehalm, in contrast, is the great soldier
and the active leader, and though, like Gyburc, he is capable
of showing another side of his nature, in his love for her or
in the excessive grief at the death of Vivianz and later at
the loss of Rennewart, his is the active, masculine role which
comes into its own above all in the battles. It will be seen
that the battles are themselves an integrating factor, supplying the sense of parallelism and balance which is so much a
part of the work, and Willehalm, as the Christian leader in
both battles, dominates much of the action. Moreover, as
Bumke has shown with effect, his role widens out, as the conflict widens from a personal quarrel between two men into a

war which is both religious and ultimately political.[11]
W. J. Schröder, in his review of Bumke's study, neatly summarizes Willehalm's development: "Ist er anfangs der Minne-
ritter in recht prekärer Lage, so wird er danach zum Fürsten,
der um Landgewinn kämpft, dann zum Führer des Kreuzheeres,
schließlich zum Statthalter des römischen Kaisers und damit
zum Führer der gesamten Christenheit".[12] The relationship
is clear, between the action of the work and its hero.

The structure of the work ensures that Willehalm is involved in the action throughout, though at times he may recede
from the foreground to give way to another character. He is
present in the two battles, of course, the focus of attention
on the ride to Munleun and at the Court itself. He is linked
with the principal events of the work and with its central
characters - Gyburc, Vivianz and Rennewart, the King and Queen
of France, Count Heimrich and his other sons - and so he links
these also with one another. As leader of the Christian army
he is linked with Terramer, as the husband of Gyburc with Tybalt. When he comes face to face with Arofel in battle, it
is as the leader of one army facing the illustrious representative of the other, and when, at the end, he meets Matribleiz,
he does so as the grief-stricken victor of the terrible war.
Even on a relatively superficial level, then, he acts as an
integrating force in the work as a whole, contributing to the
harmony of structure which has already been observed.

It has been seen, too, that Gyburc is important as the
person who harmonizes the thought of the work, but it is to
Willehalm that Wolfram gives the task of expressing her message of love and compassion in tangible terms, for this, surely, is what he does in his conversation with Matribleiz and
his gesture towards the heathen as the work ends. What the
woman has advocated and expressed in her very being, the man
expresses now in actual terms, and though the treatment of the
heathen slain and of Matribleiz is perhaps only a token of
Willehalm's esteem for his fellowmen, it nevertheless reflects
the influence of his wife and his respect for what she has
advocated. Willehalm and Gyburc join in this gesture which

is the true expression of Wolfram's message, and it is appropriate that each plays a different part, in accordance with
what Wolfram sees as the different role of men and women: the
woman inspires and supports her husband in the activity which
is his prerogative.[13]

Clearly, then, the final scene of Wolfram's work shows
Willehalm firmly related to the spiritual thought of the
whole, and thus to Gyburc herself. Physical supremacy and
victory in battle combine with spiritual greatness to produce
this moment of humanity, when Willehalm can transcend his own
suffering and his own needs in order to show his deference to
a higher ideal. This is the moment which Mergell has described as "Das Reifwerden zur höchsten Menschlichkeit"[14] and
which has led other scholars, too, to speak of the 'development' of Willehalm and to draw attention to the contrast
between his behaviour now and his actions, sometimes reprehensible, elsewhere.[15] It is true that one sees here a different
side of Willehalm, yet it seems impossible to deduce from the
text that Wolfram wished to imply an actual development in
his hero. This is, after all, the first occasion which Willehalm has had to show the effect on him of his wife's plea.
Until this time his concern has been to defend the cause to
which he is committed, and no-one, least of all Gyburc herself,
would have expected him to withdraw from the battle: this is
certainly not what she urges in her plea for mercy. Just as
Gyburc accepts her responsibility for the suffering she sees,
so does she accept the necessity for her husband to inflict
suffering, even death, and, in this context, it is the positive duty of Willehalm to act in the defence of their faith.
When he frees Matribleiz and grants burial to the heathen
slain, he does so, not because he undergoes a sudden change
of attitude towards the Saracens, but because the opportunity
has come for him to act in accordance with his wife's appeal.
Though he recalls her specifically when he speaks of her kinship with Matribleiz and with some of the slain kings (461,26-
27; 462,26) and though one may be justified in believing that,
in this time of military victory, he may be thinking of his

wife's plea to the Christians to be merciful in victory,
Wolfram does not suggest that this is a new Willehalm, be-
having in a way hitherto not anticipated. Here Bumke seems
more realistic in his assessment of Willehalm's behaviour as
"weitgehend situationsbedingt".[16]

The Willehalm who speaks with compassion and respect to
Matribleiz is not different from the Willehalm who - under
extreme pressure and in the urgent desire to escape and return
to his wife, and remembering the death of his beloved nephew
whose body he has just left - slew Arofel and divested his
corpse of armour. Yet Willehalm's behaviour towards Arofel
is reprehensible, both in human terms and in terms of chivalry. This is an angry act of revenge upon an opponent who cannot even be held personally responsible for the death of
Vivianz, and Wolfram does not attempt to excuse it. Rather,
by his high praise of Arofel[17] and by emphasizing the fatal
misfortune which befalls him when the straps on his leg armour
snap (78,26ff), does he seem himself to be criticizing the behaviour of his hero, who uses this misfortune, as might be
expected, to defeat his opponent, but, more than that, to slay
him. Werner Schröder speaks of the slaying of Arofel as an
execution[18] an act of deliberate, revengeful murder in which
Willehalm's safety is no longer a decisive factor, for Arofel,
dreadfully wounded as he is, is incapable of doing him harm,
as Arofel himself points out in his plea for mercy (80,27ff).
Even Willehalm's desire for the armour and the horse which
will, and do, allow him to escape, is no genuine motive, since
the powerless Arofel has offered him so much in exchange for
his life and would hardly deny him these things.[19] Willehalm
seems to consider none of this, nor the fact that Arofel is
the uncle of Gyburc,[20] as he raises his sword and slays him,
adding to this terrible deed the further act of pure brutality
when he strikes off the head of the corpse, after he has removed the armour. Far from obscuring the horror of the episode, Wolfram has accentuated it, by separating two actions
which coincided in the source, where Guillaume had slain Aerofles
by decapitating him.[21] This, Wolfram would seem to be saying,

is his hero at his lowest point, pressed by exhaustion and
emotion to perform an action which can thus be explained but
not condoned.[22] Werner Schröder, who previously described
Willehalm's behaviour as "nicht bloß unchristlich, sondern
zugleich unhöfisch und unritterlich",[23] appears, in his most
recent writing on the subject, to have come closer to Bumke's
view that Willehalm's behaviour is "situationsbedingt": "Dem
geschlagenen und gehetzten Feldherrn auf dem Felde von Alischanz fehlte die Muße, darüber nachzudenken; sein Tun und
Lassen wird von seiner verzweifelten Lage diktiert".[24]

The actions themselves remain unchristian and uncourtly,
and the memory of them accompanies Willehalm as long as he
wears the armour of Arofel, carries his shield and rides his
horse. Walter Mersmann, in considering the relationship between those items which Willehalm takes from the corpse of
Arofel and his subsequent behaviour, attributes an interesting symbolic value, particularly to the shield: "Die Tötung
Arofels, gleichsam verkörpert in seinem Schild, lastet auf
Willehalm".[25] It is this symbolic value, according to Mersmann, which explains Willehalm's otherwise puzzling remark
er was ouch mir ze swære (204,4)[26]: the weight of responsibility, of regret even, for the death of Arofel rests on Willehalm. At the monastery, long before Gyburc's exhortation
to mercy, he acknowledges the deed which robbed minne of one
of her finest champions:

> ich hân der minnen hulde
> verloren durch die schulde:
> ob ich minne wolde gern,
> ich mües ir durch den zorn enbern,
> wand ich Aroffel nam den lîp,
> den immer klagent diu werden wîp.
>
> (204,25-30)

In this confession of his guilt towards Love, Willehalm seems
to be expressing regret at the deed, accepting that Love has,
in turn, deprived him of the shield. Clearly, then, the memory
of the deed is burdensome to him, though he is not yet ready
to acknowledge his crime in any profound, or even direct, way.
The active leader, who has still a great battle ahead of him,
cannot yet demonstrate that mercy which will fill him in the

Matribleiz-scene, the <u>unverswigeniu güete</u> (463,10) which so
perfectly expresses the effect of Gyburc's speech.[27] Yet
surely Wolfram is here showing that Willehalm will be sus-
ceptible to those moving words of his wife: the death of
Arofel has not left him untouched. Whether one sees Willehalm's behaviour as 'situationsbedingt' or discerns an actual
development, there can be no doubt that his speech at the
monastery is significant, looking backwards to the slaying of
Arofel yet pointing the way forward to the great peak which
is the Matribleiz-scene. Scholars who see this 'confession'
as no more than a boast on the part of Willehalm seem to be
denying the significance of the scene within the delineation
of the complex hero of the work,[28] but Mergell, rightly it
seems, describes the confession of guilt against love as
"eine wichtige Stufe seiner inneren Entwicklung",[29] while
Mersmann is more specific when he says of Willehalm at the
monastery: "Er erscheint dabei als ein gegenüber der Arofel-
szene Gewandelter".[30]

Mergell, in tracing the development of the hero, describes the Willehalm of the Matribleiz-scene as "ein Anderer,
innerlich G e w a n d e l t e r ",[31] but his behaviour towards Matribleiz is not, in fact, inconsistent with his revenge against Arofel, nor with his fury at the French Court
when, again, his behaviour may be considered reprehensible.
When he behaves so violently towards his sister, who is treating him in a remarkably heartless manner, and later abuses the
King himself for what he sees as his ingratitude and cowardice,
his need is very great and the provocations enormous to a man
already under pressure. And even then, Wolfram shows that this
man is capable of remorse and gentleness, when Alyze exerts
her calming influence on him. This scene, too, like the monastery scene, points the way forward, showing as it does Willehalm's susceptibility to the influence of a woman[32] and
anticipating the power of Gyburc to move him to serenity and
compassion.

The Willehalm who reacts tenderly to the presence of his
niece, or who speaks intimately with his horse, is the same

Willehalm who finds contentment and compensation for all suffering in the love of his wife, but Wolfram knows the complexity of the human mind, and he knows that the same man
must react differently in different circumstances. In Gyburc,
too, he shows a woman who is deeply sensitive yet prepared to
act with ruthless courage if the need is there. These are not
contradictory elements in human behaviour, but an aspect of
the fullness of all human beings, and Wolfram shows the harmonizing of such elements, just as he shows the variety of
all human experience, in which sorrow and joy, love and suffering all have a place.

The mood of conciliation which Wolfram gives to Willehalm at the end reflects his power to create rounded characters, and he shows, here, too, something more of his conception of the nature of the relationship of Gyburc and Willehalm, when he expresses in a unique and moving way his
sense of the harmony of the couple who contribute, each in a
characteristic way, to this gesture of love and compassion.
The scene itself expresses the beginnings of the harmonizing
of conflicting forces which may be seen as Wolfram's ideal
in this work, which, treating as it does so much that is dis-
cordant and destructive, nevertheless attains a quite remarkable harmony of structure and of thought.

d) Vivianz as an integrating factor

Gyburc and Willehalm, then, are the two characters who,
in their own ways, dominate the work from beginning to end,
uniting its separate episodes and contributing to the harmony
of thought. Both are, again in distinctive ways, necessarily
related to the two battles and to Wolfram's use of the two
battles as a simple structural framework, but it is above all
through a third character, Vivianz, that Wolfram links the
battles, isolating him in his death on the battlefield and
raising him to the quality of a symbol of all those who perished in the first battle of Alischanz. From the moment of
his death, Vivianz becomes the representative of his slain
comrades and as such demands revenge, and in order that he

may fulfil this role Wolfram makes of him a figure who is at
the same time unique yet typical of so many Christian soldiers.

In his activity on the battlefield, Vivianz is like many
of his comrades, bold and resolute, young and handsome, spurred on by noble thoughts yet doomed to die: it is in his
death that he becomes unique.[33] Yet the one is dependent
upon the other: it is primarily because he possesses all the
qualities of those who fight and die at Alischanz that Wolfram isolates him by giving him a unique death. From the
moment of his first appearance, in combat with Nöupatris,[34]
Vivianz is an exemplary young soldier, distinguished above
all as the nephew of Willehalm and through him related to
Gyburc (23,1; 23,6-9; 24,13-15; 41,13). Such references to
this relationship anticipate the later grief of all who hear
of the tragedy of the first battle and for whom Vivianz is
both a personal loss and the symbol of more general affliction.

At the first mention of Vivianz, before he appears in
person, Wolfram uses to describe him the adjective which is
to become associated above all with him: the adjective clâr
(13,21). Bumke has spoken of the particular significance of
this word in reference to Vivianz: "klar ist hier nicht ein
beliebiges Schmuckwort, sondern meint den in göttlichem Licht
erstrahlenden Heiligen, ähnlich der Bedeutung, die das Wort
in Veldekes Servatius hat".[35] Although the significance of
the word goes beyond the physical, it nevertheless has its
source in the external appearance of the young man, in whom,
as in Parzival and Rennewart, in Alyze and Gyburc, spiritual
purity is manifested in physical radiance. Like Vivianz,
many of the soldiers, Christians and heathens, are described
as clâr, in recognition, no doubt, of their nobility and handsome features, and their bright garments (6,24; 14,25; 46,1;
55,15; 88,4; 354,26; 381,4; 411,6), but it is Vivianz who is
most consistently characterized with this word, long after its
significance has transcended the physical.[36] Wolfram's use
of the adjective exemplifies his depiction of Vivianz, as a
character who, though his significance depends upon what is

typical in him, transcends the typical and becomes uniquely
representative of many.

This introduction of Vivianz, and the first mention of
him as clâr, is coupled with the first reference to his
approaching death, though as yet without the accompanying
suggestion of martyrdom:

> ouwê daz sîniu jungen jâr
> âne mundes granhâr
> mit tôde nâmen ende!
> von hôher freude ellende
> wart dar under sîn geslehte.          (13,25-29)

Already Wolfram anticipates the role of Vivianz: to die and
to become the object of profound lamentation.

The actual death of Vivianz is unlike the deaths of any
of his comrades. These are passed over relatively quickly,
for there is no time for detailed description of recurrent
scenes of death. Instead Wolfram allows the deaths of many
to be subsumed in the unique scene of the death of Vivianz,
one of the most significant single scenes in the whole work
and one which, as its central function, unites the two battles
and so serves to make of Vivianz another vital integrating
force. In the same way as he uses the adjective clâr to describe both Vivianz and many others who fight at Alischanz,
yet endows it in the case of Vivianz with a deeper, spiritual
significance, so does he describe the fighting of Vivianz and
his mortal wound in terms similar to those used to describe
those of other men, Christians and heathens. There the typical ends, and Wolfram sets the memorable death-scene of
Vivianz in a place apart from the battlefield which has been
the scene of so much death. At the wazzer Larkant there
occurs the miracle of the appearance of the archangel, who has
guided Vivianz there, who protects his soul from the devil
(49,10-11) and promises him that he will not die until he has
seen Willehalm again (49,23-26). It is now that Wolfram
speaks for the first time of the martyrdom of Vivianz:

> Vivîans, der marter dîn
> mag ieslîch rîter manen got,
> swenn er sich selben siht in nôt.
>                              (49,12-14)

The lines anticipate the role of Vivianz as an example to
other knights: already his significance as a great soldier
active on the field of Alischanz is giving way to the significance which he will assume, as the spiritual inspiration
of those who remain, elevated now to the role of martyr and
so, through death, influencing the events to come and the
progress of the whole work. Another miracle accompanies his
death and confirms the saintly quality of the young man, when
a fragrance fills the air at the moment of his death (69,12-
16). The sense of the miraculous, the place set apart from
the action of the battle, the spring and the linden-tree,
the nocturnal vigil of Willehalm by the body of his nephew,
all these things serve to give to Vivianz his unique significance, and the memory of this death pervades the whole
work.[37)]

Repeatedly the memory of Vivianz gives rise to lamentation, even very late in the work, when, after the second
battle, Willehalm recalls the losses of the first:

> ôwê tag, und ander tac!
> Ein tac, dô mir Vivîans
> wart erslagen ûf Alischans
> selbe sibende fürste, und al mîn her,
> wan daz ich selbe  entreit mit wer.
>                                    (459,30-460,4)

The lamentation for Vivianz begins before his death, when
Willehalm finds him mortally wounded and utters a long and
passionate speech, in which he expresses his profound grief
and remorse (60,21-64,30). In contrast, his grief when Vivianz actually dies is expressed with the utmost restraint:

> der marcrâve was mit klage
> ob sîner swester kinde.          (69,18-19)

The lamentation is taken up, however, at intervals throughout the work, by Gyburc (101,27-102,20), by the Queen in
Munleun (164,28-165,27) and again at the site of the monastery (208,9-20), and by Gyburc again in her speech to her
father-in-law (253,24-254,20). Increasingly, too, the need
for revenge comes to the fore, not, of course, in the speeches
of Gyburc, but expressed for the first time by the Queen:

> mînen jâmer den grôzen
> ræch ich, möht ich, schiere.     (165,12-13)

> sint die mit manlîchen sitn,
> daz richet unser ungemach.      (165,26-27)

Bertram takes a little further the theme of revenge when he
speaks of his own readiness for battle:

> ich hân starken lîp und fürsten guot,
> und ze mîme gebot die rîterschaft
> der gêrt sol sîn diu gotes kraft:
> daz mac mich allez niht entsagen,
> ine müeze in mîme herzen tragen
> leit, daz immer twinget
> unz mich mîn bruoder bringet
> an die stat dâ ich râche tuon
> umbe Mîlen mîner swester suon
> und umb den clâren Vivîanz.      (171,4-13)

It is taken up then by Irmschart, when she urges Loys to aid
Willehalm:

> 'hêrre und ouch mîn hœhster suon,
> iwerm kinde ze êren sult irz tuon,
> und durh mîn tohter, iwer wîp,
> daz ir Vivîanzes lîp
> rechet.' sprach frou Irmenschart.
>      (183,11-15)

The echo comes in the declaration by the King:

> al die durh mich in râche sint
> umbe Vivîanzes sterben,
> die lâz ich gein mir werben.      (184,8-10)

Most explicit of all is the statement by Wolfram himself:

> nu wart ûf Alyschanz gebiten
> Vivîanzes râche zîte.      (240,2-3)

In these two lines he unites the two battles through Vivianz,
as he does in the course of the second battle:

> dâ wart gerochen Vivîanz
> mit den swerten sêre.      (418,24-25)

Yet the _idea_ of revenge for Vivianz had emerged very
much earlier, when Willehalm came face to face with Arofel,
and, having wounded him, still refused to grant him the mercy
he craved: the reason given for an action which is brutal and
which Willehalm recalls with something like regret[38] is that
he thinks now of the death of Vivianz:

> er dâhte an Vivîanzes tôt,
> wie der gerochen würde,
> und daz sîn jâmers bürde
> Ein teil gesenftet wære.      (79,28-80,1)

Willehalm's anger in the recollection of the death of his

nephew is increased by Arofel's revelation that he is the
brother of Terramer, and the motive of revenge widens, as
Willehalm declares that Arofel must pay for the grief inflicted on him in the deaths of his dearest kinsmen (80,17-
21).

Already, then, Vivianz has come to represent all the
Christian slain of the first battle, and when Willehalm
comes to Gyburc and tells her that they have cause for lamentation, it is of Vivianz that she thinks first:

wâ ist der clâre Vivîanz ...?          (93,9)

It is his name which heads her list as she enquires after
their kinsmen, and Willehalm, too, epitomizes the extent of
their losses in the brief statement:

in kan dir niht gesagen
von ir ieslîches sunder nôt.
bärlîch Vivîanz ist tôt.          (93,26-28)

In her lament for those slain, Gyburc again singles out
Vivianz (101,27-102,9). When Willehalm is recounting his
losses at the Court of Loys, his speech culminates in the
simple statement:

Myle und Vivîanz sint tôt.          (151,30)

That it is above all the last name which gives rise to the
excess of lamentation which follows is implied by its
repetition soon after in the lines:

von herzen frœlîch lachen
durch Vivîanzen wart verswigen.          (152,8-9)

The name of Vivianz recurs in the grief of the Queen of France
when she hears of the losses at Alischanz (164,28-165,1), and
again she singles him out in her more protracted lament:

mirst ze fruo misselungen
an dem clâren jungen,
den diu küngîn Gyburc mir benam
und in rezôch als ez ir zam.
diu süeze von sîm blicke
noch manegem wîbe dicke
sol füegen klagehafte nôt.
ey wie getorste dich der tôt
Ie gerüeren, Vivîanz,
unt daz er lât mîn herze ganz?
          (167,23-168,2)

The name of Vivianz echoes again and again during the

interval between the battles, and with increasing frequency
during the second battle.[39] Sometimes it is coupled with
the name of Mile,[40] and the notion of revenge is often explicit. Always when the name is used in rhyme, the rhyme is
with Alischanz:[41] Vivianz is emphatically linked, even verbal-
ly, with the battlefield. He has come to stand for all the
Christians slain in the first battle, and as such is seen as
the impetus, through revenge, to the second battle. The
memory of him, and the repeated references to him are powerful factors in uniting the two battles, and, like Willehalm
and Gyburc, in drawing together distinct events in the work.

Bumke suggests that the grief for Vivianz is ultimately
superseded by grief for Rennewart: "... Rennewart, vor dem
schließlich ganz direkt die Klage um Vivianz verstummt".[42]
This is not entirely just: although for a time Willehalm's
lament for Rennewart seems to exceed all other grief (454,4-8),
the memory of Vivianz nevertheless returns and the loss of
Vivianz is not subordinated to that of Rennewart, but set
side-by-side with it:

> ôwê tag, und ander tac!
> Ein tac, dô mir Viviâns
> wart erslagen ûf Alischans ...
> (459,30-460,2)

The second battle has achieved one of its aims, in avenging
the death of Vivianz, and Rennewart, the principal means to
the victory, may justly be placed beside Vivianz for whom he
has achieved revenge. Yet the sorrow of Willehalm remains,
unalleviated by the military victory, and the loss of Rennewart now is the confirmation of the loss of Vivianz.

Indeed, it is possible to see Vivianz and Rennewart as
parallel figures, a further aspect of the structural framework of the work.[43] To do so is not to deny the differences
in Wolfram's depiction of the two young men, for the variety
of his presentation of all his characters is evident also in
his treatment of these two, who, with much in common, are
essentially individualized. It is true, as Lofmark has said,
that Rennewart occupies a much larger portion of the narrative
than Vivianz does,[44] but, in contrast, the role of Vivianz

remains significant for the work as a whole, not least for
the major part of it when he is no longer physically present.
Like Gyburc, though in a different way, and for a different
reason, he dominates the work with his spirit and, like her,
he draws together its events.

e) The relationship between the two battles

It is stating the obvious to say that the two battles
of Alischanz balance one another and form a simple structural
framework for the whole work. As has been said, the first
battle, and the defeat of the Christians epitomized in the
death of Vivianz, demand a second battle in which revenge will
be taken. It has been seen, too, that revenge is bound up
above all with Vivianz and that the very name of Vivianz is
often linked with the name of Alischanz. To the second battle
Wolfram devotes considerably more time than to the first. For,
although both structurally and thematically the second battle
does balance the first, its significance is different. The
battles are two major periods of activity, linked with one
another but distinct in mood and in narrative treatment.

Between the first battle and the second, the motivation
changes: the religious conflict, itself based on the personal
loss by the heathens of their Queen, and by Terramer of his
daughter, widens into a political one, with Terramer's expressed intention of gaining the crown of Rome (339,30-340,11).
Bumke observes: "Die Vernichtung des Christentums und die heid-
nische Weltherrschaft sind Terramers Ziele":[45] these are immense aims indeed, and the second battle is consequently big-
ger in scope, with more men fighting an even fiercer battle.
The memory of the great spiritual appeal by Gyburc pervades
the second battle, too, and though her entreaty that the Christians should spare their heathen opponents for the sake of
their Christian honour and her assertion of their common source
as the creatures of God are not given tangible expression until after the battle in the gesture of Willehalm towards
Matribleiz and the heathen slain, the awareness of Gyburc and
her conception of the precious nature of all human life gives

to the second battle a greater depth and a surer sense of
direction. Where the first battle, for all its brilliance,
was little more than the account of dire conflict between two
noble races of opposing creeds, there is about the second the
profoundly sad realization that, whatever its outcome, it
must be tragic, since through the mouth of Gyburc the message
has been propounded that the destruction of life is not only
wasteful in human terms, as was made clear before, but that
it is above all immoral and transgresses the law of God. Thus,
though the place remains the same, and though Wolfram links
the two battles in many ways, the tone is completely different. The second battle is indeed the counterpart of the
first, but it is also an extension of it, deepening its sense
and introducing new and vital motifs.

Despite their differences, however, Wolfram ensures that
there are reminders in the second battle of the first. The
same names occur: Halzebier, who dealt the mortal blow to
Vivianz, leads one of the heathen divisions in the second
battle; Ehmereiz, with whom Willehalm declined to fight, is
taken captive in the second battle and for a time the narrative lingers on him; men like Josweiz and Poydwiz, who have
been mentioned only briefly in the course of the first battle,
now emerge into full activity. Side-by-side with the name of
Vivianz are the names of others who died in the first battle:
Mile, Tesereiz and Arofel. These three men assume differing
roles in linking the two battles. Mile is frequently coupled
with Vivianz: both young men are nephews of Willehalm (14,21-
22; 23,1), related to the family of Heimrich and mourned by
all (223,24-25; 450,10-11; 454,12-14). Like Vivianz, Mile
becomes significant because the second battle represents the
attempt of the Christians to gain revenge for him.

Another name is linked with that of Vivianz and the
motive of revenge: that of Tesereiz. Wolfram comments specifically of the second battle:

> Thesereiz und Vivîanz
> gerochen wart ze bêder sît.          (334,12-13)

Tesereiz, indeed, occupies on the heathen side the position

of Vivianz on the Christian: he too is mourned by all and
although his name is linked in mourning with those of many
others who perished in the first battle - Pynel, Poufameiz,
Eskelabon (106,22-24), Tenebruns, Arofel, Fausabre, Kalafre
(255,5-13), Nöupatris (337,25), to name just a few whom Wolfram names - it seems to occur most often and most prominently.
Indeed, at one point, Wolfram states that it is the name of
Tesereiz which heads the list of the noble heathen dead
(254,28-29) and he who should be praised above all (347,16-
20). These latter lines occur in the speech by Terramer to
his armies before the second battle, and in this speech he
has recalled the glory of Tesereiz, whose men have lived to
avenge him (346,26-347,13). The name of Tesereiz recalls the
vivid description of the young man who died, quite specifically, in the service of Love:

> daz was Thesereizes her,
> der ie gein schanden was ze wer,
> unt dem diu minne nam den lîp.     (378,13-15)

This reminder of him comes in the middle of the second battle,
but it brings with it the memory of the early references to
him as the knight of Love (36,20-22; 83,6-14; 86,3). When
Tesereiz died, he died as der minnær (88,1), sent there by
Love itself (88,14) and his death is accompanied by a miracle
similar to the one which occurs at the death of Vivianz:

> der clâre kurteise
> möht al den bîen geben ir nar:
> sît si der süeze nement war,
> si möhten, wærns iht wîse,
> in dem lufte nemen ir spîse,
> der von dem lande kumt geflogen,
> dâ Tesereiz für unbetrogen
> sîn rîterlîchez ende nam.     (88,4-11)

The spot is sweetened by the body which lies upon it, and the
whole scene is pervaded by elements of legends of martyrdom:[46]
in the context of the whole work, the significance is increased
by the likeness to the death of Vivianz. The Christian knight
dies in the service of God, brought to the wazzer Larkant by
the archangel and sustained by the Sacrament: he assumes,
then, the role of the Christian martyr who inspires the Christians in the second battle. Tesereiz stands for all the

heathen who, as Wolfram so often tells us, are urged into
battle by Love and die in its service: he is, as Bumke describes him, the 'minne Märtyrer'[47] and as such the counterpart of Vivianz, der junge helt vor gote erkant, like Vivianz linking the two battles and setting the tone of the
fighting, in which revenge will be taken on both sides.[48]
In Tesereiz Wolfram has taken from his source a figure of
little individual significance and, by giving to him, as to
Vivianz, a unique feature, he has deepened the sense of his
purpose for the work and shown, as he does so often in so
many ways, that each side in this terrible conflict has its
own motivation which must be respected.

Arofel, too, is remembered for his allegiance to Love:
when he dies, Wolfram comments

> da erschein der minne ein flüstic tac.
> (81,20)

He, too, is related to Vivianz, though in a different way
from Tesereiz. Willehalm slays him in personal revenge for
his nephew and subsequently speaks of how he deprived Love
of one of her most faithful servants.[49] Terramer, too, in
urging his sons into battle, speaks of the courage and fame
of their dead uncle (345,14-30) and later these men are described as taking revenge for Arofel (374,8-30). Kinship and
allegiance, love and grief, are again shown to link the two
battles, this time through Arofel who is not, like Vivianz
or Tesereiz, the representative of many who have died, but
the highly individualized, colourful knight who dies as a
victim of the necessity of battle and is mourned not least
by the man who killed him.

Other names link the two battles, though less prominently than these. Pinel is mentioned specifically as one for
whom revenge must be taken (337,23-24; 341,12; 362,9), and
one of the additional explicit aims of the second battle is
to release Bertram from captivity (299,2; 301,14-16; 374,4).
The name of Gyburc's son, Ehmereiz, links the two battles,
with Terramer's address to his grandson (342,24-30) recalling
the young man's bold activity in the first battle, when he

had fought so bitterly against the army of the man who had
abducted his mother, even though Willehalm himself refused
to fight with his wife's son, and anticipating the young
prince's brilliance in the coming battle.

More subtly, Wolfram links the two battles, once more
through the memory of Vivianz specifically, but through him
in recollection of the scene of the first battle, when he
shows the second battle moving towards the wazzer Larkant:

> gein der funtâne,
> dâ bî Vivîanz lac tôt,
> des endes sich der strît erbôt.
> nu was diu schar ûz manegem lant
> über daz wazzer Larkant,
> und die karrâschen mit den goten.
>
> (398,22-27)

The memory of that vivid setting ensures the significance of
the moment and provides, too, the confirmation of the relationship between the two battles.

The progress of the second battle is, in the simplest
terms, the reverse of that of the first. Where the first
battle had seen the Christians apparently heading for victory
until a gradual reversal of fortunes brought the heathen to
victory, in the second battle Wolfram shows, in contrast,
the heathen as the dominant force who are nevertheless defeated by their opponents. The outcome of the two battles,
so different in military terms and yet so similar in terms
of personal loss, is expressed by Willehalm himself when,
after the second battle, he speaks of his two experiences:

> ôwê tag, und ander tac!          (459,30)

he laments, not distinguishing between the day of defeat
and the day of victory, for the latter, too, has wrought
defeat in his heart (459,26-27), and as he continues, the
days remain linked in his mind:

> von den beiden ich wol sprechen mac,[50]
> daz mîn vreude ist verzinset dran,
> swaz der mîn herze ie gewan.          (460,12-14)

It is perhaps these lines which, above all, point to the
relationship between the two battles and their joint
significance for the prevailing mood of the whole work.

## 2. The Compression of the Narrative

The harmony of thought of <u>Willehalm</u> is furthered by a
number of aspects of Wolfram's narrative means. The work is
remarkably single-stranded, in thought and in the manner of
its relation, and there is an overriding sense of compression
which can be attributed to distinct features of the narrative.
These may not, of course, be divorced from the features already treated - the internal relationships achieved by means
of the three central characters and the essential balancing
of the two battles - but the concern here is rather with Wolfram's choice in his presentation of events, their ordering and
the relationships among them. Such factors, as will be seen,
strengthen and support the integrity of the thought and give
to the poem as a whole its characteristic sense of unswerving
direction.

In his chapter on <u>Willehalm</u>, Hans-Hugo Steinhoff stresses
one of the essential qualities of the work in a very apt sen-
tence: "Konzentration and Kontinuität bestimmen die Struktur
von Wolframs <u>Willehalm</u>",[1] and, as Steinhoff is well aware,
these qualities go beyond the actual structure of the work and
are a significant aspect of Wolfram's narrative art. Steinhoff's precise concern is with the element of simultaneous
action, and in his perceptive analysis he shows what brilliant
use Wolfram makes of this technique, although he necessarily

restricts his treatment to certain parts of the work, notably
to the battles.

Simultaneous action, then, is one of the features to be
considered in the following section, for it is indeed one of
the dominant means by which Wolfram achieves the narrative
compression so characteristic of the work (a).

Allied to the technique of depicting simultaneous action
is Wolfram's juxtaposition of distinct activities by showing
one character or group of characters viewed at a distance by
another group of characters who are themselves engaged in some
activity (b). This feature of his narrative contributes, also,
to the dramatic quality of the work as a whole.

There are four other distinct means by which Wolfram
achieves the compression of his narrative, in the close relationship among the events he depicts. These are considered
under four headings and deal with his use of interpolated
action (c), his drawing together of events which also contributes to the maintenance of suspense (d), and his use of
recapitulation (e) and anticipation of events (f).

Finally, there is an examination of a further feature
which has a part in the overall compression of the work. This,
however, concerns not so much Wolfram's arrangement of events,
but his attitude to the situation it depicts. In the examination of his treatment of the past (g), it is seen that this,
too, furthers the sense of economy and compression in the
structure of the work. Much of the past he takes for granted,
assuming it to be known to his audience, while other aspects
of the past are revealed during the course of the work, often
as an almost casual item of information contained within matters of present concern.

## a) Simultaneity of action

An early example of simultaneity of events is in the
course of the first battle, when Vivianz has been led by the
archangel to the place where he will die. Wolfram leaves him
there, unconscious, and returns to Willehalm and the battle.
The fighting ends and Willehalm makes his way from the battle-

field. Yet, during this time, the memory of Vivianz and his
plight remains. Assessing the losses of Willehalm, Wolfram
refers to Vivianz:

> wære im niht wan Vivîanz
> ûf dem velde Alischanz
> beliben, er möhte iedoch wol klagen
> (53,11-13)

and we recall the young boy lying helpless, sustained by the
promise that he will see his uncle before he dies. When Willehalm pauses to survey the battlefield, the reference to
Vivianz is implied in the mention of the Larkant (58,11).
Meanwhile, Willehalm makes his way to the Larkant (59,21-22)
and the memory of Vivianz is strengthened when he finds his
shield (59,28-29). The two men, the active leader and the
passive nephew, come together now:

> der marcrâve ersach
> daz ein brunne unde ein linde
> ob sîner swester kinde
> stuont, dâ er Vivîanzen vant.    (60,14-17)

Two separate threads join in this meeting of the two men.[2]

Already, however, Wolfram has made use of the impression
of simultaneous activity, when he described Vivianz lying unconscious on the ground, beneath the horses' hooves (47,24-25).
He thus achieves an awareness of the battle which continues to
rage as the young man recovers and makes his way with difficulty on the wounded horse towards the Larkant. The simultaneous
activity of the battle is implied as the constant background
to the specific events described.

Still earlier in the first battle, Wolfram retards the
narrative by means of a personal intervention and so, again but
by different means, gives the impression of the battle continuing to rage all the while. Yet his actual stress is on the
bright clothing of the heathens:

> sold ich si zimieren
> von rîcher kost, als si riten,
> die mit den getouften striten,
> sô mües ich nennen mangiu lant,
> tiure phelle drûz gesant
> von wîben durh minne
> mit spæhlîchem sinne.    (19,18-24)

Though he seems to be concerned in these lines with the
apparel of the heathens and its source, there is no lessen-
ing in the awareness of a battle continuing throughout: it is
simply that the emphasis has shifted, from the prowess in
fighting of the men to the beauty of their dress.

In the second battle, Wolfram reminds his audience of
the background of general fighting by returning intermittent-
ly to generalized comments (e.g. 408,30-409,6; 409,10-12;
410,4-16). Such examples show how Wolfram sums up the magnitude of events which he cannot relate in full and sustains
the sense of a background of continuous fighting. Indeed,
the second battle depends to a considerable extent on the impression of simultaneous activity. Wolfram thus attains the
sense of enormous numbers and barely controlled confusion
giving way to total chaos.

Wolfram's technique in describing the first half of the
second battle ensures the vivid impression of the action, of
a strictly maintained order of events and, at the same time,
a growing awareness of simultaneous activity. The ten ranks
of Terramer's troops are brought into the action in succession
to one another: the division under Halzebier (362,3ff), that
of Tybalt (364,1ff), Synagun (368,6ff), Gyburc's ten brothers
(372,6ff), Poydjus von Griffane (375,12ff), Aropatin von Gan-
fassasche (381,18ff), Josweiz (388,1ff), Poydwiz von Raabs
(389,20ff), Marlanz (393,26ff), and, finally, Terramer himself (398,20ff). Wolfram's focus of attention at this stage
is on the heathens, who seem to have the upperhand. It is,
at this time, the heathen combatants who dominate the foreground, and there are numerous examples throughout Book VIII
of Wolfram's descriptions of their brilliant clothing, the
force of their combat and their personal qualities (e.g. 365,8-
11; 366,4-13; 368,22-25; 371,17-20; 376,6-18; 378,23-30). In
contrast, as Mergell has demonstrated, the Christians are
seen in fleeting pictures - Augenblicksbilder, as he calls
them -[3] vivid but essentially subordinated to the more dominant picture of the heathen action. Thus, for example, Wolfram shows Gandaluz riding towards Tybalt and fighting bravely

with him (366,16-22), and later Willehalm and Arnalt fighting
together at the head of one division (369,5-11); Bernart von
Brubant and Buov von Kumarzi are described as riding under
one flag (372,19-22) and the account rests for a short time
with this pair of Christians. In general, though, one must
look for references to individual Christians, amid the wealth
of heathens named in the conflict; yet clearly, of course,
the Christians are there all the time, bearing the brunt of
the heathen attack.

By a quite different means, Wolfram indicates simul-
taneous activity on another occasion in the second battle.
Having anticipated the coming battle in the long speech by
Terramer, he conveys the movement of events in a single line:

> Nu wârn ouch die getouften komn.     (351,21)

All the while, we are to understand, then, the Christians
are approaching.

A different use of the impression of simultaneous activity occurs when Willehalm has returned to Orange with his
new forces and with Rennewart. After the meal, when Gyburc
has attended to the needs of her father-in-law, Wolfram turns
to the tender love scene between Willehalm and Gyburc (279,1-
280,12). He concludes the interlude, however, with a return
to Willehalm's men, reminding us that they, too, are at last
restored to peace:

> der marcrâf kurzwîle pflac.
> al sîn her ouch schône lac,
> sô daz si heten guot gemach.     (281,17-19)

There is, moreover, a third activity taking place simultaneously: that of Rennewart:

> wan Rennewarten man noch sach
> mit arbeiten ringen.     (281,20-21)

When, overcome by exhaustion, Rennewart makes his way to the
kitchen, his uncomfortable sleep -

> sîn lindez wanküsselîn
> daz was sîn hertiu stange -     (282,16-17)

proceeds while, as we recall, Willehalm is resting in the
arms of his wife. For both the night comes to an end, and
the two are brought together when someone informs Willehalm

of the singeing of Rennewart's beard and Willehalm asks Gyburc to go to him and console him (289,10-17).

When, in Book VII, Rennewart forgets his pole for the third time, Wolfram's use of simultaneous activity is very important. Rennewart finds his pole at last and Wolfram assures us that, charred though it is, it is tougher than ever before: he tugs it out of the ashes and launches once more into action:

> er zuctes ûzem fiure
> und lief gein âventiure.                    (319,3-4)

In the very next lines, however, Wolfram is back with Willehalm:

> der marcrâf was sô nâhe komn:
> ûf einen berc het er genomn
> sîner helfær vil durch schouwen:
> an halden unde an ouwen
> hiez er stille habn sîn her.    (319,5-9)

So, while Rennewart is returning with his pole to rejoin the army, Willehalm is addressing the men, urging them to consider whether they have courage to face the heathen army set out below them (319,29-320,30). We hear how many of them do indeed decide to return to France and Wolfram tells us:

> si begunden wider trecken.        (321,24)

Yet their way back leads them into the path of Rennewart who is hurtling back into action. Such instances of Wolfram's use of simultaneous action, simple in themselves, contribute to the sense of compression of this work in which no activity is irrelevant and in which there is an outstanding impression of constant movement.

A dramatic use of simultaneous action is Wolfram's treatment of the fire at night in Orange. This is first mentioned, briefly and without comment, at the end of Book IV, when Wolfram has for some time concentrated on Willehâlm and the assembling of the forces. Suddenly we are told:

> die nôt gap im bî naht ein fiur    (214,30)

and the next Book opens with a return to Gyburc and her desperate peril. Yet the reference to the fire is not taken up until the vital conversation between Gyburc and Terramer:

before Terramer withdraws temporarily with his army he insti-
gates a final terrible attack on Orange at nightfall:

> des wart Glorjet in angest brâht,
> ze Oransche der liehte palas.    (223,16-17)

This, then, is the fire which brings suffering to Willehalm:
man and wife are linked by the glow in the sky and on the
sea:

> nu ersach die herzebæren nôt
> der marcrâve under sîme her,
> daz der himel unt daz mer
> beidiu wâren fiuric var.    (223,26-29)[4]

In these powerful lines Wolfram achieves a perspective on
the fire in Orange, which becomes now the symbol of the peril
of Gyburc.  It is towards the fire where, as we have been
told, Gyburc is still defending the inner city with her tiny
army (223,20-21) that Willehalm rides:

> Der marcgrâve gâhte
> ze vorderst, unz er nâhte
> dem fiwer daz im herzenleit
> gap.    (226,1-4)

It is through the smoke of this fire that he sees his beautiful palace still standing (226,8-11).  What Gyburc's men see
through the smoke, however, is an army approaching:

> duo kurn si durch den rouch her abe
> daz kom des marcgrâven her    (226,22-23)

and a third action is taking place simultaneously, the with-
drawal of the heathen force.

   In Gyburc's mind, however, the two are not distinguished:
she believes that this army coming towards them must be her
father's army returning to renew hostilities, and so she puts
her armour on once more.  With the kind of simplicity at
which Wolfram excels in time of great drama, one is made
aware of so much happening at once.  The potential confusion
is resolved, once more with the utmost simplicity:

> wan ir kom genendeclîche
> vil helfe ûz Francrîche,
> de besten rîter die man vant
> in der rehten rîterschefte lant.
> (228,29-229,2)

   When Terramer and his army are preparing for battle,
arming themselves and establishing the strategy to be pursued,

Wolfram allows several brief glimpses of the Christian forces,
assuring us that they, too, are preparing to fight. His
method is not always the same, of course. The spy who returns wounded to Terramer's camp tells of the activity which
he has witnessed on the other side:

".... die Franzoyser rîtent zuo ..." (334,24)

and he expands on these words a little later (336,7-21). The
result is that, though Wolfram lingers now on the preparations and the speeches of the heathens, there is the consciousness of activity on the other side, confirmed when his earlier
words are echoed in the steady progress of the heathens:

> der heiden schar sint nu zwuo.
> Franzoyser riten sanfte zuo:
> Halzebier durh strîten kom gein in.
> dâ wuohs dem jâmer sîn gewin.     (343,27-30)

The single line which speaks of the Christians is inserted
within those which relate to the heathens and so, once again,
the sense of simultaneous activity is reasserted.[5)]

When the battle begins (351,21-23), Wolfram remains with
Terramer, speaking of his grief so sharply contrasted with
the extravagant array which is now brought to him. Terramer
and this period of passivity are linked with the activity
which has continued all the time when Wolfram tells us

> ûf saz der von Tenabrî     (360,19)

and again more emphatically

> Nu lât Terramêren rîten:
> hœret wie die êrsten strîten.     (360,29-30)

Now the Christians and the heathens come together:

> sus samelierte sich der strît.
> die tjostiure ûz fünf scharn
> und der schêtîs kom gevarn,
> und der künec von Tandarnas,
> und swer dâ mit in beiden was,
> an den künec von Falfundê.     (362,2-7)

Steinhoff arrives at a significant conclusion regarding this
part of the battle and draws attention to the skill of Wolfram in handling his material here: "Bei genauem Hinblick
stellt sich also heraus, daß die Kämpfe der ersten neun Scha-
ren mit der Wappnung Terramers und seinem Ritt gleichzeitig
zu denken sind. Wolfram greift, obwohl er die Aufstellung

der beiden Heere streng nacheinander geschehen läßt und sie
sukzessiv schildert, obwohl auch die Massenschlacht selbst
in analysierend-desultorischer Weise zwar in sich gleichzeitig, in ihren Teilen aber nacheinander sich entwickelt,
zweimal zurück, ohne es dem Hörer ganz deutlich zu sagen.
Dadurch erreicht er zweierlei: 1. die Aufstellung der Heere
konnte ohne Unterbrechung berichtet werden und die Massenschlacht dann in der gleichen Reihenfolge ohne Pause an-
laufen - so bleibt der viellinige Bau überschaubar; 2. aus-
serdem aber werden Aufstellung und Schlacht so ineinander-
geschoben, wie es dem realen Verlauf entsprechen mag: jede
einzelne Gruppe der Heiden wird den angreifenden Christen, so-
bald sie aufgestellt ist, entgegengeworfen."[6]

This is a subtle and complicated instance of Wolfram's
use of simultaneous activity. A much simpler means is used
in the second battle, when Willehalm, having emerged from
the confused activity to dominate the narrative for a very
brief period in his fight with Oukin, sinks back into the
general fighting in order to leave the foreground for Rennewart. Wolfram comments:

> innen des ruowte ouch Rennewart     (423,15)

and so turns his attention directly to Rennewart and the
next series of onslaughts.

In the examination of the way in which Wolfram keeps
Gyburc very much within the work when she is physically absent from it, it has been seen that the memory of her is
constantly present, and another significant example of simultaneity of events is the period of separation of Gyburc and
Willehalm. The awareness of two separate strands of activity, the one belonging to Gyburc and the other to Willehalm,
is present already as they agree to part, when Gyburc declares:

> ich belîb in disen pînen
> sô daz ich halde wol ze wer
> Oransch vor der heiden her
> unz an der Franzoysære komn,
> oder daz ich hân den tôt genomn,
> ob noch græzer wære ir maht.     (103,16-21)

It is implicit in the oath of Willehalm that, while he is
away, he will eat only bread and water, in remembrance of her
suffering and privation at home, and again in the simple
lines which speak of their parting:

> alsus in von ir sante
> Gyburc diu künegîn.                    (105,14-15)

Though Book II ends with the sight of Willehalm riding away -

> unverzagt er marcte unde sach
> eine strâze dier rekande,
> gein der Franzoyser lande -           (105,28-30)

Book III opens with the huge heathen army's siege of Orange
(106,1-3) and Wolfram remains with Gyburc and her plight
while he tells of Terramer's grief and of his determination
to punish his daughter. Husband and wife are brought together again, however, when Wolfram speaks of the strength
of the heathen army and the courage of Gyburc's men:

> si heten werlîchen sin,
> die der stet dort inne pflâgen,
> swie zornic de ûzern lâgen.
> Der marcrâve ist durh si komn
> âne schaden.                          (108,28-109,2)

Wolfram, in these lines, has followed Willehalm on his way,
but the narrative is with Gyburc, for, although in thought
one travels with the Margrave, Wolfram ensures, by using the
motif of the exchange of hearts, that the action can remain
in Orange (109,6-16).[7] When, a little later, Wolfram wishes
to turn to Willehalm and his activity, he can do so by a
somewhat similar means:

> der marcgrâf sorgen rîche,
> swie balde er von Gyburge streich,
> sîn gedanc ir nie gesweich:
> der was ir zOransche bî.             (111,26-29)

The events in Orange are vivid in our minds, as in the mind
of the man who can only imagine their actual course, and Wolfram's realistic description of Gyburc's defence of Orange and
the terrible affliction by her father ensures that we are fully conscious of these events in Orange while Wolfram turns to
Willehalm. Moreover, a single line serves to suggest that,
though we leave Orange for a time, events there do indeed
continue and will be taken up later. Wolfram is speaking of

the conversation between Terramer and Gyburc and he says:

> diu rede ergienc bî einer naht
> und wart sît anders volbrâht.    (110,9-10)

It is some time before the promised resumption of the conversation at the beginning of Book V. Meanwhile the memory
of Gyburc serves to imply the vague activity at Orange which
Wolfram has suppressed in favour of the more significant
events at Munleun. What exactly she has been doing must be
imagined and is only briefly implied in Wolfram's opening
words:

> Ez næht nu vreude unde klage
> und dem helflîchem tage
> und der kümfteclîchen zîte,
> und daz der sorclîchen bîte
> mit freude ein ende wart gegebn,
> dâ Gyburc inne muoste lebn,
> diu selbe dicke wâpen truoc.    (215,1-7)

Steinhoff comments in relation to this period: "In Oransche
herrscht, solange Willehalm abwesend ist, Zeitlosigkeit, wie
sie der überzeitlichen geistigen Auseinandersetzung entspricht,
und für Willehalm geht die reale Zeit weiter, in der sehr
reale Dinge geschehen."[8] Bumke observes rather similarly:
"Die exakte Zeitrechnung des abreitenden Willehalm löst sich
von dem zurückbleibenden Geschehen um Orange, wo die Zeit in
ein unbestimmtes Dämmerlicht zerfließt."[9] Despite this lack
of precision in terms of time, the sense of simultaneity remains as a vivid element in the narrative.

b) _The viewing of events from a distance_

An aspect of Wolfram's use of simultaneous activity demands close consideration as an important means by which
Wolfram furthers the total sense of compression and economy
of the narrative. This is the technique of showing one group
of characters engaged in one activity, watching the actions
of another group and sometimes commenting on them. Steinhoff
describes this technique as _Fensterschau_ and notes that it is
akin to that of teichoscopia in drama: he goes on, however,
to reject the idea implied that the effect is a dramatic
one.[10] In fact, however, as the following examples will

show, this technique, apart from performing the function of
drawing together events into a vivid, compressed whole, contributes markedly to the dramatic qualities of a work which
is in so many respects dramatic in its impact.

A simple example occurs when Willehalm surveys the
immense forces of Terramer below him on the plain of Alischanz:

> zwischen dem gebirge und dem mer
> bî Larkant lac Terramêr,
> der kreftige von arde hêr
> und von sîner hôhen rîcheit:
> ûf Alischanz dem velde breit
> sîne kraft man mohte erkennen.
> solt ichs iu alle nennen,
> die mit grôzem here dâ lâgen
> und sunder ringe phlâgen,
> liute und lant mit namen zil,
> sô het ich arbeite vil.
> so beherberget was daz velt:
> niht wan mer und gezelt
> sâhen die des nâmen war.          (319,10-23)

A little later he watches the 'army' of Rennewart:

> der marcrâf sah die wârheit:
> Rennwartes her dem velde breit
> gap manegen stoup von storje grôz.
> er sah vil swerte blicken blôz,
> und manegen gezimierten helm
> sah er glesten durch den melm,
> manc banier, wol gemâltiu sper
> sah er gein im füeren her,
> dâ bî manc scharfe lanze.          (330,11-19)

These are brief pictures which supply a perspective on the
events and emphasize the sense of simultaneity. Though the
potentials of a dramatic situation are there, in the awareness of movement and of relationship between the watched and
the watcher in each case, there are more obviously dramatic
instances of Wolfram's use of a similar technique.

On an important occasion, Gyburc's men see Willehalm and
his army approaching through the smoke (226,22-23), and Willehalm himself has glimpsed his palace through the smoke
(226,8-11). The moment of reunion is approaching but as yet
the smoke divides husband and wife: it nevertheless constitutes a definite, almost geographical, feature in the movement towards reunion. A little later Wolfram places Gyburc

and Willehalm in a position of advantage, at the windows of
the palace, watching for the approach of reinforcements. This
is not a new technique in Wolfram: Belakane had sat in the
window with her ladies watching the combat between Gahmuret
and Hiuteger (Parzival, 37,10-11) and acclaimed Gahmuret for
his bravery (Parzival, 38,14-15); Herzeloyde, too, had watched the tournament from the window (Parzival, 61,3-5) and
presumably saw Gahmuret approaching; Ginover and her knights
and ladies are at the windows to witness the arrival of Parzival at the Court, and the ill-treatment of Cunneware by Kei
(151,7-10); with the aid of the magic pillar, Gawan sees
Orgeluse approaching Schastel Merveil. These are interesting
examples of Wolfram's linking of two events, or two groups of
people, and of suggesting, in the case of Belakane, for
example, the involvement of the one with the other. Yet none
of them has the sense of sustained drama which attaches to
the present example in Willehalm, as Gyburc watches the
assembly of the separate forces. She sees first the army of
Buov von Kumarzi (234,30-235,2), then that of Bernart:

> unlange daz dô werte,
> unz si von manegem swerte
> und von den schilden blicke
> durh grôzen stoup sah dicke.      (236,11-14)

In both cases what she actually sees is the dust thrown up by
the hooves of so many horses, and it is Willehalm who is able
to identify his brothers. When Heimrich arrives with his men,
Gyburc herself recognizes her father-in-law (238,5), but before that Wolfram has described at some length the approach
of the old Count and his men:

> Willehalmes her sich breite.
> gewâpent dar zuo leite
> mange storje strîteclîche
> Heimrîch der rîche,
> von Narbôn der alte,
> der ie sîn dinc sô stalte
> daz sîn habe was gemeine.
> er kom ouch dâ niht eine.
> sich muosen stûden neigen,
> dô der begunde zeigen
> wie rehte strîteclîch er reit
> mit verdrungener schare breit.      (237,15-26)

This is a vivid picture, made the more impressive by the
knowledge that two people are watching from the windows high
above and that these new forces are added now to those already amassed below. The awareness of Gyburc and Willehalm
watching is heightened by their brief conversation (238,6-
10), before the arrival of three more divisions, headed by
Bertram, Gybert and Arnalt, and strategically spaced in order
that each can come to the aid of the other in case of need
(238,23-30). Again there is the awareness of Gyburc surveying the vast assembly, summed up this time in the simple
statement:

Gyburc nam ir aller war.　　　　　　(239,1)

What she sees is described fully; the preparations of the
knights, eager for battle, and the arrival of the last division under the command of Schilbert von Tandarnas and Heimrich der Schetis, then the meeting between the latter and his
old father, Count Heimrich (242,7-15). All this Gyburc wit-
nesses, and we are reminded of the perspective which she has
on the proceedings below:

> dort oben sprach de künegîn
> 'wes ist diu sunderstorje grôz?
> ir schiltriemen sind nacket blôz
> und unverdecket von den breten:
> si sint ze strîte etswâ gebeten.' (242,16-20)

Even Willehalm is at a loss to identify his brother at this
distance (242,21-30), but Wolfram's concern for the moment
moves away from the soldiers below, to the couple watching
them:

> diu künegîn in dem venster lac,
> diu der geselleschefte phlac:
> des marcgrâven umbevanc
> an sîne brust si dicke twanc. (243,17-20)

The military activity continues, but briefly Wolfram turns
back to the intimate scene and ends the period of watching
from the window:

> der marcrâve ûzen venstern trat. (244,4)

This long and visually impressive period gives way to a new
kind of activity, as Willehalm goes to greet his father, but
the whole double scene is an outstanding example of Wolfram's

use of this technique which he uses less prominently but
equally effectively on other occasions.

At Munleun Wolfram uses the same vivid technique of the
picture in the framework of the window:

>Eins âbnds der künic komen was
>zen vensteren ûfem palas,
>und diu künegîn und sîn tohter.
>al die wîle enmohter
>niht bezzer kurzwîle sehen:
>des muose der margrâve jehen,
>der dâ bî Alyzen saz. (187,1-7)

The picture comes to life:

>sich huop ie baz unde baz
>zwischen dem palase und der linden
>daz man sah von edelen kinden
>mit scheftn ûf schilde tjostieren,
>dort sich zweien, hie sich vieren,
>hie mit poynder rîten,
>dort mit pûschen strîten (187,8-14)

and from the picture there emerges Rennewart:

>dô nam der marcgrâve war
>Daz ein knappe kom gegangen:
>der wart mit spotte enphangen:
>der truoc ein zuber wazzers vol. (187,30-188,3)

Wolfram's description of the activity of the pages gives way
now to the passive description of the boy, at this, his first
appearance, and this in turn is followed by the account of
his ill-treatment by the other pages and his final response
to it. Only now does Wolfram return to the onlookers, and in
the lines which follow we are made aware once more of the
group at the window:

>der marcrâve zem künege sprach
>'sâht ir, hêrre, waz geschach
>ûf dem hof an dem sarjant
>der treit daz küchenvar gewant?'
>der künic sprach 'ich hânz gesehen ...' (190,21-25)

An impressive example of this technique of showing the
watchers at the window occurs at the end of Book VI, as Gyburc watches the Christian army depart for Alischanz:

>Gyburc diu kom schiere
>in diu venster durch schouwen
>mit maneger juncvrouwen,
>wie mit fürstenlîcher krefte

> maneger geselleschefte
> daz velt wart überdecket.
> allenthalben zuo getrecket
> ûf die strâzen gein dem mer
> kom ein sô kreftigez her,
> daz ez die engel möhten sehen,
> kunden si zimierde spehen.
> si heten an den stunden
> ûf die helme gebunden
> manec tiwer zimierde clâr.
> ouch sah man her unde dar
> daz velt al überglesten
> mit phellen den besten
> an den hôh gemuoten werden.
> ûf al kristenlîcher erden
> wart manlîcher zuo komn
> von wirtes friwenden nie vernomn. (313,6-27)

Perhaps what Wolfram achieves above all by this description
is perspective on this great force, seen as it is by Gyburc
and her ladies from the vantage-point of the window. The
converging of many separate divisions can be seen distinctly
from this distance, and the magnificence and colour of the
whole scene are apparent in this impressive mass in a way
which, in the crush of battle, will not be possible again.
Moreover, as on other occasions, the significance of the
scene is increased by the awareness of the involvement of
the onlooker with the scene below: this is Gyburc, who has so
recently delivered her magnificent speech to the men about to
enter the battle, watching them depart into that battle which,
as she hopes, will demonstrate the ideals of Christian mercy
which she has advocated. Thus, in the final words of this
Book, Wolfram links the watching woman with the God whom she
and the army serve:

> got waldes, sît ers alles phligt.
> der weiz nu wol wer dâ gesigt. (313,29-30)

The technique of 'watching from the window' succeeds here,
not just as a physical device, but in linking the watcher and
the watched, and all of them with the Almighty, who alone
knows what the outcome will be.

A few moments early in the work are significant in other
respects[11] and also have a place in this context. It is not
from a window that Willehalm surveys the field of Alischanz

from which he has just escaped, but, as it seems, from a
distant hill:

> Er enthielt dem orse und sach hin wider,
> dez lant ûf unde nider. (58,1-2)

Again, then, Wolfram gains perspective, this time on the
battlefield and on the vast numbers of the enemy:

> nu was bedecket berg unt tal
> und Alyschanz über al
> mit heidenschefte ungezalt,
> als ob ûf einen grôzen walt
> niht wan banier blüeten. (58,3-7)

As in the case previously discussed, the impression is a
vivid one, of immense numbers and bright colours, and, as
before, the technique is increased in effect by the awareness
of the essential relationship between the person watching and
the scene watched.


c) Interpolated action

The compression of the work is occasionally also furthered by Wolfram's use of interpolated action. A slight example
occurs at Munleun, when the Queen has fled to her room from
the wrath of Willehalm (147,28-148,2). In the great hall the
scene continues, with the indignant anger of the King and the
embarrassment and fear of those who have witnessed the events
(148,3-17). Then Wolfram returns to the room, with the brief
conversation between Alyze and her mother (148,19-28). The
words of Alyze are important as a reaction to the behaviour
of the Queen, only part of which she has witnessed, while
those of her mother anticipate the reconciliation to be effected by the young girl. Outside, events continue, unbroken
by this private interchange between the two women:

> der fürste ûz Narbôn dô gienc
> alrêrst da er sînen sun enpfienc
> (148,29-30)

and they are broken only by the arrival of Alyze herself
(154,1-2). This entry of the young princess is treated in
another connection,[12] but it is relevant to notice here the
link which Wolfram has forged between her principal appearance as the reconciler of her mother and her uncle and the

hasty plea, uttered by her mother, that Alyze should seek his favour on her behalf. After the central scene of Alyze's appearance in the great hall and her conversation with her uncle, Wolfram again returns to the kemenâte:

> Alîze was nu wider komn, ...          (163,11)

Only when the Queen is sure that Willehalm is not there himself to attack her again does she let her daughter into her room, with Scherins and Buov:

> Si liez die maget wol gevar
> dar în                              (164,1-2)

and when they have informed her of the losses of the first battle, told already to the assembly in the great hall by Willehalm, she herself elects to rejoin the others:

> si gienc her ûz, dâ gein ir sprach
> der marcrâve Willalm.               (165,28-29)

This is a subtle series of changes of place, linking the private room and the great hall, intensifying the role of Alyze as intermediary, honouring Wolfram's source in the depiction of the angry scene between Willehalm and his sister, yet preparing the way for the speech of the Queen, Wolfram's own addition, and her approach on Willehalm's behalf for aid from her husband.

Less subtle but dramatically more effective is the scene of the Christian soldier who catches sight of a heathen spy and the skirmish which ensues. This brief interpolation is a remarkable example, too, of Wolfram's use of detail. For a few lines, the narrative rests with the bold soldier who slips away from Willehalm's camp and encounters the spy from Terramer's army. Little is said of him, but much is implied: he has stolen out durch sînen prîs (333,13) and later he is to be acclaimed for his courage (333,15). Indeed, though Wolfram does not linger on the combat between them, he tells us that it brought fame to both men (333,20-22). He cannot resist a few details of this isolated encounter, watched by no-one and unconnected with the main events of the second battle (333,23-334,2). The tiny scene is an interesting example of Wolfram's use of every opportunity to fill this work with contrasting details, often by interpolating actions or by switching sharply from one scene to another.

The scene when the great King Terramer receives gifts of equipment is interpolated within the military preparations for battle. This description is immediately preceded by two groups of lines which speak equally of both sides of the conflict:

> die tjostiur ze bêder sît
> mit einem buhurt huoben strît,
> Franzoys und Sarrazîne          (351,25-27)

and

> Jêsus hab die sîne:
> d'andern ûz al der heiden lant,
> der müeze pflegen Tervigant.     (351,28-30)

The impact of these first lines is considerable, despite their brevity, and Wolfram can suspend description of the action in order to interpolate the moving picture of the tragic Terramer receiving the exotic gifts. The scene is relevant to the battle, where he will himself become involved in the fighting and even engage in combat with the leader of the opposing force. Wolfram builds up gradually, however, to the battle which, though its outcome is obscured to human minds at present, will bring such humiliating defeat to the man now so elaborately attired, and the culmination of the process comes with Terramer's command that one thousand drums be sounded and eight thousand trumpets blown. The sounds signify the entry of the heathen King into battle, and Wolfram inserts his information that the trumpet was invented in heathendom (360,10-12). The immense sound is as extravagant as the attire of the King and his horse, and all of them are linked with heathen origins:

> dô zoch man Brahâne dar.
> unz ûf den huof daz ors vil gar
> gewâpent was mit kovertiur:
> ein phellel glestende als ein fiur,
> mit kost geworht in Suntîn,
> der lag ûf der îserîn.          (360,13-18)

Yet the external glamour is marred by Wolfram's ominous comment:

> swen die gote dâ betrugen,
> die drûf wârn gemachet,
> des geloube was verswachet.     (360,26-28)

The defeat of Terramer and the consequent shame of the heathen
army are anticipated in this brief comment, but the action
must continue:

> Nu lât Terramêren rîten:
> hœret wie die êrsten strîten.     (360,29-30)

Wolfram's attention has returned now equally to both sides
of the conflict. This interpolation, which contains so much
significance for the conception of the tragic heathen King,[13]
gives way now to the activity of battle which was interrupted.

d) <u>The drawing together of events and the maintenance of
suspense</u>

On a number of occasions Wolfram deliberately bridges
time and place in order to draw together distinct events, to
remind us sometimes of a relationship or perhaps to draw attention to an echo within his narrative. Like the techniques
of recapitulation and anticipation, this aspect of his story-
telling has the effect of furthering the overall impression
of concentration.

A simple example of the technique occurs in the second
battle. Halzebier's men, seeing Rennewart slay five kings
in revenge for Milon von Nivers, flee towards the sea. Wolfram observes:

> ir hêrren Halzebier man giht
> daz er des tages mit sîner schar
> alrêrst der vînde næme war,
> daz er des sturmes begunde     (414,10-13)

and draws together the beginning of the battle and the beginning of its end with this reminder that it was Halzebier
who opened the fighting. The effect is, however, not only
to imply the structure of events but to ensure also that no
blame attaches to the army of Halzebier who achieved such
success in the early stages of the battle.

The man who slew Vivianz cannot be forgotten in general
confusion and so Halzebier emerges for the last time, again
with the reminder that it was he who opened the fighting that
morning (418,28-419,1). Magnanimous as always, Wolfram has
no wish to deprive of credit this man who has been the cause

of the death of so many Christians and even of Vivianz. At
his death, he comments

> sus starp der schanden blôze
> ân alle missewende                                    (419,20-21)

and the formulation recalls his earlier account of the men
of Halzebier fleeing to their ships yet fighting all the
while (414,14-16).

I began by describing this as a simple example of Wolfram's technique of drawing together separate events, yet it
has been seen that there are complex ramifications. Twice we
are reminded of the beginning of the battle now that it is
approaching its end. Each time Wolfram recalls the fame of
Halzebier whose men are now forced to flee and who himself
now perishes. Beyond this, however, he relates the two happenings: as Halzebier's men flee, they are pursued by Rennewart and his men, uttering the cry of _Monschoy_! It is this
cry which reaches Bertram and his seven companions who lie
captive in one of the heathen ships and who are then rescued
by Rennewart, and it is in conflict with these eight princes
that Halzebier dies. The man who slew Vivianz dies in combat, not with Rennewart, in many ways the counterpart in the
second battle of Vivianz, but, fittingly, overwhelmed by
eight knights who owe their freedom to Rennewart.[14] It is
no coincidence, either, that we recall Wolfram's early assertion that Halzebier has the strength of _six_ men (46,4): only
eight can prove too much for him.

The death of Oukin brings with it the reminder of his
son Poydwiz, whose death was relatively briefly described
in the series of three to which it belonged (412,10-25). Now
it is brought vividly to mind in the lamentation of the old
father, before he too dies, at the hand of Willehalm (420,27-
422,25). Much is achieved here: Wolfram reminds us of an
earlier event, retelling it now in quite a different way,
through the poignant account in the mouth of the bereaved
old father, and so giving to it a new perspective and thereby varying his narrative texture. More than that, though,
the scene reiterates a basic awareness in Wolfram's work:

that in these two battles he is concerned, in the last resort, with the individual human being and, as here, with
the human relationships which are at stake.

In a completely different way, Wolfram employs the
technique of 'echoing' himself, when he frames the first
battle with two similar pictures of Willehalm. Before the
battle Willehalm contemplates the formidable enemy with its
magnificent tents and banners stretched out before him (16,2-
19). His stress is on the size, as well as on the gorgeous
colours and lavish materials, but at the end of the battle
Willehalm stands alone and defeated and again gazes back,
this time to realize above all the huge proportions of the
heathen army (58,1-13). The balance of the two pictures is
surely no chance: Wolfram draws together the beginning and
the end of the battle by means of the two common factors,
the great Christian leader and the mass of his heathen foe.

Similarly, but more succinctly, there is a coming-
together of events in two brief lines when Wolfram observes:
Des ze Munlêûn was ê gesworn,
daz was hie ze Orlens niht verlorn. (212,1-2)
Munleun represents many things, it has been the background of
vivid events which have been related in detail, full of people
and contrasting moods, but specifically it represents here
the promise of aid which can be fulfilled in Orleans.

At other times this technique of linking events contributes to a process of crescendo, building up towards a particular climax. When Wolfram has Willehalm assure his men that
those who fight in the coming battle will be fighting for God
(320,1-3) and entrusts their decision to the guidance of God
(320,10-12), he is preparing the way for the Pitît Punt episode, where he tells how those who are struck by Rennewart
believe that God Himself is punishing them for their flight
from His service (325,1-4). Indeed, it was Rennewart himself who first touched on the idea, when he wondered if perhaps God were testing him, when he mysteriously forgot his
pole for the first time:

> waz ob mich versuochen wil
> der aller wunder hât gewalt,
> und ob mîn manheit sî balt?        (317,28-30)

When, at Pitît Punt, the deserters come upon the idea that
it is the hand of God which is striking them down, the link
with Rennewart's weapon remains in the lines:

> swaz er ir mohte erlangen
> mit sîner grôzen stangen,
> der wart vil wênc von im gespart.
>                                    (324,27-29)

The significance of the thought is maintained by the fact
that Wolfram has Rennewart forget his pole on **three** occasions,
while Willehalm himself recalls in his speech a little later
that St. Peter was tested **three** times (332,12-14). The relationship among the separate occasions and the gradual
building-up of an idea receive a new expression in Willehalm's
lament, when he couples with his recognition of the aid of
Rennewart in the victory his awareness of the role of God:

> er sprach 'in hân noch niht vernumn
> war mîn zeswiu hant sî kumn.
> ich mein in der ze bêder sît
> den prîs behielt, dô diu zît
> kom und der urteillîche tac,
> daz ich von im des siges pflac,
> und von der hœhsten hende.        (452,19-25)

In general, in his telling of the story of Rennewart,
Wolfram links events in a way which both contributes to the
compression of the whole work and builds up the suspense which
is so much a feature of this story. When the young man takes
his leave of the princess as she sits on the grass beneath
the tree (213,9-25), Wolfram refrains from an explanation of
the nature of the kiss which they exchange: only later does
what might seem a formal parting emerge as a leave-taking
between two young lovers who have no idea whether they will
meet again.[15] It is considerably later that the kiss is
given a more precise significance in Wolfram's explicit statement of the inspiration of Rennewart in battle which he enters
in order to avenge the suffering which he has endured before
her:

> sus rach er smæhlîchez leit
> des er vor Alyzen pflac:

> ir minne an prîse im gap bejac.
> sîn dinc sol immer sus niht varn:
> Alyzen minne in sol bewarn.
> swaz man ie smæhe an im gesach,
> Alyzen minn die von im brach
> dar nâch in kurzen zîten
> in tôtlîchen strîten. (285,14-22)

Thus, when Rennewart recalls the kiss and fears that it will
be brought to shame if his return to fetch the pole is con-
strued as cowardice (318,12-17), the full significance of
that kiss is known. When Rennewart speaks to Willehalm of
a reward which he might ask if he achieved victory in the
coming battle (331,13-18), the mysterious words are full of
meaning, and, later, in the crush of battle, the reminder
comes unambiguously of the relationship between the young
couple:

> in den strît gap in geleite
> ir niftl Alîzen soldier. (418,14-15)

Thus, in retrospect, Wolfram gives to the brief parting its
true significance: beneath the controlled formality of the
meeting and the apparent ambiguity of the kiss is all the
passion of a parting between two people who may never meet
again and whose relationship in any case seems hardly capable
of fulfilment. His narrative technique here, the deliberate
withholding of information, and, even more, the incomplete
explanation which he offers, contributes to the manner of his
telling of the story of Rennewart, in which mystery and
suspense have an important function.

Similarly, and most significantly of all, Wolfram uses
the technique of suspense to tell the story of Rennewart's
origin. Here, too, his effect, a gradual building-up by
means of innuendo and often of irony, is achieved by his
linking of separate parts of his narrative. It is a story
which is told in different ways, by different people and to
different people, for Rennewart is seen in varying situ-
ations, in conversation with several people, for example, and
reacting differently to each. Yet this does not mean that
there is anything diffuse about Wolfram's account, for the
continuity is ensured by means of parallels and certain

recurrent motifs.

At the Court of Loys, Willehalm observes Rennewart and
notes the immense strength of the boy, his poor clothing and
the traces of his kitchen work in his hair. Although Wolfram himself speaks of the innate qualities of Rennewart,
these, he makes clear, are concealed:

> verdacter tugent in nœte
> Pflac Rennewart der küchenvar.
>
> (188,30-189,1)

The hints which Wolfram himself has already given, through
the images of the gold-piece which falls into the dust, the
jacinth which is thrown into soot and the eagle which flies
from its nest, receive some clarification in the King's
rather bald explanation of how the boy came to be at his
court (190,28-191,18). The explanation is decidedly one-
sided, based on Rennewart's refusal to be baptized and the
consequent ill-treatment which he has received and of which
Loys seems in no way ashamed. The compassion which is absent
in Loys's words comes with the simple, spontaneous request
from Willehalm that he should give the boy into his care:

> 'waz ob ich, hêrre, im sîn lebn
> baz berihte, op ich mac?' (191,22-23)

Some kind of intuition seems to prompt Willehalm's idea that
the boy can, by different treatment perhaps, be guided aright,
and the pleas of Alyze, inspired by love, as we know only by
hindsight, persuade her father to do what he at first refuses
to do. When Rennewart is brought before Willehalm, new
aspects of his physical appearance and his demeanour are mentioned. The fact that he has as yet no beard not only reflects his youth but anticipates the bitter incident when his
newly acquired beard will be cruelly singed by the cook. The
wretched clothing is mentioned again, but this time coupled
with the sense of shame of the boy, who nevertheless has a
natural knowledge of courtly behaviour (192,1-5). Already,
then, Wolfram is building up his picture by means of hints
and incomplete comments.

The conversation with Willehalm is the first in the
series which Wolfram gives to Rennewart and a Christian. The

stubbornness of Rennewart in refusing to respond to the
kindness of Willehalm is accentuated by Wolfram's own comments which punctuate the opening of the encounter:

> dô der marcgrâve in prîsûn
> gevangen lac dâ ze Arâbî,
> Caldeis and Côatî
> lernt er dâ ze sprechen.
> done wold ouch niht zebrechen
> der knappe sîniu lantwort:
> Franzoyser sprâche kund er hort.
> do der marcgrâve in komen sach,
> en franzoys er im zuo sprach
> mit der jungen künegîn urloup.
> do gebârter als er wære toup
> unt als ers niht verstüende:
> er het ouch guote küende,
> swaz iemen sprach, man oder maget:
> der gegenrede wart niht gesaget
> von sînem edelem munde.          (192,6-21)

More is implied here, however, than the personalities of the
two men, for by this brief and factual reference to the captivity of Willehalm, made as it seems simply to explain his
knowledge of the heathen tongues, Wolfram reminds us of Gyburc,
whom Willehalm met while he was imprisoned, and with the reminder comes, obscured as yet, the beginnings of the hints of
the relationship between Rennewart and Gyburc. Wolfram's art
is subtle, however, and now is not the time to stress this
point: instead he goes on to the conversation between Willehalm and Rennewart who is prepared to reply to Willehalm's
questions when they are put in his own heathen languages. In
his first answer, in fact, Rennewart gives his own account
of his origin which balances that given to Willehalm by Loys
(193,1-22). This is Rennewart's side of the same situation
as Loys has related: his refusal to be baptised is given here
a somewhat different reason, for the implication is that
Rennewart has been holding on to his faith in Mahomet until
he has at last begun to doubt his power to aid him and has
turned instead to Christ, though resisting still, out of
obstinacy perhaps, and perhaps the remnants of piety to his
former faith, the baptism which would have made his life at
the Court so much more pleasant. The last lines contain
the first specific reference to his birth, yet even this is

vague, prompting a question which passes unasked:

> nu ist mir der touf niht geslaht:
> des hân ich tac unde naht
> gelebet wol dem ungelîche,
> op mîn vater ie wart rîche.     (193,19-22)

Instead, Rennewart concludes his speech with another poignant
touch, which again raises a matter which is not expanded
here:

> sol iemmer wert âmîe
> mînen lîp umbevâhen,
> daz mac ir wol versmâhen:
> wan ich bin wirden niht gewent,
> unt hân mich doch dar nâch gesent.
>                                  (193,26-30)

The role of Alyze in supporting Willehalm's request for Rennewart has not yet hinted at a closer relationship between them:
these lines remain, then, like much of the story, unexplained,
to further the suspense of the whole.

Meanwhile the conversation turns to the newly formed
relationship between Rennewart and Willehalm and anticipates
the role of Rennewart in the coming battle as he pledges his
allegiance:

> sol ich in iwerm gebote sîn,
> ir muget an mir behalten prîs.
> hêr, sît irz der markîs,
> der daz geflôrierte her
> von den komenden über mer
> hât verloren in strîte,
> sô bin ich iu bezîte
> in iwer helfe alhie gegebn:
> die wil ich rechen, sol ich lebn.
> ziwerm râte wil ich phlihten.     (194,10-19)

Rennewart's position between two faiths, expressed in his
rejection of the heathen gods and his refusal to accept baptism, in no way prevents his positive commitment to the
Christian side in the conflict. Already a motivation enters
into his declaration of allegiance which will dominate the
future activity of Rennewart - that of revenge.

This first encounter between Rennewart and Willehalm
is important in establishing the bond between them and
securing the aid of Rennewart which will be so vital for the
Christians in the second battle. At the end of it, Wolfram
reminds us that they are speaking in a foreign tongue (195,1-3).

The element of mystery which is so much a part of the story
of Rennewart is preserved even in this purely external way.

Other events intervene, including Rennewart's parting
from Alyze, and the continuity of Wolfram's revelation of
the history of Rennewart is taken up much later, this time
in relation to Gyburc. The parallel with the earlier occurrence when Willehalm first noticed the boy is striking:
Gyburc observes him, like her husband before her, as he un-
consciously demonstrates his enormous strength, this time
tossing the long, thick pole from hand to hand (230,12-15).
As Willehalm had asked the King, so now does she ask Willehalm:

> si sprach 'wer ist der sarjant?
> sul wir iht angest gein im hân?
> er ist sô wiltlîch getân.'          (230,16-18)

The reply which she receives from Willehalm is strangely
unconcerned:

> disen knappen den gap mir
> der rœmsche künec, unt helfe grôz
>                           (230,20-21)

and he goes on to speak of the troops which will aid him in
the coming battle. Yet the link with Rennewart remains in
the notion of revenge, although the link is only implicit in
the words of Willehalm:

> hânts die vînde hie gebitn,
> von Franzoysen wirt gestritn
> dazz d'engel möhten hœren
> in den niun kœren
> und dazz mîn mâge rechen sol.
> wær tal unt berc der heiden vol,
> Die müesen strît enphâhen.
>                           (230,25-231,1)

Gyburc is given no indication whatever of the origin of the
boy, but Wolfram supplies a most subtle hint of the link
between them when Gyburc leads her husband into a bedroom,
giving instructions that his horse should be cared for:

> Diu künegîn des niht vergaz,
> des landes hêrren fürbaz
> si fuort zeinr kemenâten în,
> und hiez behalten Volatîn.     (231,29-232,2)

The name of the horse brings with it a vivid reminder of how

it came to be in Willehalm's possession, but Wolfram delays
comment on this while he speaks of Rennewart who remains with
the horse, ensuring that it is well cared for (232,3-5). Gyburc and Rennewart are linked, then, through their care for
Willehalm and his horse, but the horse itself is a link,
obscured as yet, between the two who are related equally to
the dead Arofel. Of this Wolfram says nothing, for such bald
statements of fact have no place in his treatment of the relationship which comes only gradually and never fully into
the mind of Gyburc. Instead he concentrates on the sign on
the horse's flank, only gradually relating this to the shield
of Arofel, like Volatin himself an object of the rêroup of
Willehalm:

> dâ von Samargône
> ein insigel was gebrant
> ans orses buoc, daz er dâ vant,
> dar nâch was Arofelles schilt.
> den knappen hete gar bevilt,
> und het er sich versunnen
> wie daz ors wart gewunnen.      (232,6-12)[16]

Wolfram goes some way, in these lines, towards an open declaration of the origin of the horse, but he resists the opportunity, increasing the element of dramatic irony as Rennewart
gazes uncomprehendingly at the spot on the horse where the
shield had hung, and passing now to the factual statement by
which he returns to Gyburc and Willehalm:

> do entwâpent sich diu künegîn.     (232,13)

Although nothing has been said, Wolfram has begun to suggest
the relationship between Gyburc and Rennewart which she herself will feel a little later. Perhaps she feels it already,
but Wolfram does not say so, even though in passing over to
her in this way he may himself be implying a cue to a likely
response in her: instead Wolfram suspends further comment
and so maintains the sense of mystery.

The third person to enquire about Rennewart is Heimrich,
and the occasion is again parallel to the two previous
occasions, for once more it is a simple question, relating to
the great strength of Rennewart:

> zer künegîn sprach dô Heimrîch
> 'wer ist sô starc, sô manlîch
> dâ her în für uns gegangen
> mit einer sô grôzen stangen?'     (271,27-30)

The answer which Gyburc gives repeats the information given
to Willehalm by Loys, and to Gyburc by Willehalm, but she
extends it, adding her own opinion that the boy should be
better treated (272,5) and commenting on his courage and good
looks (272,6-10; 272,13-17).  However, the culmination of her
reply to Heimrich comes when she speaks of her own reaction
to the boy:

> mîn herze giht etswes ûf in,
> dar umbe ich dicke siufzic bin
> sît hiute morgen daz i'n sach:
> mir sol freude odr ungemach
> vil schier von sîner kumft geschehen.
> ich muoz im antlützes jehen
> als eteslîch mîn geslähte hât.
> mîn herze mich des niht erlât,
> ichn sî im holt, ichn weiz durch waz:
> sô treit er lîhte gein mir haz.   (272,21-30)

For all her uncertainty, Gyburc here expresses for the first
time her sense of kinship with Rennewart.  This acknowledgement on her part sums up the veiled hints of Wolfram and
those of Rennewart himself in his answer to Willehalm, and it
anticipates the conversation between Gyburc and Rennewart.

Once more, however, Wolfram preserves the tension, for
he does not pass straight over to that important conversation,
though his narrative remains with Rennewart, as he describes
him eating at table with Heimrich and Gyburc, and then relates
a further instance of his response to the teasing of the
pages.  Yet Wolfram does include a further detail which adds
to the growing mass of vague evidence, when he speaks of
Rennewart sitting next to Gyburc and draws attention, for the
first time, to the striking likeness which seems to have escaped notice before (274,18-26).  Again, the remark is not
taken up, but it echoes later, when Rennewart himself speaks
of Gyburc's likeness to the young girl he remembers as his
sister in his native land.

Meanwhile, Wolfram himself gives the first precise statement of Rennewart's origin when he describes him sleeping in

the kitchen on his hard pole:

> sîner swester sun Poydjus
> was selten doch gelegen sus.
> der künec von Vrîende
> (dar zuo diente ouch sîner hende
> Griffân Trîande und Kaukasas):
> ich wæne, im baz gebettet was
> swenne er slâfen wolte,
> des œheim hie dolte
> des er gar erlâzen wære,
> swer doch diu rehten mære
> wiste, wie sîn hôher art
> von ammen brust verstolen wart
> ûz rîcheit brâht in armuot.    (282,19-283,1)

The mention of Poydjus, known to us from the first battle
and known as one of the grandchildren of Terramer (36,5-10),
constitutes the first precise reference to the origin of
Rennewart, yet Wolfram uses it almost casually: all mystery
has slipped away in this completely factual mention of Rennewart's kinship with Terramer. But Wolfram does nothing
casually, and he has reserved for this moment his own revelation of what he has been at pains to enshroud in mystery.
Without lingering on this significant moment of revelation,
he passes to his longest and most detailed account of Rennewart's story. Some of what he now tells is known already,
either from what Rennewart has said or from the hints which
Wolfram himself has let slip, but the story is now put together in a coherent sequence. He tells how the child Rennewart was bought by merchants who hoped to gain a great deal
of money because of his high birth (283,3-7). The facts of
his origin are told, not in a straightforward narrative as
though by Wolfram himself, but by means of the information
given to the boy by the merchants (283,8-20). Even now,
though the father, the brothers and the sisters are mentioned,
the name of Terramer does not occur, nor, less significantly
perhaps, that of Arabel. Wolfram tells further that the
child learnt French from the merchants who intended to bring
him to the French King, and the story of past events coincides with the present:

> dô hiez sîn phlegen schône
> von Rôme der künec Lôys.    (284,8-9)

Wolfram's story of Rennewart embraces events past, present
and future.

Now comes the first statement of the relationship between
Arabel and Rennewart, and, coupled with it, a further reference to his refusal to be baptized. This rejection of baptism
has been mentioned before, by Loys to Willehalm (190,25-
191,18), by Rennewart to Willehalm (193,1-22), but only now,
in this objective account by the narrator himself, is it
coupled with the love of the young boy for the Christian
princess and seen as an obstacle to that love. A new perspective is given to the story, with the insertion that Rennewart told his tale to Alyze, recognizing the extent of her
loyalty (284,23-26). This knowledge gives, in retrospect,
depth to the little which has been seen of the relationship
between the young couple and adds significance to Alyze's
intervention on Rennewart's behalf, at the time when Willehalm asked the King to give him the young page. Rennewart's
stubborn refusal to be baptized is related now, too, to his
menial work in the kitchen, and the previously mentioned ill-
treatment at the hands of Loys is given a further explanation.
Finally, Wolfram turns in this long account to the hatred of
Rennewart for his kinsmen (285,1-5), but he provides also the
explanation hitherto lacking of their apparent negligence of
the fate of the lost child:

> sîn haz unrehte giht:
> wand sine wisten sîn dâ niht.
> wær kein sîn bote an si komn,
> wolt iemen hort hân genomn,
> sölher gâbe wær nâh im gepflegn,
> Franzoyser möhten golt noch wegn.
>
> (285,5-10)

This explanation, given to Wolfram's audience, is denied to
Rennewart himself, and so the tragedy of the situation is
increased by the element of dramatic irony, in the fierce
pursuit by Rennewart of revenge on his kin for a crime they
have not committed.

The speech of Rennewart as he laments his singed beard
contains his first public declaration of his birth, yet even
now Wolfram's desire to maintain the element of secrecy which

has so far pervaded his story is continued in the way in
which he now handles this declaration. For Rennewart himself
this is no public statement, but Wolfram makes it clear as
Rennewart begins to speak that what is intended as a secret
lament is overheard:

> si luogeten durch die want dar în
> und hôrten wie die grane sîn
> Rennewart der junge klagete,
> und waz er al klagende sagete. (286,27-30)

When he has finished, Wolfram reminds us of those outside:

> Durch die want sin hôrten alsus klagn
>                                    (289,1)

and a few lines later he recalls the principal information
which has been given:

> eteslîche heten sîn hôhen art
> vernomen, unde iedoch niht gar. (289,14-15)

The speech itself moves away from Rennewart's distress at the
singeing of his beard and the interpretation of the action
as an insult both to Alyze and to the King himself, and as
bringing shame upon his kinsmen. Where, in his own earlier
account, Wolfram had spoken of Rennewart's ten brothers but
had given no names (283,19-20), Rennewart now supplies these
names:

> Fâbors und Utreiz,
> Mâlarz und Malatras        (288,10-11)

> Glorîax und Bahsigweiz,
> Carrîax und Matreiz,
> Merabjax und Morgôanz.      (288,15-17)

The list of names is striking, both for their intrinsic quality of sound and for the echo of the previous occasion when,
at the beginning of the first battle, the sons of Terramer
had been named (32,12-18). Surely Wolfram intends his audience
to recall that earlier occasion, as he leads up now to Rennewart's final dramatic statement:

> ich pin doch Terramêres parn.      (288,30)

This high point of the story of the young Rennewart is
followed by the dramatic conversation between Gyburc and
Rennewart, itself a central scene in the story. Ironically,
the scene depends on the ignorance of each of the true identity of the other and of the relationship between them. The

irony is increased by Wolfram's juxtaposition of the scene
with the simple statement that Rennewart is the child of
Terramer, for the whole story of Willehalm is dependent upon
the fact that Gyburc, too, is the child of Terramer. Deliberately, then, he suppresses that same information which he has
given, unembellished for the first time, to his audience and
to Rennewart's hearers.

Wolfram refrains, then, from the somewhat obvious drama
of a scene in which Gyburc and Rennewart openly acknowledge
their relationship. Though he is content to depend for much
of his story of Rennewart on dramatic irony, this clear-cut
culmination has no part in his conception of his young hero,
certainly not at this stage and perhaps not at all. Instead
the conversation with Gyburc continues on the same level of
innuendo, as she asks him about his family, and in particular
about his sister, and Rennewart resists what appears to be
an irresistible cue. When, as though to explain Rennewart's
refusal to grasp the obvious, Wolfram allows him to speak of
the poverty of Gyburc which distinguishes her from the sister
whom she resembles in other respects (293,1-2), he unites this
scene with the work as a whole, in which Gyburc herself speaks
of the poverty. This scene, then, which might have brought
the simple, dramatic conclusion to the story of Rennewart,
takes on a new proportion, assuming a place in the wider context, in the same way as Rennewart himself, for all the
mystery and interest of his story, is ultimately assigned to
a subordinate role.[17]

The link between the conversation and the battle to come
is in the armour which Gyburc gives to Rennewart. Moreover,
it perpetuates the theme of the relationship between them,
for it belonged to Synagun, her nephew, and Halzebieres
swester sun (294,24). As she explains how it came into her
possession, when Willehalm was taken captive by Synagun, Wolfram links the present with the past and bridges the lapse in
time between the earliest acquaintance of husband and wife
and the coming battle which is its consequence. He provides
Gyburc, too, with the occasion to speak of the position which

she occupied in those days:

> mîn houbet ze Todjerne
> krône truoc von erbeschaft:
> dô het in manegen landen kraft
> der milte künc Tybalt von Cler
> (er füert noch hiute grôz her),
> der gap mir krôn dâ ze Arâbî.     (294,16-21)

Again, the relationship with the present is apparent, and
in particular the contrast is implicit here between Gyburc's
picture of her wealth and position and the poverty which
Rennewart has observed in her.

The story of Rennewart is known now, after so much
secrecy and such gradual unfolding, but still the mutual recognition of Gyburc and Rennewart is postponed. This, like
the future of the love of Alyze and Rennewart, is enshrouded
in uncertainty as Rennewart goes into battle. Instead, when
so much of the story of Rennewart had looked back, Wolfram
now looks forward, as he anticipates the activity of Rennewart in the battle to come:

> sîn muot begunde im stolzen,
> gein prîse truoc er stæten muot.  (296,4-5)

Wearing the armour of the nephew of Halzebier, Rennewart goes
into the battle which has, as one of its declared objectives,
the revenge of the death of Vivianz, the nephew of Willehalm,
slain by Halzebier. Yet we have already seen that Halzebier
will die in the battle to come because Rennewart releases the
eight princes taken captive in the first battle by Halzebier,
in revenge for the death of Pinel, another nephew. [18] The
irony is complete: Rennewart, in some ways the counterpart
of Vivianz, avenges the death of Vivianz, but he does so in
the armour of Synagun.

e) <u>Recapitulation of events</u>

Another of the means by which Wolfram achieves the sense
of compression and the tight inter-relationship of separate
parts of the work is the occasional recapitulation of events.
An important example is the first battle, when events are
related as they occur by Wolfram himself, then by Willehalm

to Gyburc, and by Willehalm to Arnalt. Although these two
accounts by Willehalm are the same in substance, Wolfram
varies his means by having the first in direct speech:

> er sprach 'in kan dir niht gesagen
> von ir ieslîches sunder nôt.
> bärlîch Vivîanz ist tôt.
> in mîn selbes schôz ich sach
> daz der tôt sîn jungez herze brach.
> Mir hât dîn vater Terramêr
> gefrumet mangiu herzesêr,
> und tuot noch ê erz lâze.
> mîn flust ist âne mâze'          (93,26-94,4)

and the second in indirect speech:

> der marcrâve im nante tôt
> Mylen unde Vivîanz,
> und wie der buhurt ûf Alischanz
> sich bêde huop unde schiet,
> und was dô Terramêr geriet
> daz Oransch wart umbelegn,
> und waz er angest muose pflegn
> ê daz er durh si dan gereit.     (120,18-25)

Arnalt, in his turn, tells his men what has happened, and his
account is rather more protracted, with the signs of personal
involvement in the grief which have been absent, so far, in
the brief, factual account of Willehalm, worn by battle and
intent upon the next stage:

> Arnalt sagt in rehte dô,
> daz im die Sarrazîne
> drîzehne der mâge sîne
> gevangen heten unt erslagen:
> 'nu erloubet daz ich müeze klagen.
> die fürsten alle wâren
> almeistic von den jâren
> daz ir necheiner gran noch truoc.
> mîn bruoder ungemach genuoc
> het ân unsich erworben.
> sîn man sint erstorben,
> dar zuo sîn wîp besezzen ist:
> des enweiz er niht, wie lange vrist
> sich Oransche müg erwern,
> od welhes trôstes si sich nern.
> ez stêt gar an der hœhsten hant.'
>                                  (124,14-29)

Most moving is the brief account by Willehalm to Wimar, which
is full of the simplicity of total despair:

> lieber wirt, ich hân verlorn
> hôhe mâge und werde man:
> dar zuo hân ich in angest lân

    ein wîp, der dort mîn herze ist bî:
    mîn lîp ist hie vor freuden vrî.
                                        (135,8-12)

There are no details; the impact of Willehalm's losses is
evident to his host without his expanding on them. The longer
account by Willehalm comes before the assembly at the Court
of Loys, when he concentrates on the loss of so many of their
common kinsmen (151,6-30), and the substance of Willehalm's
account is imparted by Scherins to the Queen in her chamber
apart from the great hall:

        duo saget ir rehte gar
        den grôzen jâmer Schêrîns
        und wie mit tôde gâben zins
        ûf Alischanz ir mâge.          (164,2-5)

Though Wolfram does not report the details here, the impact
of the unreported speech by Scherins is reflected in the
passionate reaction of the Queen, a long speech (164,10-
165,27) which begins with a cry of woe:

        'ôwê,' sprach si, 'het er mir
        daz houbet mîn hin ab geslagen! ...'
                                        (164,10-11)

and rises to a peak in her outburst of grief, centred on
Vivianz:

        hân ich von Terramêre
        die hôhen flust ûf Alischanz,
        ey beâs âmîs Vivîanz,
        wie vil noch unsippiu wîp
        dînen geflôrierten lîp
        Suln klagen durch die minne!
                                        (164,26-165,1)

After the meal, Willehalm speaks again, addressing himself to
Loys, with the intention of making clear what the losses of
the first battle mean to him, the King himself (177,25-179,1).
This is a different account, slanted in a different way, without the emotional emphasis on the loss of kin but stressing
the political implications which, he hopes, are most likely to
rouse Loys to action.

    It is, however, the personal element which dominates in
Willehalm's longest account of the battle, when he speaks of
the slaying of Arofel, explaining how he killed him in revenge
for Vivianz (203,19-207,30). This is the speech when he comes

a second time to the monastery and finds it burnt to the
ground, and it is the outstanding example of Wolfram's use
of recapitulation. Indeed, the description of the period
spent there is occupied almost entirely by Willehalm's speech,
which relates what is already known to the audience but comes
as news to Willehalm's own hearers, the slaying of Arofel and
Tesereiz. The fights with the two men, and particularly that
with Arofel, are major events, yet at the time they had been
passed over relatively briefly, in order that they should
take their place in the whole narrative. Now, for the first
time, Willehalm himself gives his account, relating events
as we know them to have happened yet colouring them now with
the subjectivity which is inevitable. Only now is the terrible
action seen through the eyes of the man who perpetrated it.

The impetus to this speech, which amounts almost to a
confession and a self-justification,[19) is the reference to
the shield which has perished in the fire. Loys and his
Queen have heard from the abbot of this precious shield with
so many costly gems, and Loys queries what seems a frivolous
gesture on the part of his brother-in-law:

> 'dar zuo dunket ir mich zalt,
> daz iu ûf tôtbæren strît
> iwer muot die volge gît
> daz ir iuch zimiert alsô.'　　　　(203,14-17)

The words which are meant, surely, as a jibe at Willehalm
supply the cue to an explanation, not just of the practical
use which he made of the shield, together with the other armour
of Arofel, but they lead also to a moving account of the act
from his side, and to his interpretation of the loss of the
shield. The brutality of the action is softened a little now,
as Willehalm himself tells how he thought of Vivianz when
Arofel offered him the thirty elephants laden with gold in exchange for his life:

> der bôt mir für sîn sterben dâ
> drîzec helfande,
> die man geladen bekande
> mit dem golt von Kaukasas.
> al anders mir ze muote was:
> sîns sterben mich baz luste,
> wand ich smorgens kuste
> Vivîanzen dicke alsô tôt.　　　　(203,22-29)

His words echo, in substance, those of Wolfram at the time:

> do der marcrâve sîniu wort
> vernam, daz er sô grôzen hort
> für sîn verschertez leben bot,
> er dâhte an Viviânzes tôt,
> wie der gerochen würde,
> und daz sîn jâmers bürde
> Ein teil gesenftet wære                    (79,25-80,1)

but the effect is different. Where Wolfram had emphasized
the thought of revenge and of alleviation of Willehalm's own
grief, Willehalm himself brings vividly to mind the poignant
sight of the dead Vivianz cradled in his arms: the idea of
revenge recedes as he seems to emphasize the more appealing
one of love. At the same time, Willehalm does not seek to
obscure the reality of his action by emphasizing his motivation. Indeed his statement is quite without embellishment:

> ez half in niht swaz er mir bôt:
> Ich enthoubte den künic wol geborn.
>                                           (203,30-204,1)

Yet already his reference to the nobility of Arofel points
towards the theme which dominates his speech now and which,
in retrospect, gives colour to the figure of Arofel. Willehalm sees the shield as the symbol of Arofel's service of
Love: he himself has deprived Love of this exemplary service
and so he, in turn, has been deprived of the shield:

> des hât diu minne mir verlorn
> sînen schilt kostebære.
> er was ouch mir ze swære:
> in solte der geprîste tragen,
> den ich drunder hân erslagen.    (204,2-6)[20]

Wolfram's passing references to the nobility of Arofel culminate, ironically, in this moving testimony by the man who
slew him:

> swaz mir nu tuot Terramêr,
> ich hân im doch daz herzesêr
> an dem werden künge alsô gesant,
> dâ von im jâmer wirt bekant:
> der ze Samargône
> in Persîâ die krône
> vor den edelen fürsten truoc,
> mîn hant iedoch den selben sluoc,
> sînen bruoder den getiwerten,
> vor wîben den gehiwerten.
> ich hân der minnen hulde
> verloren durch die schulde:

> ob ich minne wolde gern,
> ich mües ir durch den zorn enbern,
> wand ich Aroffel nam den lîp,
> den immer klagent diu werden wîp.
>
> (204,15-30)

Linked in the mind of Willehalm with Arofel as the servant
of Love is Tesereiz, but his death at the hand of Willehalm
lacks the remembrance, which taints the other, of a noble
man pleading for his life. Wolfram again uses the technique
of recapitulation as Willehalm passes on to his account of
this encounter, and again the account is coloured by the
subjectivity which inevitably attends its relation by the
chief protagonist himself (205,1-21). The regret which was
implied but not expressed in his account of the slaying of
Arofel is put into words now, as Willehalm laments the necessity for the act:

> mîn hant in sluoc ungerne
> durch sîne hôhe werdekeit.      (205,24-25)

The poignancy attendant upon the tragic deed is increased by
its relation now by the man who committed it, and the personal regret of Willehalm pervades his account:

> Ouwê daz i'm niht entreit,
> dô der gezimierte
> mich vil gehardierte.
> mîn tjost was im doch unbekant,
> unz Arabele wart genant,
> bî der minne er mirz gebôt:
> dâ von was kümftic im sîn tôt.
>
> (205,26-206,2)

Again, the words recall the facts of the incident, for Tesereiz had indeed challenged Willehalm with his taunting
references to Gyburc:

> 'nu kêre, ob dich in dienste weiz
> Arabel diu künegîn'      (87,10-11)

but these are seen now from the standpoint of Willehalm, a man
determined to resist an unwished-for combat but provoked
beyond endurance.

Willehalm passes now to a rapid account of the sequence
of encounters which followed his slaying of Arofel. The
account is necessarily compressed but pervaded with the same
sense of tragic inevitability which accompanied his account
of the deaths of Arofel and Tesereiz:

> Von Boctân rois Talimôn
> was noch durch der wîbe lôn
> gezieret baz dan Thesereiz:
> vor dem bestuont mich Poufemeiz
> der künec von Ingulîe,
> unt Turpîûn, die drîe,
> der rîche von Falturmîê:
> den tet ich allen glîche wê,
> Tschoyûse dez leben ûz in sneit.
> Arfiklant ouch mit mir streit,
> und des bruoder Turkant:
> Turkânîe was ir lant.
> der newedern half sîn krône,
> ine gæbe im daz ze lône
> als ich Vivîanzen ligen sach,
> den ich sît an Arofelle rach.          (206,3-18)

His reference here to Arofel recalls, in passing, the reason
for the whole explanation - the shield itself - and when he
speaks of his flight (207,10) and of how he was saved by his
knowledge of the heathen tongue (207,2-4), he is referring
obliquely to the use which he made of the armour despoiled
from the body of Arofel. Indeed, Willehalm himself brings
the speech back, as he ends it, to the precious armour and
the shield, and to Volatin, the horse which played an important part in bringing him to safety:

> ich hân vil rehte iu gesagt
> wie diu zimierde ist bejagt,
> der schilt unt daz kursît:
> und des wâpenroc noch gît
> alsô kostebæren schîn,
> des selben was ouch Volatîn.          (207,25-30)

Several motifs merge in these six lines, however: his _rêroup_,
the memory of the radiant Arofel and his tragic death, and
the incongruous appearance of Willehalm himself which had,
one recalls, so puzzled the onlookers at the French Court.
Willehalm has, moreover, brought his speech full circle, recalling now that it began with the King's questioning of his
luxurious equipment.

This is a long speech, and the intense concentration of
the audience is suggested, as it is during the speech of Gyburc to the assembled knights, by the absence of interruption.
Its impact, too, is again implied by Wolfram: where the powerful emotion of all present is there expressed in the silent
gesture of Gybert (311,1-3), it is here conveyed in the simple

statement by Wolfram:

> Manegen dûht sîn arbeit grôz.     (208,1)

The lines which follow, too, are surely full of subtle significance:

> durch daz si smæres niht verdrôz,
> die dâ sâzen unde stuonden,
> wand si selten ie befuonden
> ze keiner slahte stunde
> lüge von sînem munde.     (208,2-6)

They give an interesting depth to the speech. No-one raises
any objection to the tale because they all have the impression
that it is true: Wolfram thus supplies a new slant on Willehalm's suffering which is evident to all who see him and
listen to his account, but, more than that, he indicates the
immensity of Willehalm's exploits anew, since, but for the
evidence of their eyes and their sensitivity to what they see
and hear, the audience might have questioned the authenticity
of his account. In this way, then, the speech serves to draw
together some of the experience of the first battle and to
summarize it in Wolfram's account by the man who has survived
to tell of his suffering.

The whole scene at the site of the monastery is important for its focus on this speech by Willehalm, which draws
together events now past but continuing still in their repercussions, not least in the mind of the speaker. It gives a
new perspective, now that there is the opportunity for repose
and meditation, on both Willehalm and Arofel, the two men who
came together in the vivid and tragic encounter, and in doing
so, it expresses one of the major concerns of the work, the
tragic dilemma of individuals linked by respect and even love,
yet separated by their creeds and the demands of circumstances.
The effect of this speech is great, too, in its impact within
the narrative, for it represents a vivid, dramatic period,
with a large audience concentrating upon the account of the
weary, grief-stricken man, intent upon his return to his wife
of whose fate he is unsure, yet thinking back to this major
encounter with a great and noble opponent. [21] In the background, too, is the monastery where he left the shield and

which is now burnt to the ground. The whole is indeed a
scene of immense narrative power which confirms the importance of the speech itself.

A different type of recapitulation is that used by Wolfram at the end of Book IV. Willehalm is approaching Orange
now and can assess the strength of the Saracen army which is
besieging the city. He contemplates the losses of the first
battle, juxtaposing them with those he now anticipates:

> zeinen sorclîchen zîten
> der marcrâve mit den sînen
> kom sô nâhe den Sarrazînen,
> daz er mit sînen ougen sach
> daz im sîn herze des verjach
> mêr flüste denne er ie verlür.
> und swaz er angest sît erkür,
> dô er von Vivîanze schiet,
> und des morgens dô sîn manheit riet,
> fümfzehen künege rîch erkant,
> die entschumphiert sîn eines hant,
> Tenabruns und der Persân,
> swaz im die hêten getân,
> und der minnen gerende Thesereiz,
> und ander manic puneiz,
> dâ wart er werlîch ersehen.     (214,12-27)

Vividly Wolfram compresses into this mental recapitulation the
most significant events of the first battle, the death of
Vivianz and Tesereiz, of Tenebruns and Arofel.

Again Wolfram recapitulates events when he sums up the
actions of Gyburc in the absence of Willehalm, when the latter
has returned to Orange:

> Gyburc streit doch ze orse niht:
> diz mære ir anders ellen giht,
> daz si mit armbrusten schôz
> und si grôzer würfe niht verdrôz
> unt ir wer mit liste erscheinde.
> ir tôtez volc si leinde
> gewâpent an die zinnen,
> und ruortez sô mit sinnen,
> daz ez die ûzeren vorhten,
> die de antwerc gein ir worhten.
> arbeit het si verselwet nâch.     (230,1-11)

We know that she has done these things; Wolfram has described
them in greater detail before; but it is apt that they should
be remembered in this compressed form and linked with the
grimy appearance of Gyburc when Willehalm brings her release.
Moreover, the recapitulation indicates a coming-together of

man and wife at this crucial point which has been achieved
by the activity of both of them during their separation.

An effective use of recapitulation opens Book VI, when
Wolfram speaks of the circumstances of the oath which Willehalm made to Gyburc before they parted and which can be
lifted from him now:

> Mac sölh gelübde ein ende hân,
> diu des âbents wart getân,
> dô der marcrâve schiet
> von Oransche, als im geriet
> Gyburc diu in selbe bat
> nâch helfe rîten ûz der stat
> in der Franzoyser lant,
> ob in dâ des rîches hant,
> vater, bruodr und mâge
> sus wolten lân in wâge,
> daz er genâde wurb an sie?
> ir helf er vant, nu sint si hie.
>   sîn dan scheiden unde ir komn
> mugt ir wol bêdiu hân vernomn.
> er mac nu ezzen mêr dan brôt.    (269,1-15)

The constant references to the oath, or more often to the
kiss he left behind in Orange[22] have been frequent brief
echoes of the occasion described now in greater detail.  In
these opening lines, too, Wolfram bridges time and place,
linking the parting of Gyburc and Willehalm and their reunion
by means of the events between, of which we have heard in full
and which he now passes over in a few words.


f)  _Anticipation of events_

Just as he sometimes recapitulates past events, Wolfram
uses a certain amount of anticipation, and the effect is,
again, to compress the events of the work.  Indeed, from the
beginning, there are references to disaster to come.  These
are simple references to coming catastrophe in the broadest
terms, and they resemble the much more frequent references in
the _Nibelungenlied_ which pervade the work and establish its
tone.

Of the marriage between Gyburc and Willehalm, Wolfram
observes:

> dar umbe unschuldic volc erstarp.    (7,28)

Of the baptism of Arabel he comments:

> waz hers des mit tôde engalt! (8,1)

More specifically, he speaks of the sorrow which will overwhelm the land of Provence:

> Provenze her unde ouch dâ
> gewan sît jâmers künde (8,10-11)

and he extends this statement with his anticipation of the vast numbers who will die:

> des meres fluot der ünde
> mac sô manege niht getragen,
> als liute drumbe wart erslagen. (8,12-14)

These and similar remarks (eg. 7,23-26; 8,2-9; 8,15-21; 8,22-23; 8,24-25) build up to the moment when he makes the factual statement which speaks of the beginning of the war:

> daz brâhte der künec Terramêr
> ûf dem mer zeinen stunden
> in kieln und in treimunden,
> in urssiern unde in kocken. (8,30-9,3)

When the army arrives on the field of Alischanz, Wolfram observes

> ûf daz velt Alyschanz
> kom manec niwer schilt al ganz,
> der dürkel wart von strîte. (12,19-21)

These lines, which seem to refer to the actual moment of arrival, speak also of the tragedy to come, in a way which sums up, before the battle commences, the many references to what will happen at Alischanz. Towards the end of the passage, as the army nears its destination, such anticipation has become more frequent, and more specific:

> Terramêr wart des enein,
> ûf Alitschanz er kêrte,
> dâ strît sîn her gelêrte
> des er nimmer mêr wart vrô. (12,4-7)

Again, a little later:

> si wârn im sippe al gelîche,
> Willalm des lobes rîche
> und Tybalt Arabeln man,
> durh den er herzesêre gewan
> vor jâmer nâch dem bruoder sîn
> und mangen werden Sarrazîn
> dem tôde ergap ze zinse. (12,9-15)

Finally, there is a more generalized comment on the nature of the story which he is about to tell:

> ein herze daz von flinse
> ime donre gewahsen wære,
> daz müeten disiu mære.          (12,16-18)

More specifically, Wolfram anticipates events on some
occasions. In Book VI he says that he will not name the
princes whom Loys sends to join Willehalm, because these men
are going to desert and bring disgrace upon themselves
(302,1-7). Briefly he observes a little later that Rennewart will aid the Christians (311,30).

Anticipation is very much a part of Wolfram's technique
in his treatment of Rennewart, where mystery and suspense are
essential features of his story. The principal example is in
the passage which is often discussed in relation to the problem of the conclusion of the work. Wolfram tells us of
Rennewart:

> sus rach er smæhlîchez leit
> des er vor Alyzen pflac:
> ir minne an prîse im gap bejac.
> sîn dinc sol immer sus niht varn:
> Alyzen minne in sol bewarn.
> swaz man ie smæhe an im gesach,
> Alyzen minn die von im brach
> dar nâch in kurzen zîten
> in tôtlîchen strîten.          (285,14-22)

The lines anticipate a change in Rennewart's fortunes, though
they do not indicate the precise nature of this change. Wolfram's work, as it stands, provides no evidence of the manner
of fulfilment of these lines, or of whether they are fulfilled at all. Whether the prîs to which Alyze's love is to
lead him is a glorious death in battle[23] or marriage with
Alyze after baptism,[24] remains untold, and despite the quality of anticipation in these lines it is perhaps not necessary
to see in them Wolfram's intention to take the story of Rennewart further than he does.[25] Moreover, the question arises:
what does Wolfram predict in these lines? He tells us that,
fighting on the side of the Christians, he will avenge the
shame which he has endured in front of Alyze and which he
blames upon his negligent kinsmen. This he does in the battle
which shows him wreaking vengeance on the heathens. Her love
indeed inspires him in battle, when he is described as Alîzen

soldier (418,15), and he has told Willehalm that he will
help him in battle in the hope of a secret reward (331,13-20).
The second element in Wolfram's prediction refers, surely in
general terms, to Rennewart's situation: the love of Alyze
will spur him on in battle and ensure that his present state
of subjection will not last. In this respect, too, the work
provides fulfilment, for Rennewart attains a role of author-
ity and respect in the battle and is prized by Willehalm himself as his zeswiu hant (452,20). Lofmark observes that
Wolfram never hints at a death in battle for Rennewart and
that the line Alyzen minne in sol bewarn "does not give the
impression that Wolfram intended him to die in battle".[26]
Equally, one might say that it does not give the impression
that he did not intend him to do so: it gives no impression
at all, beyond that which is indeed fulfilled, in the glorious
conduct of Rennewart in battle.[27] The smæhe which he has
endured is lifted from him in the fighting, by virtue of the
inspiration of Alyze's love. It seems, therefore, that the
passage need not, and perhaps should not, be given a weightier
significance.[28] It belongs with other examples of Wolfram's
technique of anticipating within his work, and resembles
another example which anticipates the activity of Rennewart
in the battle to come in more general terms and without the
distracting reference to the love of Alyze:

> sîn muot begunde im stolzen,
> gein prîse truoc er stæten muot. (296,4-5)

When Wolfram introduces Vivianz, it is to contrast his
youth and handsome features with the death in battle which
is so significant a part of the work:

> und der clâre Vivîans:
> ich wære immer mêr ein gans
> an wizzenlîchen triuwen,
> ob mich der niht solde riuwen.
> ouwê daz sîniu jungen jâr
> âne mundes granhâr
> mit tôde nâmen ende!
> von hôher freude ellende
> wart dar under sîn geslehte:
> daz tâten si mit rehte. (13,21-30)

Already, before the start of the battle even, Wolfram focuses

his attention on that feature of the young Vivianz which will
be the centre of his story: the grief of all people for him
which will constitute a motivating force of the second battle.

After the death of Nöupatris, the grievously wounded
Vivianz launches back into battle:

> der junge lobesbære
> Hurte fürbaz in den strît.     (25,30-26,1)

At this vital point Wolfram sees fit to assess what has happened in a brief statement and to anticipate worse to come:

> Tybaldes râche und des nît
> ist alrêrst um den wurf gespilt.
> swen noch des schaden niht bevilt,
> der mag in fürbaz vernemen.     (26,2-5)

When Vivianz has found the wounded horse and swung himself with difficulty upon it, he makes his way towards the
Larkant, and Wolfram prepares the way for the appearance of
the cherubim and the approaching martyrdom of Vivianz by
speaking of the baptism of Christ which gave to all baptized
the name of Christian:

> der uns ime toufe wart
> und Jêsus an der süezen vart
> ime Jordân wart genennet Krist,
> der nam uns noch bevolhen ist,
> den die der touf bedecket hât.     (48,15-19)

The general statement gives way to the specific, as he returns to Vivianz, who did not forget his baptism and fought
for Christ until his death (48,20-23). The approaching death
is anticipated with increasing certainty:

> mich jâmert durch die sælde mîn
> und freu mich doch wie er restarp,
> der sêle werdekeit erwarp     (48,28-30)

and then

> Der junge helt vor got erkant
> reit gein dem wazzer Larkant     (49,1-2)

until Wolfram appeals to Vivianz as a martyr:

> Vivîans, der marter dîn
> mag ieslîch rîter manen got,
> swenn er sich selben siht in nôt. (49,12-14)

Wolfram thus approaches the single most important event of
the first battle, the death which, in a sense, represents the
culmination of all those deaths described so briefly in the

battle, and he approaches it with an increasing certainty
that Vivianz is the elected one.

The actual death of Vivianz, so long expected and short-
ly to come about, is anticipated by Wolfram in Willehalm's
grief as he accepts that he must leave his slain men:

> wære im niht wan Vivîanz
> ûf dem velde Alischanz
> beliben, er möhte iedoch wol klagen. (53,11-13)

The words increase in irony in the knowledge, which Willehalm
himself lacks, that Vivianz is lying dying at the <u>wazzer
Larkant</u>.

When Willehalm takes the horse of the dead King Talimon,
he foreshadows the way in which he later takes Volatin, the
horse of Arofel, but the fate of the horses is different, for
so are the circumstances. Willehalm has his own horse, Puzzat,
and he needs no second one. As he makes his way through the
spear thrusts of the heathens, the horse becomes a burden to
him, and his killing of the horse, so factually related by
Wolfram, perhaps sums up the horror of the battle:

> hindern büegen stach erz tôt:
> ern gunds der heidenschefte niht.
> (57,16-17)

There is no place here for sentiment, and this man, who only
a few lines later is shown in affectionate conversation with
his own horse, prefers to kill the animal rather than give
any potential advantage to his enemy. Perhaps the action is
not unconnected with the slaying of Arofel, when, enraged by
events, Willehalm goes against humanity and the code of chivalry itself. The element of anticipation seems to be present on
several levels, even perhaps on a negative one, as Wolfram
highlights the difference side-by-side with the similarities
in the events.

More specifically, Wolfram anticipates the second battle,
not as he did the first one with words, but in the events
which precede it. The result is that, during the period before the battle, we never lose sight of the fighting to come.
The arming by Gyburc of Rennewart has another, more important
purpose,[29] but this, like the scene in which Terramer receives

the gifts of armour and equipment,[30] looks towards the battle.
Wolfram's own reference to the Mass points also towards the
battle (296,25), while perhaps the most powerful factor in
pointing forward to the events of Alischanz is the great
speech by Gyburc before the assembled forces. Similarly, Wolfram has Terramer speak of the strategy which he will adopt and
of the multitude of the heathen forces:

> swie vil mir hers sî tôt gevalt,
> ich hân noch hers ungezalt,
> daz nieman wol geprüeven mac.     (340,27-29)

By focusing his attention on father and daughter, in these
different ways, Wolfram anticipates the quality of the coming
battle: the fierce military encounter with a vast heathen
force and with the Christians fighting, in response to the
words of Gyburc, in order to defend their Christian honour and,
in victory, to preserve it.

Anticipation, then, exists in Wolfram's work in different
forms and producing different effects, but always conserving
the sense of compression of the whole poem, and the close
inter-relationship of events.

g)  Wolfram's treatment of the past

After his brief, though very significant, prologue, Wolfram embarks upon his narrative with remarkable directness.
The compression of the work as a whole characterizes its beginning, as he passes quickly over the events which lead to
Willehalm's meeting with Arabel. Indeed, he assumes in his
audience a knowledge of the events which need not be repeated
here:

> ir habt ouch ê wol vernomen
> (es endarf iu nu niht mære  komen),
>                                                 (7,23-24)

and he passes to his simple, factual reference to Willehalm's
winning of the heathen princess. Yet even this is coupled,
more significantly, with a reference to events to come:

> Arabeln Willalm erwarp,
> dar umbe unschuldic volc erstarp.     (7,27-28)

We learn, too, of Gyburc's baptism and her new name, but again with the utmost simplicity and directness:

> Gyburc si sich toufen liez. (7,30)

Not many lines later, however, the consequences of these facts
are told in more emotional terms, when Wolfram says of Terramer:

> sîme liebsten got Mahmeten
> und andern goten sînen,
> den liez er dicke erschînen
> mit opfer mange êre,
> und klagete in ouch vil sêre
> von Arabeln, diu sich Gyburc
> nande, und diu mit toufe kurc
> was manegen ougen worden
> durch kristenlîchen orden.
> diu edel küniginne,
> durch liebes friwendes minne
> und durch minne von der hœhsten hant
> was kristen leben an ir bekant. (9,8-20)

Even here no details are given, and Wolfram moves straight on
to the account of the first battle, with his mention of the
relatives of Terramer who come to his aid:

> Terramêr was ir vatr:
> Arofeln sînen bruoder batr,
> und den starken Halzebier.
> die zwêne manec urssier
> in sîne helfe brâhten. (9,21-25)

Already, then, Wolfram is deep in his narrative, and even his
terse comment -

> wol si des gedâhten - (9,26)

refrains from judgement. Only Tybalt, who plays a somewhat
subdued role in the work which follows, is described as reacting to the events with any passion:

> ir man, der künec Tybalt,
> minnen flust an ir klagete:
> ûz freude in sorge jagete
> mit kraft daz herze sînen lîp.
> er klagete êre unde wîp,
> dar zuo bürge unde lant.
> sîn klage mit jâmer wart bekant
> unz an die ûzern Indîâ. (8,2-9)

The time lapse is implied, but left undefined:

> swaz dâ enzwischen sît geschach,
> des geswîg ich von in beiden,
> den getouften und den heiden,
> und sage des hers überkêr (8,26-29)

and with remarkable economy Wolfram launches into his account of the first battle of Alischanz.

The past of Gyburc is clearly an essential feature of the
story, for it has given rise to the present situation, yet
Wolfram is not concerned to tell, save in the broadest outline, of the events which have led to the current state of
war. There is, moreover, a significant absence of comment on
the emotional dilemma which one can only imagine to have
existed in the mind of the wife and mother torn from her family by a new and uncontradictible force. This, indeed, is of
no concern to Wolfram, for whom, as for Gyburc herself, the
claims of the Christian faith are supreme, and one is left to
wonder about the past suffering of this woman which is not
even suggested in the course of a work concerned with her
present grief. Yet this is no casual omission on the part
of the narrator, nor is it meant to imply the indifference
of a Kriemhild to the fate of her child: rather is Wolfram's
omission deliberate, like everything else in his narrative.
He is not the man, as we know, to ignore the ordinary human
claims of the woman separated from her loved ones, but by the
time the work opens, such suffering lies in the past, transcended perhaps, though certainly not forgotten.

By the beginning of the first battle, then, the facts are
told, in outline, and the remainder of the work does little to
fill in the details. Yet Wolfram does supply a few snatches
of information, though he does so, it seems, almost casually,
with no sense of obligation to supply a complete picture of
past events. When, after the first battle, Willehalm needs
to escape, once away from the battlefield and then away from
Orange, Wolfram mentions without comment that he is able to
do so because he has command of the heathen tongue (83,18-19;
105,27). He does not explain how he comes to have this knowledge - indeed the question does not seem to arise - and this
additional information is supplied, again almost casually, in
a quite different context, when Willehalm is questioning
Rennewart:

> do der marcgrâve in prîsûn
> gevangen lac dâ ze Arâbî,
> Caldeis und Côatî
> lernt er dâ ze sprechen.                     (192,6-9)

Still the connection with the significant events of the past
is not made until Gyburc herself, in conversation with Terramer, tells of how she came to know Willehalm when he was
taken captive (220,14-20). She goes on to give, yet still
in the simplest, factual terms, a brief account of their elope-
ment together:

> von boin und anderen sîm versmidn
> macht ich in ledec an allen lidn,
> unt fuor in toufpæriu lant. (220,27-29)

Yet these three lines, which give some of the most colourful
information in the whole work of the events leading to the
war, belong within their context: this is not Gyburc deliberately telling of her romance but speaking simply of the circumstances of her baptism. More important, in fact, are the
lines which follow these and supply the context:

> ich diente im und der hœsten hant.
> Mîns toufes schôn ich gerne.
> (220,30-221,1)

The other details fall back into place, nonchalantly mentioned by Gyburc as a part of a much broader account.

When, later, Gyburc speaks again of the battle between
Willehalm and King Synagun, it is again for a purpose quite
different from that of providing Wolfram's audience with
further vivid details of the story of the love of Willehalm
and Gyburc. She gives to Rennewart the armour which Synagun
wore in that battle and explains to him:

> ez truoc der künec Synaguon
> in dem sturme do er den markîs vienc,
> dâ diu grôze schumphentiure ergienc,
> Do der künic Tybalt wart entworht.
> (293,28-294,1)

This moment provokes the longest account of the past in the
whole work, as Gyburc speaks of that time, of the captivity
of Willehalm, of her own status as queen and her marriage
with Tybalt (294,2-30). Yet at the end of the speech she
returns to the armour which has given rise to the account:

> daz harnasch und der markîs
> sint mit mir beide entrunnen.
> sus diz harnasch wart gewunnen. (294,28-30)

The past is significant, it seems clear, in its relationship

with the present, and for Wolfram this passage represents,
surely, a step towards the unfulfilled recognition of Gyburc
and Rennewart,[31] rather than a deliberate account of past
events.

When Gyburc speaks later in her great speech to the rât
of the wordly goods which she has mentioned in her speech to
Rennewart, she couples with them something which she mentions
now for the first time, indeed for the only time:

> dêswâr ich liez ouch minne dort,
> und grôzer rîcheit manegen hort,
> und schœniu kint, bî einem man,
> an dem ich niht geprüeven kan
> daz er kein untât ie begienc,
> sîd ich krôn von im enpfienc.     (310,9-14)

Here then, but muted and barely explicit, is the regret for
which one will search in vain in the rest of the work. And
even here, in the context of her magnificent credo, the passing references to her husband and children give no impression
of lasting suffering: her declaration of the innocence of
Tybalt -

> Tybalt von Arâbî
> ist vor aller untæte vrî -     (310,15-16)

gives way to a more significant declaration:

> ich trag al ein die schulde,
> durh des hœhsten gotes hulde,
> ein teil ouch durh den markîs
> der bejaget hât sô manegen prîs. (310,17-20)

If one seeks, and one is perhaps tempted to seek, for the
signs of ordinary human feeling, then one finds it in these
lines, yet quite transcended, the commitment of a mother and
a loving wife replaced by the superior commitment to the
Christian God.

One feature remains to be mentioned in Wolfram's handling
of Gyburc's past. This is the figure of her son, Ehmereiz,
a colourful young knight who emerges as an individual in both
battles. In the first, he meets Willehalm who declines to
fight him, for the sake of his mother, but he accuses Willehalm for bringing disgrace on his mother, and the forthright
terms of his attack suggest something of the grief and bewilderment of the vulnerable young man, left as a child by his

mother, the living victim of past events (75,4-20). Wolfram
himself does not pass any comment, leaving his audience to
ponder on the tragic rights and wrongs of a situation for
which, as he sees it, there was no alternative. In the second
battle, Ehmereiz again comes to the fore, briefly, and this
time without complication of an encounter with his mother's
husband: yet he is an outstanding figure and in his splendid
cloak he recalls the colour and extravagance of his heathen
homeland, the kingdom which she sacrificed to live in 'poverty'. Other heathens are mentioned as relatives of Gyburc
(76,15; 461,25-26); Willehalm's gesture towards Matribleiz
and the heathen kings at the end of the work is specifically
in remembrance of her (462,24-463,1).[32] The all-important
origin of Gyburc is constantly remembered, but it is Ehmereiz
who supplies that link with the past which is, in other respects, somewhat obscured in a work which deals above all with
the present.

    Wolfram's handling of the past, then, is subtle, a facet
of the texture of his narrative and, in the way he telescopes
past events within those of the present, an aspect of the
compression of the whole narrative.

3. <u>The Texture of the Narrative</u>

In this section attention is paid to details of Wolfram's narrative means within the general structure treated so
far. As might be expected from a fairly superficial acquaintance with the work, the 'texture' is varied, but recurrent
features emerge. Wolfram's use of contrast and his power of
economic, pungent expression, which may at times verge on
understatement, are, for example, characteristic features of
his style in telling his story. His use of parallels, too,
is a marked element in this work which deals in conflict and
in which, as has already been seen, the framework of the whole
is dependent on basic parallelism, of the two great forces,
and the two battles of Alischanz. Inevitably the features of
Wolfram's narrative may overlap at times: an image may, for
example, have the effect of drawing attention to a contrast,
or the pungent use of contrast at which Wolfram is adept may
contribute to the economy of his expression. Inevitably, too,
he uses certain of the common tools of the narrative poet -
direct speech and imagery, for example - and his use of such
features is often distinctive.

a)  The use of contrast

Although, in its basic terms, Willehalm is the account
of two great battles fought between Christians and heathen,
Wolfram has laid stress on the motivation of the conflict and,
above all through Gyburc, he has given expression to a standpoint not even hinted at in his source. He is concerned with
the outcome of the battles, but he is more concerned with the
wider implications of his subject. It is not enough, therefore, that he should narrate the progress of the battles with
acute attention to details, but he probes also the depths of
the human mind in search of the reasoning behind the action
and, more important still in view of his concept of the conflict, he examines the relationship which lies, for him, at
the core of the strife.

Immediately, then, the substance of the work has two
contrasting components, although these are closely related
and fused, as has been seen, into an overriding harmony, and
Wolfram's art is correspondingly one of contrast and, at other
times, of a merging of contrasts.

A basic contrast exists in Wolfram's treatment of the
love of Gyburc and Willehalm. This he does not, of course,
leave implicit but, by including two tender love scenes, he
shows the deep personal relationship in proportion to the
great battles and expresses once more his essential belief
that human love is an aspect of divine Love and may show the
way to it.[1]  Further, he deepens the characters of the two
principal protagonists, contrasting the personal and intimate
with the broad impersonal of the context, and he allows the
gentle harmony of the brief meetings between these two people
to contrast with the chaos of the strife which surrounds them
and of which they and their love are the cause. It is this
latter effect which is important here, for it is one of the
clearest examples of Wolfram's blending of contrasting and
seemingly incompatible moods in a work which is outstanding
for its artistic integrity.

The two scenes of the physical reunion of husband and
wife are beautiful manifestations of the love which pervades

the work. The first, when Willehalm comes back to Orange
after the defeat at Alischanz, is a brief interlude, a pause
in the action yet shown to be closely related to that action.
There is an actual pause in the hostilities, and Gyburc leads
her husband, who is exhausted from the battle, into the
chamber which is to bring respite and privacy:

> Gyburc den marcrâven dan
> fuorte, den strîtes müeden man,
> dô daz ûzer her verzabelt was
> und daz inre wol genas
> sô daz in niemen stürmen bôt
> und daz gestillet was diu nôt.
> in ein kemnâten gienc
> Gyburc, diu ez sus an vienc
> mit ir âmîse. (99,9-17)

Much is contained in these lines: the memory of Alischanz,
the awareness of the enemy outside the city wall, contrasted
with the sense that the scene which follows takes place in
a room set apart from the main action, and the love between
husband and wife expressed already in the single word âmîse.
As Gyburc proceeds to tend the wounds of Willehalm, we recall
again the battle which produced them, and the wounds are
juxtaposed now with the woman who, throughout the battle,
was spoken of as its cause.

As the couple lie together, Wolfram further contrasts
the peace which they now have with the hostility outside and
the battle just lost:

> mit Terramêres kinde
> wart lîhte ein schimpfen dâ bezalt,
> swie zornic er und Tybalt
> dort ûz ietweder wære.
> ich wæn dô ninder swære
> den marcrâven schuz noch slac.
> dar nâch diu künegîn dô pflac,
> si dâhte an sîne arbeit
> und an sîn siuftebærez leit
> und an sîn ungefüege flust. (100,14-23)

The brief period of rest is in no way divorced from the main
action, yet there is a pause and a distinct change in the tone
of the narrative.

From this respite there arises the prayer of Gyburc as
she appeals to God in her grief at the loss of so many and
above all of Vivianz (100,28-102,20). The short period of

inaction ends, however, when her tears awaken Willehalm and
he gives to her the decision whether he should remain or ride
away for help. Her response is the inevitable one, and the
work reverts to the account of action.

In the second love scene, Wolfram relates the suffering
of Willehalm more explicitly to his wife:

> Des landes hêrre (ich mein den wirt)
> kom wider ûf, der niht verbirt
> ern neme ouch die gesellekeit
> dâ von er liep unde leit
> ê dicke het enpfangen.           (279,1-5)

Here he couples with the suffering the joy which Gyburc brings
to Willehalm, and in the lines which follow he expresses,
again more explicitly than in the earlier scene, this basic
contrast, that their love compensates them for their suffering
and their losses:

> an ein bette wart gegangen,
> dâ er und diu künginne
> pflâgen sölher minne,
> daz vergolten wart ze bêder sît
> daz in ûf Alyschanz der strît
> hete getân an mâgen:
> sô geltic si lâgen.           (279,6-12)

In these lines Wolfram expresses unambiguously the duality of
their love, its power to compensate in full for the suffering
which it brings. When, a little later, he speaks again of
the power of Gyburc's love to compensate Willehalm, he does
so without mention of her responsibility for that suffering:

> Gyburc mit kiuscher güete
> sô nâhe an sîne brust sich want,
> daz im nu gelten wart bekant:
> allez daz er ie verlôs,
> dâ für er si ze gelte kôs.
> ir minne im sölhe helfe tuot,
> daz des marcgrâven trûric muot
> wart mit vreuden undersnitn.
> diu sorge im was sô verre entritn,
> si möhte erreichen niht ein sper.
> Gyburc was sîner freuden wer.           (280,2-12)

All emphasis now is on the perfection of her love and its
power to dispell his sadness. The awareness of her role in
this sadness remains, but by now the stress is totally on the
positive power of her love for him, and his for her.

These two scenes are brief but powerful: they represent

moments of harmony achieved within a work which, though it
may give promise at times of harmony, is concerned essentially with conflict and destruction. The scenes have several
functions. They give tangible evidence of the love of the
couple which is shown as an abstract force throughout the
work; in the midst of the conflict they constitute a reminder
of the human relationship which is its cause and which should,
at all cost, be defended. The memory of the love scenes will
remain to give validity, above all, to the magnificent speech
by Gyburc, when she will speak of her responsibility for the
fighting and of her love for God and for Willehalm.[2]  On
another level, they introduce a new tone into the narrative,
the peace and harmony of these short periods contrasting with
the dominant mood of conflict. This is a work of an essentially serious nature, yet Wolfram knows that an account of un-
mitigated gloom will lose its impact. Accordingly he con-
trives, by a variety of means, to heighten the tragedy by the
use of its opposite, and in these two scenes he allows the
gentle moods of love and consolation to stand in juxtaposition
to those of warfare and death. The effect is remarkable:
Wolfram does not attempt in this way to obliterate the memory
of the reality outside, but in showing this love in relation
to its opposite and in allowing this period of respite within
the framework of relentless conflict, he accentuates the tragic
context and endows the fundamental human tragedy with a new
reality.

   A single moment of rest within the activity so characteristic of the work comes when Rennewart takes leave of Alyze.
Once again, Wolfram reveals his understanding of youthful love
and a delicate awareness of the importance of his setting,
when he describes the parting:

            de junge künegîn sunder was
            under boumen anme gras:
            dar begund er durch urloup gên
            und eine wîle vor ir stên.....     (213,9-12)
The moment of parting passes quickly, but it is full of significance never fully explained,[3] and it remains in the
memory as Rennewart launches into the conflict. As in the

case of the love scenes between Gyburc and Willehalm, Wolfram
achieves here by this brief scene a vivid contrast with the
prevalent mood and so enhances the dramatic effect.

The memory of Alyze remains, then, as she sits on the
grass beneath the trees, but there is another, perhaps more
striking, picture of her earlier in the work. It occurs when
she enters the assembly at the Court of her father, and I have
noted elsewhere[4] that this is the longest and most intensive
description which Wolfram gives, in all his praise of women.
The description of the young girl, virtuous and beautiful, in
her splendid clothes, is outstanding in this work, which,
though it often lingers on the magnificent array of the soldiers,
rarely concerns itself with feminine beauty. Nor is the intention in the present case only the objective description of
a lovely woman, though he speaks of the radiance of the girl
which is seen by all who look on her (155,1-17) and is a manifestation of the virtue sensed by everyone present. Wolfram
here prepares the way for the reaction of Willehalm, who is
moved to tears when he sees his niece kneeling before him
(156,1-3). Once again, he has managed, in a single brilliant
stroke, to break into the mood of the work, to allow a moment
of rest to interrupt the action which fills the work and so
to accentuate this action.

Another moment stands out for its contrast with its context. At the beginning of Book II, Willehalm pauses and gazes
back at the field of Alischanz. The solitary figure is set
against the expanse of mountains and valleys, and now for the
first time he realizes the extent of the power of the heathens.
The contrast is perpetuated as, in his anger, he addresses the
enemy:

> 'ir gunêrten Sarrazîn,
> ob bêdiu hunt unde swîn
> iuch trüegen unt dâ zuo diu wîp
> sus manegen werlîchen lîp,
> für wâr möht ich wol sprechen doch
> daz iwer ze vil wær dannoch'

(58,15-20)

but then immediately turns to his horse:

'ouwê, 'sprach er, 'Puzzât,
kundestu nu geben rât,
war ich kêren möhte!
wie mir dîn kraft getöhte,
wær wir an disen stunden
gesunt und âne wunden,
wolden mich die heiden jagen,
ez möhte etlîches mâg beklagen.
nu sî wir bêde unvarende,
und ich die freude sparende. ... (58,21-30)

This is perhaps one of the most moving moments in the work,
achieved by Wolfram's skill in contrasting the impersonal of
the battlefield with the intimate conversation of the great
leader with his horse. As Willehalm goes on to promise his
horse a fine feast if they ever return to Orange, one recalls the desperate plight of this lone survivor and, in the
lines which follow, the dependence of the man on his horse:

ich enhân hie trôstes mêr wan dich:
dîn snelheit müeze trœsten mich. (59,7-8)

Wolfram's attention to detail, which exists side-by-side with
his conception of the whole, is reflected, too, in his description of the brown coat of the horse, covered with white
foam resembling snow, and of Willehalm's gesture in wiping
it with his own coat. In this moment of rest, between the
defeat at Alischanz and the death of Vivianz, Wolfram pauses,
too, to mention the fine silk from Triant of which the cloak
is made (59,13). Recovering soon from his exhaustion, the
horse begins to snort, and to eat the grass. The accumulation of details in this restful passage does nothing to retard the action: rather does it accentuate the activity on
either side of it.

In each of these scenes there is a concentration on the
personal: it is a human relationship which Wolfram stresses,
for in this work which deals with vast numbers and where, for
example, the protagonists can be compared with drops of rain
or the waves of the sea, he nevertheless never loses sight
of the individuals involved, nor of the ordinary human emotions
which are at stake. Similarly, in the battles, he is capable
of conveying simultaneously the sense of the mass, while
allowing individuals to emerge from it and then return to it.[5]

The essential duality of substance, then, the activity concentrated above all in the battles and at Munleun, and the love of Willehalm and Gyburc, is echoed and reiterated in other aspects of the work. Contrasts exist clearly in both substance and narrative texture: indeed the two are closely related as the above examples have already shown. There are smaller instances of contrast, too, which contribute to the texture of Wolfram's narrative and support, in their own way, the sense of the juxtaposition of opposites which characterizes the work.

Before the first battle of Alischanz, Wolfram has spoken of the vast numbers of heathen knights, best described in the picture of them covering hill and valley: he then turns to Willehalm, with his pitifully small army:

> ûf Alischanz erzeiget wart
> gein Terramêrs übervart,
> daz man sach mit manlîcher wer
> des marcgrâven Willalmes her,
> die hant vol als er mohte hân.          (13,5-9)

The lines convey the essence of the first battle: the immense forces of heathendom in conflict with the much smaller army of Christians.

A little later in the first battle the picture of Willehalm surveying the formidable enemy (16,2-19) leads immediately to his speech of exhortation to his men, as he urges them to fight in the defence of their faith (17,3-22). Passive contemplation of the battle ahead gives way, then, to the active, verbal, expression of its implications, until, with the ending of Willehalm's speech, there comes the sound of trumpets, the tangible sign of the commencement of the fighting. These are three separate narrative moods, a developing sequence yet at the same time contrasting.

Later, when the battle has been raging for some time, Wolfram allows Willehalm to assess his situation and to link his losses with his love for Gyburc:

> riweclîche er dô sprach
> 'mîner mâge kraft nu sîget,
> sît sus ist geswîget
> Monschoy unser crîe.
> ey Gyburc, süeze âmîe,
> wie tiwer ich dich vergolten hân!...'  (39,8-13)

er klagt daz minneclîche wîp
noch mêre dan sîn selbes lîp
und dan die flust sîns künnes.
'got, sit du verbünnes
Gyburge minne mir,'
sprach er, 'sô nim den trôst ze dir,
swaz der getouften hie bestê,
daz der dinc vor dir ergê
âne urteillîchen kumber.
des ger ich armer tumber.'          (39,21-30)

In the midst of so much conflict, Wolfram focuses his attention on one man, and, as so often in this work, he highlights
the solitary human being and the personal within the public
and the impersonal. Then, in a swift movement, he shows Willehalm fighting his way through the ranks of the enemy in
search of his kinsmen. The example shows, again, a development through the contrasting moods, but here the contrasts of
personal and public merge as the leader of so many men, alone
and grief-stricken, battles his way through the overwhelming
numbers of his enemy.

Contrast is, indeed, an outstanding feature of Wolfram's
account of the first battle, this conflict between unequal
forces fighting for irreconcilable causes, and contrast exists
in his handling of the description of the battle. He passes
over groups of combats very quickly, supplying no details
beyond, in some cases, the names of the individuals involved,
but suggesting consistently the high quality of the chivalry
(e.g. 26,16-19; 27,2-4; 27,6-11; 27,12-15). Yet side-by-side
with these swift, shadowy incidents are battles which he describes at greater length and in considerable detail, until
his account centres on Arofel, as he speaks of the prowess
shown by him and his ten nephews and so anticipates the death
of Arofel himself.

A further aspect of his use of contrast is in his treatment of the colour and extravagance of the heathen clothing
and the magnificence of their encampment: all this has its
darker side, for the clothes will be darkened with blood and
the beautifully adorned helmets will be pierced and battered,
and the splendid turbans are no protection for the vulnerable
heads. Equally, the exultant cries of Tervigant! and Monschoy!

must fade in the face of the sombre lamentation which is the
keynote of the battle.

At the centre of Wolfram's thought is the woman doubly
named, who returns with her advocacy of universal love the
hatred of all about her. This basic contrast pervades the
work and gives it its essential stamp, yet equally the juxtaposition of seemingly irreconcilable opposites exists within
the sense of an overriding harmony, of thought and of narrative.

Thus the figure of Rennewart, the larger-than-life figure
who occupies so much of the work and who, with so much about
him of almost burlesque humour, contrasts so markedly with
the mood of the whole, nevertheless finds a place in the
whole. This gauche young boy who appears so completely out
of place at the French Court comes into his own on the battlefield of Alischanz. Yet even there, his stange, the uncourtly weapon which he wields so ruthlessly, is in sharp contrast
to the prevailing mood of high chivalry, and only gradually
does it yield to the knightly sword, as Rennewart himself
seems gradually to find his place in the courtly context.[6]
In detail, too, there is an incongruity about what we learn
of Rennewart, even from his first appearance. Wolfram declares that he has in his own person the strength of six men
(188,4-7), yet soon afterwards he describes him enduring the
ill-treatment of the other pages als ein kiuschiu maget (190,1).
Incompatible though these two descriptions may seem at first
sight, they are, however, an essential part of Wolfram's conception of the young boy, in whom extraordinary physical
strength and a self-effacing manner unite to give depth to a
character remarkable for the sympathetic fusion of conflicting
elements. Rennewart, who can fall into a rage and behave with
extreme brutality when roused, is capable also of the tender
farewell from Alyze. The link between these seemingly irreconcilable facets is the complexity of the story of the young
prince, deprived of his heritage and profoundly embittered by
circumstances. The ultimate reconciliation of these opposites,
the harmonious picture of restored honour and requited love,

lies, of course, beyond the framework of Wolfram's <u>Willehalm</u>,
though it may be anticipated in the hints at the love between
the boy and the young Princess, and in his enigmatic conversation with Gyburc.

Wolfram supports the total impression of contrast in
<u>Willehalm</u> on a verbal level, too. When, for example, he has
spoken of the death of Cliboris, he recalls the brilliance of
the man as he lies dead:

> der clâre junge starke gast
> underm orse tôt belac. (411,6-7)

The contrast in these two lines is characteristic of Wolfram's
power of precise, economic statement: it depends upon his
juxtaposing the accumulation of three adjectives which convey
the sense of life and movement with the single unembellished
word <u>tôt</u>. In an oblique reference to the nobility of Trohaz-
zabe he again achieves his effect by the contrast of two
lines:

> swelhes tages er keinen vîent sach,
> bî vriunden het er ungemach. (365,13-14)

A further example of verbal contrast occurs when he comments
on the activity of the battle in the brief contrasting statement:

> hie der stich, dort der slac,
> jener saz, dirre lac. (19,3-4)

The two lines are effective in conveying the swift contrasting
movements which continue all the time in the clash of opposing
forces. They sum up the essence of the battle which Wolfram
is capable of expressing elsewhere by means of elaborate descriptions of military strategy. Indeed, a part of the contrasting texture of Wolfram's descriptions of battle scenes
depends upon his ability to juxtapose, for example, the lengthy
accounts of the movement of dense masses with the vivid and
pungent statement, or the sense of the clash between forces
of unnamed men with poignant accounts of individual combats.
Never for a moment does Wolfram lose sight of the individual
human lives which are at stake, although at times the awareness of the individual  recedes in face of the cause for
which he is fighting or of the sense of enormous numbers.

A further aspect of Wolfram's use of contrast reflects

his awareness of the incongruous in much of what he is telling. Very often this is most effectively summed up in a
verbal antithesis. After the second battle of Alischanz
Willehalm himself assesses the outcome of the battle in
powerful, tragic terms:

>     dirre sige mir schumpfentiure
>     hât ervohten in dem herzen mîn.  (459,26-27)

The lines contain the essence of Wolfram's conception of the
second battle, for what can military victory represent to
the man who, on a personal level, has known the loss of so
many friends and who, on the higher, more impersonal level
which is the greater concern of the work, is growing in his
respect for all human life and his abhorrence of its destruction.

The doubtful nature of the victory is conveyed, less
explicitly but with a grim humour which emphasizes Wolfram's
meaning, when, after the second battle, the Christian army
eats the exotic food left behind by their defeated opponents:

>     vil spîse ûz Orkeise,
>     vil spîse ûz Adramahût.
>     dâ wart manec verhouwen hût
>     mit unkunder spîse erschobn.     (447,26-29)

The horror of the situation is perhaps most potently conveyed in this juxtaposition of the rich food and the battered
helmets in lines which seem to pass a tacit comment on the
nature of the victory. One is reminded of a similar occasion,
when Wolfram had recalled that the good food consumed by the
company at Orange was left behind by those who died at Alischanz (264,15-19).

Earlier, in the course of the second battle, Wolfram's
awareness that this is a conflict which brings doubtful rewards is conveyed in a direct, ironic statement:

>     ir râche gap dâ sterbens lôn.        (363,9)

Of the old Count Heimrich he comments:

>     der alte hete gerbet
>     sîne süne mit sölhen urborn     (383,22-23)

and he proceeds to elaborate on this statement in words which
recall the opening of his work and draw attention to the
tragic irony without which the present conflict might never

have arisen:

> sît er ze sune het erkorn
> einen andern denn die sîne,
> des gâben unde nâmen pîne
> in andern landen sîniu kint.     (383,24-27)

Irony in the form of verbal antithesis is present in his
brief yet powerful comment:

> manec lebn [wart dâ] übersigelet
> mit des tôdes hantveste.     (391,26-27)

Such examples of Wolfram's use of verbal contrasts express his awareness of the antithesis which is basic to the
work. The woman doubly named whose love has given rise to
hatred speaks above the clamour of the battle her words of
love and reconciliation and the God whom she worships is the
One der weinen unde lachen geschuof (258,19-20). The basic
situation is one of antithesis, and this Wolfram furthers by
his technique of juxtaposing contrasting scenes and moods, of
varying the mood of his own narrative by contrasting textures
and by expressing antitheses in brief, pungent statements.

b)  The economy of the narrative and Wolfram's use of under-
    statement

An aspect of the texture of the narrative results from
Wolfram's ability to sum up events very briefly, and this he
does often at moments of great significance, indicating, it
is true, the urgency of the situation, but ensuring also the
impact of a swift and pungent statement.

Although he lingers for a long time on accounts of the
conflict, he is capable, too, of expressing the swift activity of battle in an economical manner, when he says, for
example:

> hie der stich, dort der slac:
> jener saz, dirre lac,     (19,3-4)

or when, at another point, the power of the attack is described in brief and vivid terms:

> Halzebier kom mit kraft.     (18,14)

A little later the mutual destruction is expressed in four
lines:

> beidiu geslagen und gesniten
> ûf ir wâpenlîchiu kleit
> was Kristes tôt, den da versneit
> diu heidensch ungeloubic diet.     (31,24-27)

Here, with the utmost economy, Wolfram speaks of the cause
of the conflict, the motivation of the Christians and the
totality of the destruction.

Before the second battle the inequality of the armies
is expressed in the simple question:

> was touc diu hant vol genant
> gein dem her ûz al der heiden lant?
>                                   (328,29-30)

The grief of the battle is summed up in the sighing of high
and low:

> dâ heten siuftebæren schal
> die minren und die mêrren.     (445,22-23)

On occasions such as these, the brief statement of fact has
an impact just as powerful as a lengthy description, and sometimes it can have an even more pungent effect, as when Wolfram
speaks of the death of Arofel and dismisses a lengthy account
in a terse cliché:

> war umbe sold i'z lange sagen?
> Arofel wart aldâ erslagen.     (81,11-12)

Often, of course, Wolfram has spoken at length and the
line in question is the final succinct expression of a situation. Thus, for example, the long account by Willehalm of
the losses sustained in the first battle ends with the simple
statement:

> Myle and Vivîanz sint tôt          (151,30)

and a single line can express what is, in fact, the basic
situation of the work:

> Durh Gyburge al diu nôt geschach.     (306,1)

Having anticipated the coming battle in the lengthy speech
by Terramer, Wolfram indicates the movement of events in a
single line:

> nu wârn ouch die getouften komn.     (351,21)

The final departure of the heathens is described in the most
economical terms, yet with a pungency and realism which echo
the mood of the whole battle:

> dâ wart niht langer dô gebiten,
> mit fluht ein ende nam der strît. (443,24-25)

When Rennewart has met the deserters at Pitît Punt and
has taken his revenge with his pole, Wolfram sums up with the
somewhat sardonic remark:

        do gerou si diu widervart.        (324,30)

Later in the second battle he unites the motif of revenge
with the death which comes to those who seek revenge, in the
single ironic statement:

        ir râche gap dâ sterbens lôn.        (363,9)

Elsewhere, too, this technique leads to something of an
understatement, as, for example, when Wolfram concludes his
account of the singeing of Rennewart's hair and his furious
reaction with the rather subdued comment:

        zornic was der junge man.        (198,28)

This reduction in the status of events is, of course, only
apparent, for Wolfram's command of his material is the decisive factor. When he says, for example, of the knights
fighting

        sine spilten niht der tocken        (222,18)

he can be sure that the incongruous suggestion will do nothing
to harm the sense of the magnitude and force of the battle,
that, indeed it may well increase it, as when he compares the
magnificently attired knights with the doll of his daughter
(33,24-26). Far from distorting the proportion of events,
such technique can establish the real proportions very firmly.

Two impressive lines during the course of the second
battle suggest effectively the scope of the fighting:

        von maneger hurte enge
        wart ûf dem wîten plâne.        (441,28-29)

Again, much is said by these lines, which stress both the
large numbers of the soldiers and the vast field where they.
are fighting. In the contrast of _enge_ and _wîte_, Wolfram
suggests the impossible: the narrowing of the broad plain by
the multitude of knights. It is such moments, perhaps, which
show Wolfram at his most powerful as a narrator: he has no
need of the long, brilliant descriptions of which he is capable when his meaning can be conveyed with economic pungency.
Thus he can express the horror and suffering in the simple
statement that the men's clothing is made of blood and sweat

(443,21-22), where the two lines express in a new manner the
trials of battle described equally effectively at greater
length elsewhere.

In this work in which so much is on a large scale, Wolfram frequently achieves a powerful effect by understatement,
or by using the negative to convey something essentially positive. Thus, for example, he says of the courageous men who
fight in the second battle:

ez wârn niht kinder.     (352,8)

Of the dead men whom Gyburc sets up on the battlements he
comments:

diene wancten niht durh zageheit     (111,23)

and the starkness of the reality loses nothing by the touch
of grim humour, either here, or a little later, when he says
of the judge who detains Willehalm:

des houbtes er dô kürzer wart.     (113,29)

Sometimes, as in this case, a certain superficial lightness
covers, but in no way obscures, the reality of what Wolfram
is saying. Thus on the field of Alischanz he says:

blanke bluomen und daz grüene gras
wurden rôt von sîner slâ     (384,8-9)

or, at greater length, he conveys the same sense of grim
reality:

den getouften henden man des giht,
von Frîende ab den gesten
ir tiweren pfellel glesten
manec swertes ekke aldâ begôz,
dazz pluot über die blicke flôz:
si wurdn almeistic rôt gevar.     (381,12-17)

Of the first battle he tells us that prisoners are not taken
there (10,27-29). What he does not say is the truth which is
nonetheless evident: that death takes the place of captivity.

At the end of Book I two separate lines stand out as
examples of the kind of directness at which Wolfram excells:
these are two vivid lines which convey, for all their simplicity, the totality of the horror. He is speaking of Willehalm making his way from the battlefield and he comments:

sîn ors durch manne bluot gewett.     (56,14)

Here the reality of physical death and mutilation is expressed

without elaboration. When, a little later, he says of Willehalm

   daz gewunnen ors er liez durch nôt  (57,15)

Wolfram is adding to the impression already achieved of
physical suffering the mental anguish of the vanquished
leader who may not grant his enemy a potential advantage and
so, in the very next line, is seen to kill the horse. This
moment of acute human suffering is passed over by Wolfram
with a final comment which unites it, for all its intensity,
with universal experience:

   ern gunds der heidenschefte niht
   als noch en vîentscheft geschiht.
            (57,17-18)

  When Wolfram tells of Rennewart that he does not take
prisoners he is again telling us something more: that the
powerful Rennewart kills his opponents in this terrible battle.
There is no need, of course, for Wolfram to spell out that
fact: instead, he offers a simple explanation:

   Berhtram was im sippe niht   (388,25)

and no more is said.

  Sometimes this technique of understatement takes a slightly different form. To make his point more emphatically, Wolfram directs his attention towards something seemingly unconnected. For example, when he says that Heimrich's men have
ridden so fast that the fish in the fords lie dead (212,28-30),
he is not, of course, concerned with the fish but with the
speed of the horses' hooves which have trampled them, and
later, when he is telling of the loss of life in the second
battle, he again tells of the fishes in the Larkant, though
his actual interest is in the blood which stains them:

   E truogen vörhen rôtiu mâl:
   rôt wurden vische über al
   von dem strîte in Larkant.   (439,1-3)

When, in speaking of the cloak of Ehmereiz, he moves away
from the cloak to the ostrich which might have hatched its
eggs by its brilliance and warmth, he is not seriously di-
verting attention to this whimsical idea, any more than when
he says that his daughter's dolls are not so beautiful as
the heathen knights he is earnestly proffering a comparison

of the two. These are subtle examples of a technique akin
to that of understatement, not quite identical in effect,
but all showing the mastery by Wolfram of his material which
makes it possible for him to introduce a fleeting subsidiary
notion which does not detract in the slightest from his
central narrative.[7]

c)  The use of parallels

The broad parallelism of the structure of Willehalm -
with parallels of time and place underlining the essential
parallel of the two battles, the second explicitly in revenge
for the first - is supported by Wolfram's use of parallels
within the texture of his narrative. Like his use of contrast,
this frequently draws attention to the conflict of opposites,
or sometimes rather to the fusion of opposites which is the
ultimate theme of the work.

Very early in Wolfram's account of the first battle the
parallelism of action is suggested in the parallel of the
battle cries:

>die heiden sich berieten:
>ir herzeichen wart benant,
>si schrîten alle Tervigant.
>daz was ein ir werder got:
>si leisten gerne sîn gebot.
>Monschoy was der getouften ruof,
>die got ze dienste dar geschuof.
>
>(18,26-19,2)

Though he is fully conscious of two opposing forces, governed
by irreconcilable beliefs, and though his narrative at all
times makes his audience aware of this, he succeeds also in
conveying the sense of the inextricability of the two sides
as they become involved in this tremendous struggle:

>die ze bêder sît dâ tohten
>gein strît, die warn geflohten
>in ein ander sêre.                    (19,5-7)

In these lines Wolfram expresses something which is basic to
his description of the battle: the merging in an indistinguish-
able mass of two forces which are known at all times to be
distinct.

At an early stage, too, Wolfram gives parallel accounts

of the motivation of the two sides in the battle. Yet there
is variety within the parallel, for while he speaks at some
length of the bright adornments of the heathens and recalls
the ladies who gave them and in whose service they have gone
into battle (19,18-27), the motivation of the Christians is
quickly stated:

> nâch dem êweclîchem prîse
> die getouften strebten.                    (19,28-29)

Similarly, when, in a passage a little later, attention is
focused on the heads of the knights on both sides, it is to
emphasize the mutual annihilation, for the vulnerable heads
of the heathens are matched by the heads of the Christians
whose helmets are battered through:

> mit swerten was vil ungespart
> ir hôh gebende snêvar:
> drunde âne harnasch gar
> was dâ manec edel houbet,
> daz mit tôde wart betoubet.
> ouch frumten si mit kiulen
> durh die helme alsölhe biulen,
> dês under der getouften diet
> vil maneger von dem leben schiet. (20,22-30)

Wolfram extends this sense of the parallel fates of un-
identified men to his treatment of named individuals. Thus,
for example, the death of Mile has elements of comparison
with that of Pinel. Both are described in the simplest terms
which stress their nobility (21,10; 21,24). Like Pinel, Mile
is mourned by all the land and both men die at the hand of the
leader of the opposing force. These are not remarkable features, but they contribute to an example of the way in which
Wolfram devotes attention equally to both sides in the conflict.

Similarly, but on a larger scale, Wolfram makes a deliberate parallel, when he speaks of Vivianz slaying seven
kings:

> und daz er sluoc Libilûn,
> Arofels swester sun,
> Eskelabôn und Galafrê,
> Rubîûn und Tampastê,
> Glorîôn und Morhant.          (46,17-21)

With them he links Pinel, the nephew of Halzebier, and much
mourned by him, when he tells how, specifically by way of

revenge, Halzebier takes captive eight princes, whose names
he gives also (47,2-6). This parallel does not end here,
however, but extends into the second battle when Rennewart,
in many ways the counterpart in the second battle of Vivianz
in the first, releases these eight men: it is in conflict
with them that Halzebier dies. This is already a complicated pattern, sustained by Wolfram through this series of
parallels and extending from the first battle into the second.
Obscurely, and by means of these parallels, one may see how,
at the last, Vivianz is directly responsible for the death of
Halzebier. Yet with the irony which is so much a part of the
work, it was Halzebier who dealt the mortal blow to Vivianz.
At the time the motif of revenge was explicit:

> nu wart gerochen Pînel
> von Halzibier dem künge snel,
> do er an Viviâns ersach
> daz er die schar mit hurte brach. (46,13-16)

The nephew of Willehalm pays the price for the death of the
nephew of Halzebier. Moreover, to complete this complicated
and subtle pattern, it is Arofel, whose name was coupled at
its first mention with the name of Halzebier (9,22-23) who
dies at the hand of Willehalm, incensed by the death of
Vivianz. Wolfram's use of parallels has extensive effects
in this chain of events. It confirms the sense which is expressed so often of losses equally endured on both sides, and
it underlines the notion of revenge basic to his conception
of the two battles. More than that, however, it has a function
within the structure of the work, contributing to its characteristic compression by the drawing together of events wide
apart in the narrative.

Quite different in technique and in effect, is an example
of Wolfram's use of a verbal parallel in the second battle
when he juxtaposes the fortunes of the two great forces:

> diu kristenheit sich rêrte,
> diu heidenschaft sich mêrte
> ûf Alitschanz dem anger.        (392,25-27)

In these lines the parallel construction, with the rhyming of
the contradictory verbs, serves to give the full force to the
third line, emphasizing the place of the conflict, rather as,

throughout the work, the rhyming of Vivianz and Alischanz
points to the place as the scene of the revenge for the man.[8)]
Here the parallel construction draws attention to the antithesis which is so much a feature of the work as a whole and
a keynote of the battle scenes. Contrast is achieved by the
emphasis on the parallelism, as it is when Wolfram speaks of
the two forces, their motivation and their fates in similar
terms.

There are specific instances of Wolfram's use of parallels
which contribute to the overall effect of balance within the
narrative. In the encounter between Willehalm and Arofel, for
example, there is a certain parallelism in the speeches of
the two men:

> er sprach 'ich pin ein Persân.
> mîn krône aldâ der fürsten pflac
> mit kraft unz an disen tac:
> nu ist diu swacheit worden mîn.
> ey bruoder tohter, daz ich dîn
> mit schaden ie sus vil engalt!
> Arable unde Tybalt,
> lægt ir für mich beide erslagen,
> iwern tôt man minre solde klagen.' (80,6-14)

> der marcrâve mit zorne sprach
> 'du garnest al mîn herzesêr,
> und daz dîn bruoder Terramêr
> mîne besten mâge ertœtet hât,
> und daz dîn helfeclîcher rât
> dâ bî alz volleclîchen was.
> ob alz gebirge Kaukasas
> dîner hant ze geben zæme,
> daz golt ich gar niht næme,
> dune gultest mîne mâge
> mit des tôdes wâge.' (80,16-26)

Both situate themselves firmly within their respective fami-
lies, and Arofel's own implied assessment of himself as the
representative of Terramer confirms Willehalm's resolve to
make him his representative in death, and to take his life in
compensation for the death of his own kinsmen.

There is a balance, too, of husband and wife, as Wolfram relates the addresses of Willehalm and Gyburc to the
assembled knights before the second battle. Gyburc takes her
place, and the whole company sits, leaving only Willehalm on
his feet. As Willehalm moves from his formal address to

those who are about to fight for him to a statement of the
issues, both personal and impersonal, which are at stake,
Wolfram concentrates, as he so often does in this work, on
the single human being, against the background of wide and
public matters. Although he appeals to his men to defend
their baptism and their faith, he draws attention to himself
and his desperate plight:

> er sprach 'ich tuon iu allen kuont,
> die mîne genôze hinne sîn,
> mîn vater und die bruoder mîn,
> und die mir ze mâgen sîn benant
> und die srîches hêrre hât gesant
> ze wern den touf und unser ê.　　(297,6-11)
>
> ich bite iuch al gelîche
> daz ir mich freuden armen
> iuch alle lât erbarmen.　　(297,28-30)

Very soon afterwards Wolfram will allow the full focus of
that great assembly to rest on Gyburc as she stands up, a
solitary figure, too, speaking of her personal affliction and
her personal faith, in order to urge the men to exercise compassion for the increase of their Christian honour. There is
a balance here, quite clearly, of husband and wife, the one
the active leader inspiring his forces to fight and the other
the advocate of the abstract ideal of mercy and love. The
two meet, however, in the desire for the protection of Christianity, and the tangible expression of this merging is in the
Matribleiz-scene, when Willehalm, the man who has led his army
to victory, demonstrates his compassion towards the defeated
survivors and his reverence for the heathen slain, the kinsmen of his wife. This consummation lies, however, far from
the present scene, yet there is certainly its seed in Wolfram's parallel structure, in which Willehalm's opening address
to the _rât_ is matched by the speech of Gyburc which closes it.
The men go into battle remembering the exhortation of their
leader, but equally they must recall the extension of his
words in the plea of his wife:

> die rœmschen fürsten ich hie man,
> daz ir kristenlîch êre mêrt,
> ob iuch got sô verre gêrt,
> daz ir mit strîte ûf Alischanz
> rechet den jungen Vivîanz

> an mînen mâgn und an ir her:
> die vindet ir mit grôzer wer.
> und ob der heiden schumpfentiur ergê,
> sô tuot daz sælekeit wol stê:
> hœrt eins tumben wîbes rât,
> schônt der gotes hantgetât. (306,18-29)

As Gyburc will do after him, Willehalm speaks of his personal
situation and of the events which have led up to the present
conflict (298,1-13). Like her, too, he speaks of their love
which he, too, links with her baptism:

> dar nâch ich bat
> in gevancnisse ir minne
> sîn wîp die küneginne.
> ir güete mich gewerte
> al des ich an si gerte
> daz tet si, durh den touf noch mêr,
> mit mir danne ir überkêr,
> denn durh mîne werdekeit. (298,16-23)

The lines anticipate, indeed, the words of Gyburc herself
when she, too, emphasizes that the power of baptism exceeds
that of the human love which has led to it:

> ich trag al ein die schulde,
> durh des hœhsten gotes hulde,
> ein teil ouch durh den markîs
> der bejaget hât sô manegen prîs. (310,17-20)

It is fitting that Willehalm's exhortation to fighting men
to go into battle prompts a wholly active response, in
contrast to the silent expression of sympathy which follows
Gyburc's appeal a little later. In turn, Heimrich, Bernart,
Bertram and Buov stand up and declare their allegiance to
Willehalm's cause, echoing their own promise made at Munleun
(170,23ff). Indeed, Wolfram himself reminds us of this when
he says:

> des ze Munlêûn si swuoren
> und ze Orlens vor dem rœmschen vogt,
> daz enwart niht lenger für gezogt.
> (304,14-16)

Only Gybert, of those who had spoken on that earlier occasion,
does not now respond to Willehalm's speech: for him remains
the task of expressing the reaction of them at the end of
Gyburc's speech, when he alone goes forward to embrace her,
in silent acknowledgement of the effect of it on all present.
The balance of Wolfram's narrative is subtle here, with this

balance of husband and wife in speeches which, while distinct and characteristic, have much in common. There is
balance, too, in the reaction of their audience, with Heimrich, Bernart, Bertram and Buov expressing in words what
Gybert alone expresses in a gesture of emotion and affection:
all five men have pledged themselves, in that earlier scene
at Munleun which anticipates the reality of the present one,
to the service of Willehalm and the defence of Gyburc herself. The presence of Gyburc now recalls how, on that earlier
occasion, she had been present as a powerful abstract force,
though separated from them physically. Once more, Wolfram
has shown, by a subtle use of parallels and balance, the
harmony of the whole which rests on the harmony of the couple.

d) <u>The function of details within the narrative</u>

    <u>Willehalm</u> is a work of large proportions and it is clear
that these proportions are both held in check and emphasized
by Wolfram's handling of such features of his narrative as
his use of parallels and contrasts, his mastery of the sense
of place and time and of the relationships among events, and,
perhaps above all, by the consistency of the thought, which
gives to the whole an outstanding harmony. On this distinctive basic texture Wolfram superimposes other strands, by his
handling of details of his narrative, his use of colours and
sounds and his isolation at times of minute features which together contribute to the exciting variety of his work.

    Already some of the details within Wolfram's narrative
have been discussed, those which themselves demonstrate his
sense of contrast or his power of economic expression, for
example. The present concern is with tangible details on
which he focuses attention and these are very often details
of physical appearance. Such details perform a variety of
functions in their own right, but the examination of them
draws attention, also, to the manner in which Wolfram integrates the sense of detail into that awareness of the whole
which is so vital a feature of the work.

    One may have felt in <u>Parzival</u> that Wolfram was sometimes

indulging his fancy and that not all the descriptions were
important in the work as a whole. In <u>Willehalm</u>, on the other
hand, the impression is that even seemingly irrelevant details have a significance, though sometimes this does not
become apparent until later in the work.

Thus, when Wolfram spends some time on the description
of the magnificent cloak of Ehmereiz, this is not just a description of clothing to rank with similar ones elsewhere, but
it gains in its function when Ehmereiz is taken captive and
the rich silk is again mentioned:

> der tiure phellel pôfûz
> gap gein der sunnen sölhez prehen,
> daz des küneges kumber muosen sehen
> diu fluot der Sarrazîne:
> doch beschutten in die sîne.     (367,26-30)

The seemingly impending fate of the beautiful cloak, whose
colour and brilliance were so vividly described before, is
not to be realized, for those same qualities ensure that it
is easily distinguished and its wearer released from the
ignominious captivity which would have been as inappropriate
for the princely son of Gyburc as the destruction of the fine
cloak.

Similarly, when Willehalm comes for the first time to
the monastery, Wolfram lays stress on his rich apparel and
particularly on the shield:

> dâ ze Samargône
> in der houbetstat ze Persîâ,
> sîn schilt was geworht aldâ:
> des buckel was armüete vrî.     (125,8-11)

The description is important, emphasizing as it does the
exotic origin of the shield and its great value, but at this
stage its particular function is not developed, as Wolfram
goes on to speak of the richness of Willehalm's clothing
(125,12-23). It is only then that he recalls how this finery
came into Willehalm's possession:

> er nam dem Persâne
> Arofel, der vor im lac tôt,
> daz friwendîn friwende nie gebôt
> sô spæher zimierde vlîz.     (125,24-27)

Already the future significance of the shield is anticipated,

yet still Wolfram's stress is on the value of the shield and
the clothing rather than on their association with the slaying of Arofel. Indeed, the comparison with the rich gifts
which Secundille gave to Feirefiz (125,28-30) introduces a
slight digression and the shield as a motif is allowed to
drop - but only for a short time. It is mentioned again as
Willehalm departs from the monastery on the next day, and
this reference is a brief and factual one:

> aldâ bevalh er sînen schilt
> und reit er gein Munlêûn.                    (126,6-7)

It is when Willehalm returns to find the monastery burnt to
the ground that the shield takes on a new stature, linking the
two visits and so contributing to the parallelism of place,
but provoking also the long account by Willehalm of his slaying of Arofel (203,19-207,30).[9] The shield and Wolfram's
description of it are in no way gratuitous details, then, but
perform an important function within the narrative.

When Willehalm arrives at the French Court after his desperate ride there, the negative reception and his isolation
are accentuated again by a small detail which becomes the focus
of attention: the costly helmet which he removes from his head
and places beside him. The suspicion and the puzzlement of
the people are conveyed with remarkable effect, as Wolfram
describes them scrutinizing him, even the ladies at the windows.
The isolation of Willehalm is increased by the sense of so
much speculation directed towards him while the movement of
the crowd is so deliberately away from him. The deliberate
action of Willehalm, as he jerks off his coif becomes the
focus of attention now, the one clearly defined action. Again,
Wolfram's description of his rust-stained face and tousled
hair and beard suggests that the eyes of the crowd are riveted
now on that (127,29-30). It is not until one of the onlookers
goes to the King with the news that a fuller description is
given, of the lavish armour and the strange, heathen garments.[10]
Where, just before, Wolfram's description had been restricted
to the head of the man, one now realizes that nevertheless all
the details had been taken in by the stunned and uncomprehend-
ing onlookers. The contrast between the economy of that first

description and the much fuller account in the report to the
King is an effective means by which Wolfram conveys the sense
of bewilderment of the crowd and the estrangement of Willehalm himself from them. This sense of estrangement is intensified, moreover, by the image applied to Willehalm, of the
wolf peering into the sheepfold (129,14-17), as Loys and his
wife go to see who the visitor is and then as the order is
given by the Queen for the doors to be closed on him. All
this adds up to a remarkably powerful visual impression,
despite the economy and restraint of Wolfram's actual description, and much is present in his brief summing-up:

> der marcrâve, der trûric man,
> het etz ors in sîner hant.          (130,4-5)

The dejection suggested here changes, on the following day,
to a mood of anger and defiance, but, again, Wolfram does not
need many words to imply this change. It comes in the sudden
gesture of Willehalm in tying up his horse to the olive-tree
(138,27-28). The gesture, which links the rejection of the
previous night with his decision now to break through the in-
hospitality of the assembly, paves the way for Willehalm's
uncourtly behaviour in the presence of the King.

The instances of Wolfram's use of detail show how he
integrates the sense of detail into his awareness of the whole
and how, too, small details, whose significance appears to be
purely descriptive, can increase the impact of the narrative.
Similarly, the recurrent stress on the clothes of Arofel is
in no way purely descriptive. The distinctive clothing aids
Willehalm's escape and subsequently prevents Gyburc from recognizing him: in these two instances it has an actual role
to play in the progress of events. Later his appearance contributes to the puzzlement of the onlookers at Munleun, who
observe both that he is armed when there is no tournament
(127,18-21) and that his clothing is rich and unfamiliar to
Christian eyes:

> tiwer unde rîche
> ist swaz er ob dem îser hât.
> sô liehtiu wâpenlîchiu wât
> wart ougen nie bekennet.
> die pfelle unbenennet

> sint al der kristenheite.
> ein heidenisch gereite
> lît ûf dem râvîte.          (128,10-17)

These lines contain already the reminder of the origin of the
clothes and so recall the battle with Arofel which will become the centre of Willehalm's explanation to his brother-in-
law who marvels that, in the midst of such dire trouble, Willehalm should have dressed himself so lavishly (203,14-17).
Willehalm retains the armour of Arofel in the same way as
Parzival for a long time continues to wear the red armour of
Ither,[11] and in both cases the apparel carries with it the
reminder of how it was won: the parallel is a clear one, for
both men bear the burden of the death of a kinsman, together
with the terrible crime of _rêroup_. The armour of Arofel, like
that of Ither, is by no means only an external factor, but it
fulfils also this function as an abstract symbol of responsibility and guilt.[12] The same is true of Volatin, the horse
of Arofel, which is mentioned repeatedly (e.g. 82,4; 85,25;
87,12; 88,29; 89,14; 109,7; 114,21; 138,16; 225,8; 227,3;
232,2) and recalls also the action which brought it into Willehalm's possession.

In the passages which precede the last meeting between
Willehalm and Vivianz, Wolfram includes details which accentuate the parallel here, as the two men make their way towards
the scene of their farewell. In both cases, he stresses that
each is going towards the _wazzer Larkant_ (49,2 and 59,22); and
in each case he stresses the horse which takes its rider there,
the unnamed horse which Vivianz finds, wounded, when he recovers consciousness after the fight with Halzebier, and Willehalm's own horse Puzzat. Significant, too, is his more
subtle use of the shield of Vivianz. When Vivianz drags himself with difficulty on to the horse, Wolfram deliberately
mentions that he does not forget his shield (48,2-3), but it
is this shield which Willehalm later finds as he rides towards
the Larkant (59,26-29). Vivianz has been forced to abandon
this symbol of himself in battle, and Wolfram develops it as
a symbol when he continues to speak of the shield and of its
role in the battle:

> ûf dem was strîtes sus gespilt,
> Hâtschen, kiulen, bogen, swert,
> mit spern gein dem man tjoste gert,
> zefuort an allen orten.          (59,30-60,3)

As Willehalm looks at it and recognizes it from its jewels,
the reminder comes of Gyburc, who gave it to Vivianz:

> der marcrâve die borten
> erkande, als er geriemet was,
> smârâde und adamas,
> rubîn und krisolte
> drûf verwieret, als si wolte,
> Gyburc diu wîse,
> diu mit kostlîchem prîse
> sande den jungen Vivîanz
> ûf daz velt Alischanz.          (60,4-12)

The symbolism of the shield has widened in these lines: it
remains the symbol of Vivianz, his literal defence now no
longer needed, but because the role of Vivianz himself will
broaden, so, too, in this association with Gyburc, does the
shield bring with it the reminder of the cause of the entire
conflict, of the woman who sent not only him, but all the
Christians, into battle.

Here a detail takes on the role of a symbol, and something similar happens in the case of the star on the flag of
Willehalm, towards which the knights ride and which comes to
represent Willehalm himself. Wolfram mentions it first quite
factually:

> si kêrten dâ der sterne
> schein ûz des marcrâven vanen          (364,4-5)

and on the next occasion with greater emphasis:

> Synagûn strebte allez dar
> da der sterne mit sîm glaste
> sô rîlîchen vaste
> ûzes marcrâven vanen schein.          (369,12-15)

Already the star is dominant as the goal of Synagun, and very
few lines later it seems to be used in place of the Margrave
himself:

> dirre stern alhie bereite
> vil tjost die Sarrazîne.          (369,20-21)

The kiss which Wolfram says Willehalm has left behind
in Orange (149,5) is, clearly, a symbol of his separation
from her.  There is, however, one instance which seems particularly relevant to the present discussion of Wolfram's accentu-

ation of detail. When Willehalm returns to Orange to bring
aid to Gyburc, Wolfram speaks of the kisses which they exchange:

> sine het ouch niht sô liehten schîn,
> als dô er von ir schiet,
> als im ir süezer munt geriet,
> der dâ vil geküsset wart.
> ouwê daz ein sô rûher bart
> sich immer solt erbieten dar!          (229,20-25)

His description contains details which increase its significance beyond that of a loving reunion. The reference to
the unshaven state of Willehalm sums up his past activity and
his suffering, but the description nevertheless centres on
the kiss which has become the symbol of their separation and
now of their reunion. Similarly, Wolfram's mention of the
appearance of Gyburc is no mere external factor, for, like
the rough cheek of her husband, it epitomizes the physical
privations of the last days. Thus, now that she is confident
of release from her immediate hardship, she can, in a deliberate gesture, put off her armour:

> Gyburc moht ir wâpenroc
> nu mit êren von ir legn:
> si unde ir juncfrouwen megn
> dez harnaschrâm tuon von dem vel.

> (246,24-27)

Wolfram is interested in external appearances, and he is concerned here to make it clear that Gyburc is a beautiful and
very feminine woman, but more is implied in this gesture, for
she herself instructs her ladies-in-waiting to dress themselves, too, in their finest array, in order to delight their
menfolk, in accordance with their duty, and so to make light
of their trials (247,1-248,8). The ladies, who are not forgotten by the Christian knights who fight above all for the
love of God, have their positive role in the conflict, and
this Wolfram makes clear in this important reasoning of Gyburc's,
which culminates in the appearance of the ladies in their
finery and above all in the picture of Gyburc herself (249,3-7).

The examination of Wolfram's use of details has shown
already that Wolfram frequently concentrates on something
which seems, on first consideration, to be external. When,

on several occasions, he interpolates a detailed description
of the colour and lavish array of the knights within his
account of dire battle, his reason is not always only to draw
attention to the startling contrast of the finery and the
grim struggle for survival, although this is certainly often
the effect.[13] As we know from <u>Parzival</u>, Wolfram loves bright
colours and delights in extravagant accounts of rich apparel,
but in <u>Willehalm</u> these accounts rarely seem to exist for their
own sake. When he speaks early in the work, for example, of
the rich clothing of the heathens, he does so, above all, to
indicate its origin:

> sold ich si zimieren
> von rîcher kost, als si riten,
> die mit den getouften striten,
> sô mües ich nennen mangiu lant,
> tiure phelle drûz gesant
> von wîben durh minne
> mit spæhlîchem sinne.
> die heiden heten kursît,
> als noch manec friundîn gît
> durch gezierde ir âmîse.                          (19,18-27)

The emphasis is rather in these last lines, which stress the
motivation of the heathen in battle, compared with the Christians who strive

> nâch dem êweclîchem prîse.                         (19,28)

The elaborate comparisons of the heathen apparel with maytime
and summertime, with flower-strewn meadows, stress, too, the
incongruity of the beautiful clothing within the context of
this terrible battle, and often too there is an accompanying
hint that the motivating force is the love of a lady and that
a woman has supplied the finery (e.g. 46,12; 54,28-55,14).
Although for a brief period such descriptions of gay and extravagant clothing and brightly shining armour break into the
dominant descriptions of battle, their more potent effect is
to heighten the sense of reality, to draw attention to the
irony, that such beautifully dressed men with their lofty aims
are doomed to perish in the all-devastating conflict. A specific instance is the brilliant description of Tenebruns and
Arofel (76,16-21) which precedes their terrible deaths at the
hand of Willehalm. Even more outstanding for its subtle over-

tones is the earlier description of the snow-white turbans
and the brightly coloured garments which brings with it the
realization that the men have gone into battle without armour,
careless of their lives. (20,13-26). Once more, then, the
function of details is both the superficial one of description and the more subtle one of expressing in a tangible way
a fact of considerable importance in the advancement of the
narrative.

e)  The role of direct speech in the work

In a brief paragraph, Carl Lofmark draws attention to
the abundance of direct speech in <u>Aliscans</u> and to the fact
that Wolfram frequently avoids direct speech, when the substance is unimportant or when it can be imparted in another
way, as reported speech or as a thought.[14] Yet there are, of
course, lengthy passages of direct speech in <u>Willehalm</u> and, as
has already emerged in the examination of the spiritual thought
of the work, much of the significant thought is contained in
the speeches of central characters, above all of Gyburc. The
love of Gyburc and Willehalm, too, is expressed in the brief
but moving conversations between the couple, while the Rennewart story is advanced by the conversations of Rennewart with
other characters, which have been considered already as vital
stages in the gradual revelation of his history.[15]

Such speeches, with their distinctive and evident significance in other respects, are not, however, the focal point
of interest in the present chapter, which is concerned rather
with the contribution of Wolfram's use of direct speech to
the narrative texture.  The less obviously significant speeches,
it emerges, have a vital function in this respect, contributing to the characterization, advancing the narrative and
attaining perspective on events.

The first speech of the work is given, for example, to
an unnamed <u>emerâl</u>, who urges his heathen companions to help
their gods to annihilate the race of Heimrich (43,1-30). The
speech epitomizes the tone of the battle, with its emphasis
on the totality of the hoped-for victory and the bitterness

which has prompted the conflict. It reiterates, too, at this
early stage and in the mouth of one closely concerned, the
motivation for the war in the relationship between Willehalm
and Gyburc, and it points, though without emphasis, towards
the duality of the consequences of the relationship which
will be taken up by Gyburc in her great speeches later:

> swaz der marcgrâve hât getân
> mit Arabeln der künegin,
> was daz ir freudehaft gewin,
> daz möht ein trûren undervarn. (43,12-15)

It is appropriate that this fairly short but powerful speech
should be put into the mouth of an otherwise insignificant
character, for this suggests the involvement of the lesser
men, who, after all, constitute the majority of those who will
die in the two battles. The total commitment to the cause is
suggested by this man, who places himself firmly on the side
of Tybalt and Terramer and the heathen gods, and who, in this
speech, expresses the conviction that together they will deal
a mighty blow to the French, and above all to the proud Margrave himself. The speech has in common with Wolfram's depiction of the entire battle, and indeed of the work as a
whole, a fusion of the sense of scope and vast numbers and
the awareness of the individual and the role of the individual:[16)]

> helfet unseren goten ir rehtes,
> daz des Heimrîches geslehtes
> immêr iht mege beklîben. (43,3-5)

> nu mac der künic Tybalt
> al sînen goten danken wol:
> die Franzoys uns gebent zol,
> den si ungerne möhten lân. (43,8-11)

> nu sulen wir niht langer sparn
> die kriegen fruht von Narbôn.
> Heimrîches toten lôn,
> sol den verzinsen unser lant?
> sô manec werlîchiu hant
> ist komen mit Terramêre:
> si megens uns jehen zunêre,
> komen sis hin genozzen. (43,16-22)

> nu wænent die Franzoyser dort,
> daz uns der marcgrâve hie
> twinge als er uns twanc noch ie. (43,26-28)

In all these examples the individual, whether Christian or

heathen, is isolated against the broader background of the
whole of the fighting.

This speech by an anonymous prince, who stands for so
many unnamed heathens who fight in the first battle and perish
in the second, is followed immediately by one by Terramer, who
urges his men similarly to take revenge for the contemptuous
treatment of their gods by Arabel:

> ir helde von der heidenschaft,
> nu rech et unser altiu kraft,
> die wir hêten von den goten,
> daz sô verre ûz ir geboten
> Arabel diu verfluocht ist komn.     (44,5-9)

But Terramer is more personally involved, of course, and he
speaks of the loss which he has sustained in the abduction
of his daughter:

> mir und den goten ist benomn
> der ich ê jach ze kinde,
> von taverne ingesinde:
> von salsen suppierren
> sich Tybalt muose vierren
> von sînem wîbe und alle ir kint
> die hie durh rehte râche sint.     (44,10-16)

Again, the personal and the public issues are fused, above
all in the reminder that the children of Gyburc, made mother-
less by Willehalm, are present now, and determined to annihilate the Christian army. His declaration which closes the
speech, that Arabel will be forced to renounce her new religion or be burned to death (44,20-30), anticipates his long
debate with his daughter when he confronts her with the choice
of three means of execution.[17]

These two speeches, of the emerâl and of Terramer, stand
alone within the first battle and the activity which dominates,
but they supply the keynote to it, representing two stand-
points, which are similar yet contrasting, between two men of
very different status, both in the heathen army and in the
context of the work.

The next speech, a short and comparatively insignificant
one in the context of the mighty conflict, is the intimate
words of Willehalm to his horse, which show another, quite
different, side of the fighting man from that shown by the

revengeful speeches treated above. Here the solitary man,
profoundly dispirited by events, speaks to his only companion,
not words of war but of comfort, promising good food if ever
they are released from their present hardship. Like the
speeches of Terramer and the emerâl, this one, too, is effective in conveying a mood and the impression of one aspect of
a personality and a situation. Unlike them, however, it does
not rise out of the situation and merge with it again, but it
is in sharp contrast to the activity which Willehalm has just
left and that which he must now enter into, in his ride to
Orange. Where they had expressed vividly the mood of the
battle, this speech looks forward rather to the reunion with
Gyburc and the period of rest at Orange.

The first major speech of the work is the long soliloquy
of Willehalm when he finds Vivianz, as he believes, dead.
This is the first of a number of laments in the work, and it
is balanced, both aesthetically and from the point of view of
substance, by the lament for Rennewart at the end of the
work.[18] It is supported, one might perhaps say, by the brief
conversation just discussed: in the words to Puzzat, Wolfram
has shown the fearless knight and the mighty leader dejected
and alone, with only his horse to talk to after the deaths
of so many of his army. The speech has shown him at a very
low point, and so the grief which overwhelms him as he finds
Vivianz is in some degree expected. Willehalm's sense of
loss and near-despair was contained, in that previous speech,
in the simple address to his horse:

> nu sî wir bêde unvarende,
> und ich die freude sparende.          (58,29-30)

The restraint of those two lines gives way now to an emotional lament, as he addresses his nephew:

> ey fürsten art, reiniu fruht,
> mîn herze muoz die jâmers suht
> ân freude erzenîe tragen.          (60,21-23)

With the release of emotion comes now an outburst of grief
when he expresses the wish that he had been slain with his
nephew (60,24-61,17). Overwhelmed with grief, Willehalm
loses consciousness and the second stage of the lament begins

when he regains his senses. This next stage is concerned
with the virtue of Vivianz and his relationship with Willehalm himself, and with the grief which Gyburc will know
through his death (62,1-63,1). Again Wolfram juxtaposes joy
and sorrow in Willehalm's lament that this boy who was born
to bring him happiness now brings him suffering through his
death:

> mir wart dîn tugenthafter lîp
> ze freude an dise werlt erborn:
> dâ hân ich siuften für erkorn.          (63,2-4)

The contrast is maintained as Willehalm continues to speak
of the way in which his palace was enhanced by Vivianz
(63,5-6) and of how he had one hundred pages knighted for his
sake (63,7-9). The sense of past joys and honours, contrasted
so sharply with the present grief, persists and is heightened
by Willehalm's description of the elaborate clothes and exotic
equipment which Gyburc gave to Vivianz and his followers:

> und diu künegîn
> ieslîchem drîer slahte kleit
> ûz ir sunderkamern sneit,
> daz ich der kost nie bevant.
> von Thasmê und von Tyrant
> und ouch von Ganfassâsche brâht
> manec tiwer pfelle, des erdâht
> was dîner massenye
> (Gyburc mîn âmye
> het dich baz denne ir selber kint);
> brûnez scharlach von Gint,
> daz man heizet brûtlachen,
> daz hiezs iu allen machen;
> daz dritte kleit scharlachen rôt.
>                          (63,12-25)

The lines are full of significance, for they recall a glorious past and so contribute some greater depth to Vivianz, who
tends in other respects to be a somewhat unreal character: in
stressing what has gone before and, above all, the relationship with Gyburc, Wolfram ensures that this idealized figure,
who is to represent all the Christians slain and whose great
moment comes in his dying speech to Willehalm and the miracle
which takes place at his death, can nevertheless be appreci-
ated as a human being who has commanded love and honour in
his life and who merits the lamentation which follows his
death. The references to the gifts of Gyburc recall the

shield which Vivianz refused to abandon in his agony and
which Willehalm later found on the ground.[19] The references to the foreign parts which furnished the materials for
the clothing recall the vast regions of heathendom, contrasted here, at this moment of the intimate encounter between two men, with the Christian Lowlands associated with
the scarlet of Ghent: this brief period of respite is placed,
then, within its context of time and place, and of the circumstances which have given rise to it.

However, it is, as so often, a single line which sums up
the irony of the situation when Willehalm says:

in dirre wirde bistu tôt.          (63,26)

All the glory of the past of Vivianz and the magnificence of
his array are set against the single reality, that he is dead,
and in the final section of the lament Willehalm turns to the
sorrow of those who will hear of his death. He speaks of his
service to Love, and of how many ladies will mourn him (64,5-
17). The idea that the death of Vivianz has inflicted a great
loss on minne gains in significance if one recalls how Arofel,
too, will be mourned as the servant of Love and that, explicitly, Arofel is slain in revenge for Vivianz.[20] As he ends his
lament, however, Willehalm narrows down the grief to those
kinsmen who will learn of the death of Vivianz and themselves
grieve for it. Finally he returns full circle to his personal
sorrow, when the loss of Vivianz has intensified the grief
which he previously felt at the loss of so many of his men
(64,25-30). The significance of this long speech is not les-
sened by the fact that, soon afterwards, Vivianz rouses and
opens his eyes. The lamentation before his actual death means
that, at the moment of his death - at a moment, that is, of
great tension - Wolfram can refrain from further comment:

waz hilfet ob ichz lange sage?          (69,17)

and the anguish of Willehalm can be expressed, not in words,
nor in tears (69,24-26), but in the action which is, in a
sense, the most appropriate response to the slaying of his
beloved nephew on the field of Alischanz.

The tone of the two speeches by Vivianz is, of course,

quite distinct. The incident stands alone in the work, and
it has a very special function. Vivianz is to become the
martyr, whose death will inspire his kinsmen to revenge and
whose name will ring out through the second battle. Because
he is to take on the role of a saintly martyr, his words to
Willehalm before his death are of the utmost importance, particularly since, in addition, these words, together with the
brief prayer when he asks God to spare him from death just
long enough for him to see his uncle again (49,16-22), constitute all that Vivianz ever says. The conversation with Willehalm is, therefore, vital to the depiction of the young man,
whose death is one of the most important single incidents in
the whole work. Already in the appearance of the cherubim to
Vivianz, Wolfram has elevated the figure of the dying man;
and in the pious acceptance of his death, the faith and love
which radiate from him, as he speaks of his love for Gyburc
and his devotion to the Margrave and as he confesses his sins,
Wolfram justifies the view of Vivianz as a martyr who dies
for the cause and for whom vengeance must be sought. His reference to what may have been his guilt of cowardice (66,30-67,2)
gives rise in Willehalm to a profoundly sad lament and self-
accusation:

> wê mir dîner clârn geburt!
> waz wold ich swerts umb dich gegurt?
> du soltst noch kûme ein sprinzelîn
> tragen dîner jugende schîn
> was der Franzoyser spiegelglas.
> swaz dînes liehtn antlützes was,
> dar an gewuohs noch nie kein gran:
> war umbe hiez ich dich ein man?     (67,9-16)

The two men are contrasted in this scene: the mature Willehalm
with the weight of so much responsibility upon him is set side-
by-side with the radiant youth who is doomed to die, in order
to further the cause for which he has fought. The older man
is left to grieve that he must live, despite the death which
has taken from him the young boy whose death he sees as his
own responsibility. Yet the link between the two of them is
Gyburc herself whose name is rarely absent for long. Though
Willehalm declares that he himself has slain the young man -

> dich ensluoc hie niemen mêr wan ich -
>
> (67,22)

he mentions also the shield of Vivianz which has not proved
a defence for him against death (67,17-20). Although the
reference to the shield is unspecific, a reference simply to
his engaging in combat, it brings with it nevertheless the
reminder that it was Gyburc herself who gave him his actual
shield. Yet this thought is far from the mind of Vivianz,
and there is no suggestion that blame attaches to Gyburc,
although in more than one sense she has sent him into the
battle which has brought his death. The link with her, however, is clear, and when, with Vivianz dead, Willehalm's
thoughts turn again towards Gyburc, this is a further appropriate affirmation of the relationship of all three people.

The incident which contains the final meeting of Willehalm and Vivianz, then, with the speeches of the two men, constitutes a complex focus of the narrative, drawing together
the events of the first battle of Alischanz into a single
event of intrinsic significance which will have also vital
repercussions in the whole work. The juxtaposition of the
two men, so different and yet united through their love of
Gyburc and their service of a single cause, is expressed in
their contrasting words. After the activity of the battle,
there comes this new mode of activity, in human speech, before Willehalm embarks on another stage of the action, in the
ride to Orange, which, with Gyburc as its goal, is the fitting consequence of the events at the wazzer Larkant.

Fittingly, then, the next significant speech is given
to Gyburc herself. This is the prayer which she utters as she
lies beside Willehalm before he departs for Munleun (100,28-
102,20), and which further confirms the link with Vivianz and
with his dying commendation of his soul to God.

Between the speeches of Willehalm and Vivianz, and the
prayer of Gyburc, lies another speech which, without having
the significance of either of these, nevertheless has its
own function in maintaining the thought of Gyburc and of her
role in the conflict. Willehalm encounters Ehmereiz who

utters a brief speech in which he accuses Willehalm of bringing shame upon his mother, persuading her to renounce the
heathen laws for the sake of Christianity (75,3-20). These
are forceful words of accusation and they cry out to Willehalm to respond to the challenge implied, but he does not do
so: for the sake of Gyburc he spares her son. The speech contributes to the vivid picture of Ehmereiz, the rich prince
with the bright cloak,[21] and, again, it points out the personal issues involved within the public one. Here is a single
man concerned, not for the abduction of his Queen, but for the
treachery of his mother to her religion and her family, and
it is Willehalm's regard for personal considerations which
permits him to spare Ehmereiz, whose only distinction from
those many heathens whom Willehalm will slay in the two battles
is his relationship with Gyburc. The incident is an example
of Wolfram's ability to see the detail and the personal within
the whole, and the speech is a clear statement of the character of the outraged prince.[22]

Against this, then, the prayer of Gyburc towards the end
of Book II stands in sharp contrast. This is the first of
Gyburc's great confessions of faith and from its opening
address -
           ˙ich weiz wol, Altissimus,
            daz du got der hœhste bist ... - (100,28-29)
it is filled with the spirit of faith and of love. Though
she speaks of the losses which she has sustained through the
battle of Alischanz, she does so in no spirit of revenge.
Like Willehalm beside the body of Vivianz, she desires death,
now that her father has inflicted such suffering upon her
(101,16-21). The link with the dying speeches of Vivianz is
reaffirmed when she addresses her lament to him:

            ey Vivîanz, bêâs âmîs,
           dînen durhliuhtigen hôhen prîs,
           wie den diu werlt beginnet klagn!
           wie moht der tôt an dir betagn?  (101,27-30)
Her wish that she might have been allowed to die instead of
him and her other friends (102,6-9) recalls the same wish
uttered by Willehalm, and her grief that her husband should
be inflicted with such loss (102,10-11) matches Willehalm's

concern for the impending sorrow of his wife. Only at the
end of her speech does she refer, yet without bitterness, to
the role of her father:

> nu hât mîns vater nâchvart
> mir disiu herzesêr getân          (102,18-19)

and in the last statement -

> daz müese Tybalt hân verlân -          (102,20)

her attitude contrasts sharply with that of her son Ehmereiz
in his bitter and revengeful speech to Willehalm. That the
mainspring of this speech is grief is manifested in the tears
which awaken Willehalm now (102,21-25) and the mood of the
opening prayer is retained throughout, to make the whole
speech into a declaration of faith and acceptance of suffering inflicted through faith. Though the immediate impetus to
the speech is grief at the death of Vivianz, as is the case
with Willehalm's lament, the speech itself assumes wider proportions, as the reflection of a woman profoundly afflicted
in an insoluble dilemma. It is not the most significant of
Gyburc's speeches, but its position early in the work and
within this brief period of respite from activity ensures that
it shall be remembered. It is important, moreover, as a
statement of a basic reality which has been expressed already
in different ways, by Wolfram himself, by Willehalm, Ehmereiz, the unnamed **emerâl** and by Vivianz: that Gyburc is the
source of the conflict and that with her must rest therefore
the responsibility for the suffering and the death of so
many. Much remains to complete the picture, but this is a
powerful part of it, with the juxtaposition of this confession of faith and acceptance of responsibility within a scene
which depicts, above all, the love of the couple which is
shown to be the core of the dilemma.

If the speeches of Gyburc belong to the spiritual thought
of the work, uniting personal love and faith with the broad
theme of universal compassion and the unity of mankind as the
creatures of a single God,[23)] then those of Willehalm are
concerned above all with the activity of battle. From that
activity they emerge and to it they return, yet it has been
seen that the activity of battle cannot be divorced from the

spiritual thought.[24]  Thus, too, the speeches of the great
Christian leader are linked with the abstract thought which
prompts the actions of the man and the words of the woman.

Four speeches by Willehalm belong together, but it has
already been observed that the first of these, his address
to the assembled forces before the departure for the second
battle, is balanced by the address of his wife to the men.[25]
Although, in speaking of the love which has given rise to
the present conflict, Willehalm anticipates the words of
Gyburc, his prime intention is to urge his men into battle,
and his speech returns towards the end to this immediate
purpose, as he urges the men to fight for the twofold reward
which awaits them:

> ... der himel und werder wîbe gruoz.
>
> (299,27)

This coupling of the distinct inspirations of the men in
battle ensures that the thoughts of the whole assembly return to the present, away from the references to past events
which have led to them, and his brief but vivid evocation of
the sound of battle recalls Wolfram's descriptions of the
first battle and anticipate those of the second:

> ... dâ man lernet sölhen dôn,
> wie sper durch schilde krachen,
> wie diu wîp dar umbe lachen,
> wie vriundîn vriunts unsemftekeit
> semft.                          (299,22-26)

The juxtaposition in these lines is effective, for the incongruous rhyming of the cracking of spear against shield and
the laughter of ladies nevertheless unites the objectives of
prowess in battle and the reward of a lady's love, while the
final idea extends that of the pleasure of the ladies in the
knowledge of the courage of their knights, to the intimate
vision of the woman tending her beloved and bringing solace
in his suffering both mental and physical.  Behind this general
picture, with its relevance to all present, is, surely, the
reminder of the specific one, of Gyburc dressing the wounds
of Willehalm after the first battle and afterwards giving him,
in the active demonstration of her love, consolation for his
grief.  Although Willehalm's reference here is to a general

comparison, the vividness of that poignant scene, which has
ensured that it should be remembered throughout the separation of Gyburc and Willehalm, means that it comes to mind now
also and gives to Willehalm's appeal to a vast force the
additional power of a personal involvement, so that his speech
can appropriately end with his completely personal declaration:

> bin ich sô frum, dâ nâch ich muoz
> ûf Alischanz nu werben,
> oder ich wil drumbe ersterben.
>
> (299,28-30)

It is fitting that this exhortation to fighting men to go into battle for such high intentions should prompt a wholly
active response, as Heimrich, Bernart, Bertram and Buov stand
up and declare their allegiance to Willehalm: these are names
which will be associated with the activity of the second
battle of Alischanz.

On the battlefield, Willehalm again addresses his men,
now with a greater awareness of the proximity of the enemy.
The setting is important, as Wolfram himself introduces the
idea, which will dominate Willehalm's address, that some of
those due to fight may be having second thoughts, now that
the battle is so imminent:

> so beherberget was daz velt:
> niht wan mer und gezelt
> sâhen die des nâmen war.
> des begunde zwîvelen etslîch schar,
> die vil genendeclîche
> ê dicke in Francrîche
> bejageten prîs und ungemach.     (319,21-27)

Willehalm makes no attempt to disguise the facts, as he speaks
of the power of the enemy, evident to all through the vast
number of tents spread out on the field of Alischanz. He
emphasizes the nearness of the great army and the approaching
need to fight:

> dort lît der Kanabêus suon,
> Terramêr der rîche,
> alsô krefteclîche
> daz wir für wâr dâ vinden strît     (320,4-7)

and he stresses, too, that the moment of decision has arrived:

> nu muoz ich vrâgen (des ist zît)
> wer vehtens welle ernenden.     (320,8-9)

Though Willehalm seems to leave the decision to the individual man, there is no doubt in his speech that the only right
decision is that to remain, and his words are chosen to strike
at the most responsive chords in the hearts of the men assembled
before him:

> ein ieslîch man durch sîne zuht
> spreche als erz im herzen weiz.
> als uns nu vil manec puneiz
> ze gegenstrîte dringet,
> swen denn sîn herze twinget
> wider hinder sich und niht hin für,
> der hât hie baz ander kür,
> daz er nu wider kêre,
> danne er die fluht dort mêre.          (320,16-24)

After this direct appeal to their courage he ends his speech
with a reference to the spiritual rewards of the coming
battle (320,26-30). The ambiguity of Willehalm's speech is
only apparent: his hearers can be left in no doubt of their
responsibility as knights and as Christians, hence Wolfram's
comment

> die wurdn almeistic dâ geschant
>                                          (321,4)

and the ignominy which the deserters will suffer at the hands
of Rennewart.

The corresponding speech is the one which Willehalm
addresses to those who remain with him. In this he extends
the theme of spiritual reward which ended his previous speech
(322,4-13). The overriding impetus to the battle is asserted,
then, in this declaration that the reward of God will be
theirs, and suddenly we are reminded of the imminence of
battle:

> noch hiute sule wir lernen
> wie diu gotes zeswe uns lônes gieht.
>                                          (322,16-17)

Yet before Willehalm turns to the strategy to be adopted, he
speaks of those who have forsaken the battle, relating their
desertion to the validity of the cause:

> dehein sterne ist sô lieht,
> ern fürbe sich etswenne.          (322,18-19)

This is the leader speaking, whose duty it is to sustain the
courage of his men in the face of the cowardice of their
comrades, and he reminds them, too, of the worldly reward for-

feited by those deserters yet available to those who remain:

> sint diu wîp dâ heime in rehten siten,
> si teilnt in drumbe sölhen haz,
> daz in stüende hie belîben baz.
> wir mugen hie sünde büezen
> und behalten werder wîbe grüezen.
>
> (322,22-26)

The lines remind us that, like the heathens, the Christians
are inspired by their ladies at home, that, though human love
may not be the overriding impetus to battle, it is a factor
which weighs heavily with the Christian knight, who, though he
wears the Cross on his armour, fights also for the love of a
lady, whose favour does not conflict with the spiritual goal
but supports it.

All these speeches by Willehalm on the battlefield further
the impression of the relationship between the leader and his
men in the tense period which precedes the battle. They are,
of course, related to the Pitît Punt episode, in which Rennewart deals with the deserters in his characteristic fashion,
but, more significantly, they are related to the battle which
follows, in which their allegiance to the dual claims of God
and human love will be tested to the full.

To complete the group of speeches, Wolfram has Willehalm
greet the deserters when they return under the leadership of
Rennewart. This final speech is related both to those other
speeches and to the battle which will now very soon begin.
Willehalm refers to their courage, previously forsaken and
now returned to them:

> ir sît an zwîvel ê gesehen:
> nu muoz man sælde und ellens jehen
> durch reht ieslîchem Franzoys.    (332,5-7)

Tactfully he refrains from mentioning the role of Rennewart
in their change of heart, referring instead to St. Peter who
was three times tested with doubt and yet defended Jesus with
his sword when the time came. [26] Like St. Peter, these one-
time cowards can come now to the aid of God (332,18-20).
Again he speaks, as before, of their opportunity to assure the
salvation of their souls in the coming battle. These men, too,
will fight under the sign of the Cross, undistinguished in
future from those who stood firm in the face of temptation:

> nu bindt die marter wider an:
> mit rehte sol des rîches van
> daz kriuce tragen, dar nâch gesniten,
> dâ unser heil wart an erstriten.
>
> (332,21-24)

But they <u>are</u> to be distinguished by their battle-cry, for
these returned deserters are to be gathered under one banner
and one leader, the same man who effected their return:

> Rennwart sî undr iwerem vanen:
> ir sult ein ander ellens manen:
> iwer herzeichen sî bekant
> als Rennewart ist genant.          (333,5-8)

The speech merges quickly with the continuing preparations
for the battle now so near:

> dane wart von knehten niht gespart,
> si schrîten lûte 'Rennewart,
> du solt die flühtegen haben dier.'
>
> (333,9-11)

It is in the final speech of the work as it stands, in Willehalm's words to Matribleiz, that the activity of battle, the
sense of the victory just achieved, and the abstract power of
the thought of Gyburc merge, in a speech which expresses
the contrasting yet harmonizing moods of the work as a whole.
The active leader speaks now, not words which urge activity
in battle, but those which express the possibility that abstract ideals, love and compassion, may in the end find their
expression in deeds. Like almost all the speeches in <u>Wille-
halm</u>, this last one is a vital part of the action.

### f) The occurrence of imagery in Wolfram's narrative

Although the close and comprehensive study of Wolfram's
imagery is a large and certainly very fruitful subject, the
concern here is rather with the way in which Wolfram uses his
imagery, the actual choice of imagery and the relationship to
the narrative context. The abundance and complexity of the
imagery in <u>Parzival</u> are not to be found in <u>Willehalm</u>. Here
even an initial survey of the images used reveals a remarkable economy and restraint, and there is hardly any sign of
the elaborate convolutions of thought which had sometimes
strained the imagination and even defeated understanding in

the earlier work.[27] Rather is the single-strandedness of
Willehalm as a whole reflected in this very important feature
of Wolfram's style.

In his use of imagery in Willehalm Wolfram shows a subtle
sense of the appropriate. Imagery is used, not in the sometimes rather wilful manner of Parzival, where it might even
detract from the train of thought,[28] but in a way which
contributes forcefully to the narrative.

Many of the images are concerned with the battle, brief
and telling comparisons which add force to Wolfram's description of the mass of knights, for example, or of the brilliance of their apparel. To speak of such concepts which recur
in the work, Wolfram uses recurrent comparisons, and this represents certainly no decline in inventiveness in his fertile
mind, but a sense of the need for continuity and an awareness
that the overriding demands of the work may not be blurred
by elaborate or superfluous language. Very early in the work
he speaks of the many people who will die as a result of the
grief of Tybalt at the loss of his wife:

> des meres fluot der ünde
> mac sô manege niht getragen,
> als liute drumbe wart erslagen.   (8,12-14)

This very basic image of the waves of the sea needs no explanation: it is clear and powerful, and it is one which Wolfram uses on a number of occasions, in variations which retain
the force of simplicity:

> diu heidenschaft in über bort
> an allen orten ündet în.   (32,2-3)

> ob Nôê in der arke
> grôzen kumber ie gewan,
> den selben mac Gyburc wol hân
> von rîterschefte überfluot.   (178,14-17)

On another occasion the comparison is stated even more clearly:

> seht wie des meres ünde
> walgen ûf und ze tal:
> sus fuor der strît über al,
> hie ûf slihte, dort ûf lê   (392,6-9)

while soon afterwards the verb alone carries the full weight
of a now evident analogy, when Wolfram says of Terramer:

> er umbefluot ot al daz her.   (404,27)

Wolfram again finds his source in the elemental when Poydwiz
speaks of himself coming into battle like a hailstorm over
a field of straw:

> ich bin ze disem strîte komn
> sô der schûr an die halme     (390,26-27)

and he compares the noise of battle with a thunderstorm:

> dâ wart gegeben und genomn
> donrs hurte als diu wolken rîz.   (389,18-19)

Among these images may be included another early in the work,
when Wolfram again makes a comparison with the elemental, comparing the vast number of tents with the stars in the sky
(16,16-19). In all these cases, he achieves his effect because
he uses a very basic comparison, whose significance is immediately apparent and in no way interrupts the narrative.

In contrast to these examples, where the effect of the
image rests on the fact that it is so immediately comprehen-
sible and merges perfectly with the direction of the narrative, is a group of images which succeed largely because of an
element of surprise. Wolfram is adept in this work at high-
lighting the sombre tone with flashes of a contrasting quality,
and the same contrast exists very often in his use of imagery.
Even when one cannot describe this contrasting tone as humour,
it has a lightness which draws attention to the serious context and thus, far from detracting from the prevailing mood,
furthers the intention of the author. An example early in the
work demonstrates this aspect of Wolfram's art:

> die wîle daz si lebten,
> Die heiden schaden dolten
> und die getouften holten
> flust unde kummer.
> man gesach den liehten summer
> in sô maneger varwe nie,
> swie vil der meie uns brâhte ie
> fremder bluomen underscheit:
> manec storje dort geblüemet reit,
> gelîch gevar der heide.     (19,30-20,9)

The appropriateness of Wolfram's descriptions is evident:
the brilliant colours of the clothing and the banners do indeed suggest the colours of the summer and the flowers of May.
Yet the force of the comparison lies in the irony of its use
here, in the tension between the joys of springtime and the

horror of the battle. Once more, Wolfram's sense of timing
is perfect: he revels in the lavishness of his comparison,
yet it retains a subsidiary position, bringing into relief
the expression of grief which precedes it, and that which
follows it:

> nu gedenke ich mir leide,
> sol ir got Tervigant
> si ze helle hân benant.  (20,10-12)

In this case, too, the irony goes further, for we learn that
the splendour of the heathen attire has another aspect, for
it means that these men are not wearing armour or helmets,
that this brilliant comparison with the flowers in the field
is the prelude to the realization of the carnage which ensues.

Later Tenebruns and Arofel, who will die so terribly at
the hand of Willehalm, are described in similar, idyllic terms
which contrast ironically with the grim reality of their
deaths:

> ist in dem meien towec gras
> geblüemet durch den süezen luft.
> dise zwên durh prîs und durh ir guft
> wârn baz geflôrieret
> und alsô gezimieret
> daz es diu minne hête prîs.  (76,16-21)

As in the previous example, a considerable part of the effect
of this description depends on its timing, for it is followed
at once by the account of the combat with the two kings. The
death of Tenebruns, and the longer and more momentous account
of the killing of Arofel, are therefore accompanied by the
memory of their gorgeous attire, and the immediacy of this
memory increases the irony which is, in other respects, too,
an essential feature of the episode.

A similar incongruity of imagery is used by Wolfram elsewhere and always with considerable effect. On several occasions
he merges the banners of the army with the natural setting and
speaks, for example, of the field of Alischanz as of a great
field 'blossoming' forth only with banners:

> nu was bedecket berg unt tal
> und Alyschanz über al
> mit heidenschefte ungezalt,
> als ob ûf einen grôzen walt
> niht wan banier blüeten.  (58,3-7)

Similar is another description:

>           sölch was der banier zuovart,
>           als al die boume Spehtshart
>           mit zendâl wærn behangen          (96,15-17)

and later:

>           hie an bergen, dort an taln
>           sah man rotte brechen für,
>           die banier in der mâze kür
>           als al die stûden sîdîn
>           wærn.                             (225,18-22)

Wolfram uses the same idea when he speaks of the battlefield
itself 'blossoming' with knights (393,20-25). A rather similar
image, which once more has its source in natural description,
comes, in its context, as something of a surprise: Wolfram
says that it seemed as if it were 'snowing' knights (425,10-11).
Though not conventional, the image is remarkably appropriate,
and not less so because it breaks into the sombre narrative
with a characteristic touch of fun. Yet this is only for a
moment, and, again, far from cutting across the dominant mood,
it serves to confirm it. The same is true of a similar image
which Wolfram uses earlier:

>           Oransch wart umbelegen,
>           als ob ein wochen langer regen
>           niht wan rîter güzze nider.       (99,1-3)

In these last two examples, as in many of those already given,
a large part of the effect arises from Wolfram's ability to
handle what might seem a somewhat daring idea - daring in that
it is surprising and apparently incongruous. Yet the incongruous succeeds and in no way detracts from the prevailing
mood, because the narrator is completely in control of this
mood.[29]

An aspect of this control is in the economy of much of
the imagery. Wolfram uses in <u>Willehalm</u>, not the lavish, in-
tricate image so characteristic of his style in <u>Parzival</u>, but
the vivid, brilliantly-timed comparison which expresses the
very essence of his thought. An example which stands out is
the remarkable comparison of Rennewart with the young eagle
(189,2-21). This is, it is true, a long description, and some
critics have maintained that its details are not appropriate
to Rennewart,[30] yet it is surely the description which

dominates the impression of Rennewart, combining as it does
physical and mental attributes into an effective picture of
nobility and independence. The idea of the young eagle which
stands the test and looks straight into the sun is a powerful
one, reflecting the fearless strength of the young man which
will be displayed so fully in the second battle. As Wolfram
goes on to speak, however, of how the eagle flew down from
the nest, not falling from it like its lesser siblings who
failed the test and were cast out by their parents, the comparison with events becomes blurred, for, as we know, Rennewart did not willingly leave his home but was stolen away by
merchants.[31] We know, too, that Rennewart did not volun-
tarily assume the lowly position in the kitchen: his position
on the bare branch (189,21) is not of his own seeking and con-
flicts with the impression of power and independence which
Wolfram has created by means of the comparison with the brave
young eagle. There is some incongruity, too, in his use of
the image of the bird on the bare branch, for elsewhere he
uses this to speak of the widowed dove.[32] However, this is
not the only time that Wolfram surprises us by using of Rennewart a description more appropriate to a woman,[33] and it contributes to the sense of a unique character. Discrepancies
are resolved in the total effect of this outstanding image,
of the young man, powerful and resolute, yet, as we are told,
possessing qualities of shyness and tenderness which justify
the implied comparison with the mourning woman as he finds
himself apparently deserted by his family and powerless to
right the wrong which is done to him.

Later Wolfram again uses of Rennewart a comparison which
he uses elsewhere to describe a woman:

> sîn blic gelîchen schîn begêt,
> als touwic spitzic rôse stêt
> und sich ir rûher balc her dan
> klûbt: ein teil ist des noch dran.
> wirt er vor roste immer vrî,
> der heide glanz wont im ouch bî. (270,19-24)

The comparison with the rose-bud recalls Wolfram's description
of Condwiramurs (Parzival, 188,10-13) and his refusal to apply
it to the dark beauty of Belakane (Parzival, 24,10). In its

echo of those former occasions, the image is surprising, yet
here Wolfram's stress is on beauty emerging unscathed from an
unattractive covering: the passage is thus double-edged, containing a description of the young Rennewart and his tender,
handsome features, and a reference to the circumstances which
obscure his true nobility.

Following on from this is another, briefer image, which
has not the element of surprise but which is effective precisely because it is so brief:

> der starke, niht der swache,
> truoc ougen als ein trache
> vorm houbte, grôz, lûter, lieht. (270,25-27)

There is nothing subtle, or even particularly original, about
this comparison, but it succeeds because it is direct and
striking. A more complex description of Rennewart is an
earlier one, where, as in the image of the rose-bud, his beauty
is shown to be temporarily obscured: again, Wolfram expresses
his meaning in two vivid images:

> etswâ man des wol innen wart,
> unt viel daz golt in den phuol,
> daz ez nie rost übermuol:
> der ez schouwen wolte dicke,
> ez erzeigt etswâ die blicke
> daz man sîn edelkeit bevant.
> swer noch den grânât jâchant
> wirfet in den swarzen ruoz,
> als im des dâ nâch wirdet buoz,
> errzeiget aber sîn rœte.
> verdacter tugent in nœte
> Pflac Rennewart der küchenvar.
>                                (188,20-189,1)

This remarkable description, which stresses the two central
features of Rennewart's physical appearance at this time -
the signs of innate nobility obscured by the dirt of the
kitchen - is followed immediately by the great image of the
young eagle. It is significant that in this work where Wolfram is somewhat restrained in his use of images, he nevertheless gives to Rennewart a relative abundance of imagery,
drawing attention to the strange, exotic quality of this
character, who is best described in imaginative, vivid and
sometimes incongruous terms.

In contrast, Wolfram is very restrained in his description

of Vivianz, who in some respects appears as a counterpart to
Rennewart. Where Rennewart is highly individualized, Vivianz
is rather a conventional figure, the representative, the
prototype of the martyr. This distinction is reflected also
in a comparison of the imagery used in connection with the
two young men. In fact, Wolfram confines himself to a single
description of the radiance of the dying Vivianz, when what
seems at first to be a simple, conventional image -

> sîn glanz was wol der ander tac -  (254,3)[34]

leads in fact to an expression of the miracle which takes
place at the death of the saintly knight:

> swâ sîn lîp ûf Alischanz belac,
> dâ möhten jungiu sünnelîn
> wahsen ûz sîm liehten schîn.  (254,4-6)

The element of imagery remains, but what Wolfram is describing
here is a single, miraculous event, which expresses in itself
the nature of the life and death of Vivianz. In its vivid
economy, it belongs very much to Wolfram's depiction of the
young man who becomes now the representative of all who died
in the first battle of Alischanz, and whose individuality is
sacrificed to his more important role as the representative
of the Christian knights who perish in this battle and will
become the impetus of the second battle. The claim of this
passage to a place among Wolfram's images is expressed by
Bumke when he says of it: "Das ist nicht manirierte Metaphorik
eines alternden Dichters, sondern Poesie gewordenes Wunder,
und als solches ernst zu nehmen, denn es gehört zum Wesen der
Märtyrerdarstellung."[35] The distinction between this single,
poetic expression of the miraculous death of a unique and
saintly figure, and the robust and varied images which Wolfram
uses of his Rennewart, reflects the differences between the two
young men, who, in their relationship with Willehalm and with
the field of Alischanz, have so much in common and yet emerge
as so totally different in personality and in role.

It has been seen that a characteristic feature of Wolfram's imagery is its suddenness, in some cases coinciding
with an incongruity which increases its effect. Many of the

examples which remain to be discussed are isolated occasions,
when, in the midst of his narrative, Wolfram uses a sudden,
sometimes startling idea.  At Orleans, Wolfram describes the
large company of Arnalt's men:

> niht halp sô manegiu bîe
> möhten tœten einen starken bern.
>
> (117,20-21)

The comparison is vivid, and, as so often, it needs no
elaboration.  Not long after comes another vivid description,
as Willehalm watches at the court of Munleun:

> ein wolf mit alsô kiuschen siten
> in die schâfes stîge siht
> (des mir diu âventiure giht),
> als dô der marcrâve sach.      (129,14-17)

The effect here is increased by the irony of the comparison,
and the line constitutes an isolated but memorable picture.

One of the most memorable descriptions in the whole work
is surely that of Willehalm breaking through the ranks of
the enemy:

> gesâht ir ie den nebeltac,
> wie den diu liehte sunne sneit?
> als durhliuhteclîch er streit
> mit der suoche nâch sîm künne.      (40,10-13)

The force of this comparison is increased by the question,
for it draws attention to the familiarity of the experience.
Who has not seen the sun breaking through on a misty day and
who, therefore, will not understand immediately the nature of
Willehalm's movement and appreciate the dramatic effect of
his sudden appearance?  The variety of Wolfram's imagery,
despite the repetitions treated above, is demonstrated by an
image used a little later in the first Book:

> als durch die dicken mûre
> brichet der bickel
> und zimberman den zwickel
> bliwet durch den herten nagel,
> Schoyûs sîn swert, der heiden hagel,
> in den ungelouben weiz,
> unz ûf den künec Poufameiz.      (54,20-26)

These two examples show, once again, Wolfram's complete
control over his effect, the distinction between the two
movements.  Like the sun on a misty morning, Willehalm himself pushes steadily forward yet still appears with dramatic

suddenness: the effect here depends on the simplicity of the
natural image, as well as on its complete appropriateness in
the context. In the second example, he has recourse to comparisons which are alien to the context, when he speaks of
the axe hacking through a thick wall and of the carpenter
driving in the wedge: yet the effect is no less and conveys
vividly the sense of the force of the action. On another
occasion he describes the Christian army riding into the ranks
of the heathens 'like a sword into its sheath' (361,28-30)
and again the comparison reflects precisely the quality of
the movement, this time by means of a thoroughly fitting
analogy.

He describes in somewhat similar terms the attack by
Tenebruns and Arofel: they strike at Willehalm 'like smiths
at the anvil':

> ieweder künec ûf in sluoc
> sô die smide ûf den anebôz.          (77,12-13)

Brief yet vividly apt comparisons like this one are characteristic of the style of <u>Willehalm</u>. He tells how the battle
comes and goes 'like a wild boar' (418,17). Oukin is struck
down 'like a thin rod' (422,22). The bows clatter 'like
storks in a nest' (375,11).

Two vivid images which Wolfram uses close together stand
out, both for their aptness and for their somewhat startling
expression of a grim reality. In speaking of the diminishing
numbers of the Christians in comparison with the growing force
of the heathen army, he says:

> ob ie her wart swanger,
> des möht man jehen der heiden schar
>                                      (392,28-29)

and he continues the notion of the pregnant army in the lines
which follow:

> ob einiu de andern niht gebar,
> So ist wunder wanne in kœm diu fluot,
> diu sô grôze rîterschaft dâ tuot.
>                                      (392,30-393,2)

A few lines later he speaks of the knights as being thrown
down like straw for the horses:

> wie si den orsen ströuten
> mit manegem gezimiertem man!         (393,8-9)

The comparison of the beautifully equipped knights with straw
suggests precisely what Wolfram wishes to suggest: the reck-
less destruction and the total disregard for worth. In the
same battle, he speaks of the inevitability of death for the
men fighting there and again his image is clear and forceful:

> manec lebn [wart dâ] übersigelet
> mit des tôdes hantveste.                    (391,26-27)

Such examples are very much in accordance with the style of
**Willehalm** as a whole. The concentration of the work is reflected in the imagery where, in general, Wolfram refrains
from embellishments. This is not to say that he does not from
time to time allow himself a whimsical thought which is very
much an aspect of his humour. At Orange, Rennewart enjoys the
feast and Wolfram comments:

> Er verschoup alsô der wangen want
> mit spîse dier vor im dâ vant,
> dazz drîn niht dorfte snîen.              (275,1-3)

As though to draw attention to the exaggeration already
achieved, Wolfram adds the further observation:

> ez enheten zehen bîen
> ûz den näpfen niht sô vil gesogn,
> mich enhabe diu âventiure betrogn. (275,4-6)

A certain burlesque humour is rarely absent for long from the
description of Rennewart, the larger-than-life character who
obviously delights Wolfram, but there is a further factor
here: despite the impending second battle, the scene at Orange
is one of relaxation of tension, and Wolfram can allow himself
this relaxation in style. The many examples already treated
of his imagery have shown that he often introduces an image at
moments of high tension, but that such images are in no way a
detraction from the direction of the narrative: rather do they
further his intention and reinforce a concentrated thought.

Similarly, in speaking of the magnificent jewels of Poydjus, Wolfram uses a strange, slightly comic comparison, with
a duck who wanted to drink all the water in Lake Constance and
found that it did not do him much good (377,4-6). The relevance is obscure, perhaps, but the next lines make his
meaning clear:

> sus prüeve ich Poydjuses her,
> daz dar kom über daz fünfte mer:
> soltens alle ir rîcheit
> hân gelegt an ir wâpenkleit,
> sô möhten d'ors si niht getragn. (377,7-11)

He goes on to say that, since in the land of Poydjus the hills
are made of gold, it is as much like boasting for Poydjus to
display his possessions as if he, Wolfram, were to adorn himself with foliage from the Spessart in Maytime (377,22-30).
This, too, is a whimsical, picturesque idea which makes his
point very vividly, without detracting from the main-stream
of the narrative.

A certain whimsicality, indeed, characterizes a number
of Wolfram's images, for this perhaps is the tone which best
accords with the mood of the narrative, where actual humour
is rare. In describing the brilliant array of the heathen
knights he observes that his daughter's dolls are not so beautiful (33,24-26). The comparison of the mighty fighting men
with dolls does nothing to weaken his description, yet only a
great narrator could be sure that his account of dire battle
could support this intervention of a homely comparison.

In describing the cloak of Ehmereiz, Wolfram extends his
vivid picture with the whimsical idea that an ostrich could
have hatched its eggs in the radiant heat of this beautiful
garment (364,21-30).[36] He thus draws attention to the excep-
tional beauty of the cloak of Gyburc's son, but having done so
he does not linger on the cloak: what matters is not the cloak
itself, though this contributes to the many descriptions of
heathen clothing, but the fate of the cloak and its owner.
When he next mentions it, it is to speak of its radiance shining
out and ensuring that Ehmereiz, taken captive, is discovered
and released:

> der tiure phellel pôfûz
> gap gein der sunnen sölhez prehen,
> daz des küneges kumber muosen sehen
> diu fluot der Sarrazîne:
> doch beschutten in die sîne. (367,26-30)

The description of the cloak, and the strange reference to the
ostrich, recede and resume their place in the broader progress
of the narrative.

In the third Book, Wolfram uses the image of the chess-
board:

> der zende ûz zwispilte
> ame schâchzabel ieslîch velt
> mit cardamôm den zwigelt
> mit dem prüeven wære gezalt,
> Terramêr und Tybalt
> heten mangern rîter dâ,
> und Arofel von Persyâ,
> und Tesereyz, den ich ersluoc,
> het ouch rîter dâ genuoc.          (151,2-10)

The lines quoted show how Wolfram uses the image and merges
it with his account: like almost all the images in <u>Willehalm</u>,
it does not exist for its own sake but in its contribution
to the context.

In contrast, the image which he uses of Alyze, when he
says that her purity is as balm to a wound, is an isolated
one, though it is clearly related to his entire description
of her and to his conception of her as a unique figure:

> Alyz diu sældenbære,
> man möht ûf eine wunden
> ir kiusche hân gebunden,
> dâ daz ungenande wære bî:
> belibe diu niht vor schaden vrî,
> si müese enkelten wunders.          (154,20-25)

Towards the end of the work, Wolfram uses a striking image to
describe the progress of the Christians, comparing them with
the noble blood-hound which does not leave the scent and continues its hunt without shaking itself when it has swum through
water (435,10-15). Once more the comparison is not an obvious
one, but it is easily comprehended and expresses with remarkable directness the force and single-mindedness of the Christian
army.

Finally, the reality of the conflict is succinctly expressed in three lines towards the end of the second battle:

> an diu schef truoc manc rîter guot
> geparriert sweiz unde bluot:
> diu kleider wurden dâ gesniten. (443,21-23)

Wolfram uses that which is literal, the clothes drenched in
blood and sweat, as the basis for his image of clothing of
flecked material made on the battlefield. The image once more
needs no explanation and therein lies its effect: once again

its impact lies in its sheer simplicity.

This final, grim image can serve to summarize much of
Wolfram's imagery in Willehalm: without elaboration he expresses here a single thought which subsumes so much description of physical and mental suffering. It can stand alone to
express the nature of the conflict and the horror of its conclusion. It epitomizes the directness and simplicity of
Wolfram's imagery in Willehalm, and his sure sense of the
appropriate in his use of it. In this work which achieves
a large part of its impact by its single-mindedness and the
economy of its narration, the imagery is characterized by
these qualities also. Although Wolfram is capable of surprising us by his choice of imagery, the source of that imagery
is, for the most part, limited to familiar things. He takes
his images from the elemental, from nature, and from objects
close to the lives of his audience. As a result, the imagery
does not retard the narrative by the need for explanation:
on the contrary, it merges with the narrative and furthers
its progress and, in doing so, contributes significantly to
the texture of the narrative.

4. <u>The Significance of the Setting</u>

<u>Willehalm</u> is full of action, centred above all in the
two battles, as might be expected, but contained also in the
ride to Munleun, the events at the Court there, the assembly
of the troops and the return to Orange.  There, too, there
is action, even if it is the subdued and contrasting action of
the tending by Gyburc of the wounds of Willehalm, or the scenes
of love of the couple.  The activity is played out against
vivid backgrounds, and Wolfram's skill is shown in his ability
to depict these settings, both in time and place, which contribute to the strong sense of reality of the work, whose very
substance, with its source in historical events, gives a basic
credibility to the events which he relates.  The battlefield
of Alischanz, Orange, Orleans, Munleun, the Monastery, are
clearly differentiated backcloths, often associated with specific settings in time and always associated with specific and
memorable events.[1)]
   Particularly in the battle scenes, two further facets of
Wolfram's power of description contribute to the evocation of
setting: his use of sound and colour enhances the effect of
a real and vivid background.  There is, moreover, a certain
relationship between the two effects, which together help to
secure one of the lasting impressions of <u>Willehalm</u>, of the
brilliance of Wolfram's descriptions of battle scenes and his

direct appeal to the imagination.

a) Settings in place and the function of movement

The first main scene of the work is the battlefield of
Alischanz, and there are a number of references which suggest
the movement towards it. Terramer comes across the sea (8,30ff)
with his large army; Wolfram speaks of mountains and valleys
covered with heathen knights (10,11ff). Now, for the first
time, Alischanz is mentioned:

>                     des manec getoufter man engalt,
>                     ze Alitschanz ûf den plân.          (10,16-17)

The lines represent a culmination of this first movement towards the battle; but the sense of movement is one which Wolfram uses repeatedly at this stage. He speaks of Terramer's
decision to go to Alischanz, where grief awaits him (12,4-7).
Many new shields are brought to Alischanz and will be bored
through with battle (12,19-21). Wolfram anticipates the stand
by Willehalm against the heathen army when he says:

>                     ûf Alischanz erzeiget wart
>                     gein Terramêrs übervart,
>                     daz man sach mit manlîcher wer
>                     des marcgrâven Willalmes her,
>                     die hant vol als er mohte hân.      (13,5-8)

Soon after he refers to the bravery which will be displayed
at Alischanz (13,20).

These references which anticipate the battle give way
to more tangible description, as the movement of the forces
gives way to their actual presence there. The first description of Alischanz is a vivid picture of the colour of the
scene:

>                     under manegem samîtes dach,
>                     under manegem phelle lieht gemâl:
>                     innerhalp von zindâl
>                     wârn ir hütte und ir gezelt
>                     ze Alitschanz ûf das velt
>                     geslagen mit seilen sîdîn.
>                     ir banier gâben schîn
>                     von tiuren fremdeclîchen sniten
>                     nâch der gâmâne siten.              (16,4-12)

This description remains in the memory as the battle proceeds,
for, in general, Wolfram is more concerned at this early stage

of the work with activity: in the second battle there will
be descriptions which will bring into relief the horror of
the battle. The vast expanse of the field is mentioned, however, although his reason is to stress rather the magnitude
of the army of Terramer:

> was Alyschanz daz velt iht breit,
> des bedorften wol die sîne.     (36,28-29)

The very name of Alischanz begins already to take on the significance which it will bear increasingly as the work proceeds:
such significance is apparent in what is in other respects a
neutral reference to the place:

> swer durh Willalm erstarp,
> der sêle sigenunft erwarp,
> Uf dem velde ze Alitschans.     (37,29-38,1)

A vivid sense of movement re-enters the work when Wolfram
tells how Vivianz rides from Alischanz to wazzer Larkant
(40,20-23), and the river begins to replace the battlefield
as the background to the action. He refers to it again at
42,26 and later takes up the sense of movement of Vivianz:

> Der junge helt vor got erkant
> reit gein dem wazzer Larkant.     (49,1-2)

Now the description becomes more specific and fuller. For
the first time there is the awareness that this is to be the
scene of the death of Vivianz. He is now the elected one of
God, though his soul is not doomed (49,3). He is led by
angels (49,4). Exact details of the setting are given: Wolfram speaks of the spring, the poplar and the linden-tree, of
the shady spot which Vivianz seeks out for himself. In Wolfram's address to him -

> Vivîans, der marter dîn
> mag ieslîch rîter manen got,
> swenn er sich selben siht in nôt - (49,12-14)

the martyrdom of Vivianz is anticipated, so that the place
and the event which will take place there become inextricable.
In immediate juxtaposition to Vivianz's prayer that God shall
not let him die until he has seen his uncle for the last time
is Wolfram's return to the battle, and, specifically, to Willehalm. He speaks of Willehalm (50,1ff) as being now, for the
first time, aware of his loss: the irony of these lines in-

creases with the awareness of the audience that he will soon
know that his loss is even greater, by the death of Vivianz.
Thus the two places and the two men are closely linked, and
the field of Alischanz is linked with the Larkant, for at
the river will be accomplished that martyrdom earned on the
battlefield.

From Alischanz, Willehalm himself takes the direction
towards Orange (53,14-17). When, on the way from the battlefield, he becomes involved in a new struggle and escapes only
with difficulty, a single line contributes to the sense of
motion:

der marcrâve ist in entriten.      (57,30)

Thus Willehalm moves away from the battlefield, and the final
view of it is after the first battle when he looks back
(58,1ff). He sees the field covered with heathen knights,
recalling the battle just lost, but, perhaps more important,
anticipating the battle to come:

> Er enthielt dem orse und sach hin wider,
> dez lant ûf unde nider.
> nu was bedecket berg unt tal
> und Alyschanz über al
> mit heidenschefte ungezalt,
> als ob ûf einen grôzen walt
> niht wan banier blüeten.
> die rotte ein ander müeten,
> die kômen her und dar gehurt,
> ûf acker und in mangem furt
> dâ Larkant daz wazzer flôz.    (58,1-11)

With this description of the heathens spreading out over
mountains and valleys, and as far as the meadows by the Larkant, comes the reminder of Vivianz, mortally wounded and still
waiting for his uncle to come. This spot is thus connected
geographically with the battlefield, yet it is set apart from
it. The death of Vivianz, the vital bridge between the two
battles,[2] takes place in a spot specially selected for an
event which is unique in the work. The deaths of other men
can occur amid the clamour of the battle to which they belong,
but Vivianz, the chosen martyr, must die in a place selected
for its peace, where a specific natural setting can be the
background for the last conversation between the saint-like
Vivianz and the man who will achieve sanctity in the eyes

of Wolfram.

When, having made his confession, Vivianz dies, Wolfram observes that the trees give off a sweet fragrance (69,12-14); the few precise details given of the natural setting are remembered, more particularly when Wolfram points also to the linden-tree to which the horse is tied (69,20-21).

From this interlude, Wolfram turns away quickly and, as he says, Willehalm's thoughts are now on Orange (69,29ff). Larkant, then, is the link between Alischanz and Orange. Alischanz belongs to Willehalm and to his activity in battle: Orange belongs, above all, to Gyburc and to the love of the two people. Yet these two things are intimately related also to Vivianz and to his death. Vivianz dies in the service of Willehalm who was, in turn, serving God and defending both his faith and his marriage with Gyburc; it was Gyburc, we have been told, who sent Vivianz into battle and gave him his fine array, and it is in the arms of Willehalm that he dies. Such relationships are reflected also in the relationships which exist between sharply differentiated localities.

The direction of the narrative is now towards Orange, and, in the same way as the battlefield of Alischanz was anticipated, Wolfram shows Willehalm moving towards Orange. He tells his horse that he will give him good food if ever they get to Orange (59,5ff). Later Wolfram tells how his heart is urging him towards Orange:

> er moht sich dô wol umbe sehen,
> die strâze gein Oransche spehen,
> Dar in doch sîn herze treip.    (69,29-70,1)

This association of Orange with his heart is taken up more specifically a little later when, during the battle with Tenebruns and Arofel, Wolfram tells how Willehalm desires to reach Orange,

> dâ Gyburc diu künegin
> sîn herze nâhen bî ir truoc.    (77,10-11)

Later he presses his way through towards Orange:

> der marcrâve niht vermeit,
> durchz her gein Oransch er reit.    (84,17-18)

Again, Wolfram's technique is similar to that by which he

anticipated the coming-together of the armies on the field
of Alischanz. The narrative moves steadily with the rider
towards his destination, when he arrives before the gates of
Orange and in one line Wolfram recalls that Orange is his
own city, that these are his own gates:

> snellîchen truoc in Volatîn
> ze Oransch für die porte sîn.  (88,29-30)

Orange is the scene of the loving reunion between Gyburc
and Willehalm. Above all, Orange represents their love, a
firm anchor in the turmoil of the battle. Yet this love, too,
is threatened, and only by the strength of Gyburc can it be
defended. Orange is closely linked with Gyburc, and Wolfram
describes the city hardly at all, for it has assumed an abstract value which usurps its significance as an actual geographical location. It is the stronghold of their marriage,
and in defending Orange, Gyburc defends their love of one
another and of God. For Willehalm, too, it is a goal and an
impetus, united with Gyburc as his support in fighting and
also as his reason for fighting.

This means that, whereas Wolfram can concern himself
elsewhere with specific descriptions, this is unnecessary in
the case of Orange, where the very name is enough to recall
what the place stands for. When Willehalm leaves Orange, the
stress is on his parting from Gyburc. She bids him go from
her:

> alsus in von ir sante
> Gyburc diu künegîn  (105,14-15)

and the movement is also away from Orange, though the place
itself is not mentioned, so closely is it by now identified
with the woman.

With the stress once more on movement, the sense of a
specific direction which is so characteristic of Wolfram's
narrative in this work, Willehalm rides now towards France:

> unverzagt er marcte unde sach
> eine strâze dier rekande,
> gein der Franzoyser lande.  (105,28-30)

Wolfram is thus once more anticipating the next major event
of the work, Willehalm's arrival at the French Court.

The sense of the passage of time, and of movement away,
is conveyed at the beginning of Book III by the way in which
Wolfram allows a reference to Willehalm to interrupt his
description of the besieging of Orange and the threats of
Terramer. After his emphasis on the mass of the heathen army
which is assembling about Orange, he reminds us that Willehalm has had to make his way through the dense ranks, and the
sense of the two actions taking place simultaneously is
furthered by his use at this point of the motif of the exchange of hearts:

> beide er bleip unde reit:
> in selben hin truoc Volatîn,
> Gyburc behielt daz herze sîn.
> ouch fuor ir herze ûf allen wegen
> mit im: wer sol Oransche pflegen?
> der wehsel rehte was gefrumt:
> ir herze hin ze friwenden kumt,
> sîn herze sol sich vînden wern,
> Gyburge vor untrôste nern.          (109,6-14)

The device, in no way original of course, is nevertheless
skilfully used here.[3] The sense of Gyburc's active defence
of Orange is combined with the awareness of Willehalm's movement away from Orange, yet towards the Court of Loys. The two
people, and the knowledge of their physical separation, are
brought into relationship in this single metaphor which suggests
their complete spiritual harmony.

With this brief, but emphatic, reminder of Willehalm's
activity, Wolfram can return to the scene he has left, and
concentrate on the conversation between Gyburc and Terramer.
Yet the main interest is nevertheless in the progress of Willehalm and his next reference to him is again to his movement
away from the physical presence of Gyburc:

> swie balde er von Gyburge streich,
> sîn gedanc ir nie gesweich:
> der was ir zOransche bî.          (111,27-29)

Again, then, he has conveyed the sense of simultaneity of
events, as well as reiterating the motivation of Willehalm.
With this established, he can concentrate on the progress of
Willehalm, which becomes now of primary significance in the
development of the action.

Willehalm arrives in Orleans, and Wolfram's description
this time is specific. Orleans has none of the abstract significance of Orange which made precise description irrelevant.
Orleans is the place where he spends a night during this
momentous ride, and the stress is on the incident which threat-
ens to delay him when he is stopped for his toll. Wolfram's
description, brief though it is, of the little hut in the
narrow lane where Willehalm spends this night and where his
horse can hardly stand upright, does not only indicate the
privation which Willehalm is imposing upon himself, here as
throughout his ride, but it also adds colour to the incident,
providing at least some impression of a place which plays a
part in the journey. More important, of course, in defining
Orleans, is the event which takes place there, and the comple-
ment to this event comes on the return journey, when Wolfram
states deliberately that Willehalm was able to pass through
the town unhindered. When he comes a second time to Orleans,
we recall how he spent the night in the obscure little house
and accepted only bread and water, and with the memory of his
reason for this sacrifice comes the awareness that for Gyburc
release is now close at hand.

On the first occasion, however, Orleans represents a
stage in his journey and once more Wolfram indicates his
movement away:

> dô zogt er ûz gein Munlêûn. (115,6)

The conversation between Willehalm and his brother Arnalt
takes place in an undefined spot. The place is irrelevant,
and the encounter is concluded when, once more, Wolfram says
that Willehalm rode away, taking up again the direction from
Orange to Munleun. The journey is broken by another night's
sojourn, this time at the monastery. Though, like the other
places, the monastery is important as a specific geographical
point on the journey - and one to which he will return - its
function is different again. Like Orleans, it marks a stage
in Willehalm's ride, and, again as in the case of Orleans,
the night spent there is balanced by a visit on the return
ride. The symmetry is maintained, but the monastery has a

further, more important, significance, in its association
with the shield which Willehalm leaves there on his first
visit and which will then form the focal point of his explanation on his second visit.[4]

Between these two occasions at the monastery lies one
of the central scenes of the work, at Munleun. In fact, this
is rather a group of scenes, and the background is important
throughout. When Willehalm rides up to the royal court, Wolfram creates his visual effect with the kind of economy he
often uses at times of great moment. Central to the scene
are the two trees which are singled out as the only precise
features, the olive-tree and the linden-tree, but otherwise
Wolfram's description is effective because it is so negative.
No-one jumps forward to take his bridle; no-one greets him.
People greet him with hostility, says Wolfram, but even this
hostility consists rather in the way they ignore him and move
away, until he has the place to himself (127,6-8).

Before the central scene, at the Court of Loys, is another incident, which has as its background something quite
different. At the house of Wimar, the sadness of Willehalm
is brought out in its contrast to the hospitality which is
offered him and which, for the most part, he declines. The
incident, which has a setting again quite distinct, has various
functions. It constitutes, as often in Willehalm, a period
of calm before the momentous and active events which follow,
and it shows Willehalm in his loyalty to the undertaking he
gave to Gyburc. The luxurious cushions and covers which are
placed at his disposal he refuses, asking that instead grass
should be brought for him to rest on, and he declines to eat
the extravagant food and drink which is offered to him. The
place is not described at all, but, like the monastery, it is
inextricable from that which happens there and so achieves a
distinction of its own.

Similarly, the great hall itself, the scene of the central
events, is barely described. Description is, indeed, unnecessary, for it would possibly prove a conventional description of a courtly gathering. Yet one detail is mentioned:

the roses which are strewn over the carpets and, trodden in
as they are, give out a sweet scent (144,1-5). It is characteristic of Wolfram that a single, minute detail should carry
the weight of a total impression, making further description
unnecessary and yet ensuring a genuine individuality for the
scene. The luxury and extravagance which this detail suggests
contrast sharply with the crude events which are to follow,
and it is significant that, even when the roses are mentioned,
the reference is followed immediately by a reference to Willehalm who remains seated despite the entry of the royal party,
his very being a contradiction to the courtliness of which the
rose-strewn carpets are the single tangible symbol. In other
respects, the visual quality of the scene is conveyed by the
impression of movement and activity rather than by any sense
of the physical setting.

In contrast, Wolfram is more specific in his description
of the assembly of the French troops in preparation for the
march to Orange. The geographical position is precisely
described:

> man sah dâ rîlîch ûf geslagen
> anz velt, dâ der berc erwant,
> treif unde tulant,
> ekub unde preymerûn. (197,8-11)

Though the description is brief, this sense of the locality
combines with the sense of time[5] to give a vivid impression
of the setting.

Now, as before on the way to Munleun, Wolfram creates
the impression of movement:

> regen und ûf machen
> sich daz her begunde.
> an der selben stunde
> wart von den gesten,
> den êrsten und den lesten,
> al die strâzen gein Orlens beriten.
> (209,4-9)

With the unimpeded progress through Orleans comes the reminder
of the earlier occasion:

> der marcgrâve moht âne zol
> durch Orlens nu rîten wol:
> in habete nu dâ niemen zuo.
> es was von êrste in ouch ze vruo. (209,17-20)

Here Wolfram's technique is, one might say, the reverse of
that used in the case of the monastery. Where in that case
a detail - the shield of Arofel - was taken up and extended,
he here speeds the pace by this brief summary of the events
of the first occasion. Yet, as Bumke has pointed out, the
two occasions are related, for it is at Orleans that Loys
turns back and hands over his command to Willehalm: "In
Orléans kommt Willehalm, im Streit mit dem _rihtære_ (113,10),
zum ersten Mal mit der Gewalt des Königs in Berührung; auf
dem Rücktritt verabschiedet ihn der König von Orléans und
überträgt ihm seine _gewalt_ (211,11)".[6] The place is important in asserting this parallelism and in emphasizing the
irony. Moreover, Wolfram points to the connection of events
when he draws together Munleun and Orleans:

> Des ze Munlêûn was ê gesworn,
> daz was hie ze Orlens niht verlorn.
>
> (212,1-2)

The events are inextricable from the place of their occurrence,
and, as is the case with Orange, the very names bring vividly
to mind the happenings associated with them.

With Orleans now behind the army, the movement is towards
Orange:

> ieslîcher sich mit sunderr slâ
> alsô gein Oransche erbôt,
> dês vische in fürten lâgen tôt.   (212,28-30)

Five lines a little later supply an outstanding example of
Wolfram's skill in economical expression and in conveying
this same sense of movement:

> ûf velde unt in walde
> si muosen gâhen balde:
> des gert der si dâ fuorte,
> wand in grôz angest ruorte
> nâch Gyburg der künginne.   (214,5-9)

Here he speaks of the varied landscape, suggesting a great
distance, and of the speed of the army. In proceeding then
to their motivation, in the anxiety of Willehalm, he comes
to the goal of the journey, as though going ahead of the
army, to Gyburc waiting in Orange. The sense of movement at
the end of Book IV is dominant, until it culminates in the
final line, with the first reference to the fire. Yet, even

then, the full significance of this line does not come until
300 lines later, when Wolfram describes the fire in Orange.
Only then does the full impact of the simultaneity of events
become apparent, of Gyburc in conversation with her father,
desperately defending her faith and her love, and of Willehalm pressing on with his army towards Orange. Wolfram draws
the two actions, and the two people, together, by his reference to the night in each case (214,30 and 223,7)[7] and by
the glow in the sky which, with its source in Orange, extends
towards Willehalm and his army:

>nu ersach die herzebæren nôt
>der marcrâve under sîme her,
>daz der himel unt daz mer
>beidiu wâren fiuric var.          (223,26-29)

It is the fire itself which now becomes the dominant
setting, as Willehalm approaches it beneath the reddened sky,
riding ahead of his men. The excitement of this desperate
ride reaches its peak when he glimpses his palace through the
smoke and realizes that it is still standing:

>durh den rouch er innen wart
>daz dannoch stuont sîn palas,
>dâ von geflôrieret was
>Oransche und al diu marke.          (226,8-11)

In these lines the palace is seen in its physical splendour,
the adornment of the city and the whole land, but behind this
material value is implicit all that Orange stands for.

As before, the palace of Orange is hardly described at
all, but the sense of the significance of the town is as
powerful as ever. It represents the stronghold of the love
of Willehalm and Gyburc, and as such it is the background to
the second great love-scene, when Wolfram shows, as before,
that Gyburc is both the source of the grief of Willehalm, and
its alleviation. Before this, however, the great hall of the
palace is the scene of the reception by Gyburc of her father-
in-law, Heimrich, and her husband's other kinsmen, with the
forces who represent her release, yet will also be the men
who fight in the second battle.

The awareness of the grim struggle just endured and of
the battle to come contrasts with the courtly lavishness

which Wolfram describes, the luxurious cushions and covers
(244,10-17) and the abundance of good food (265,8-11). Until
the arrival of Heimrich, with the evidence she has been
waiting for of relief close at hand, Gyburc remains in her
battle attire, a reminder of her defence of the palace, and
the preparations of the two great armies point to the battle
which will soon take place. The pleasure in the reunion is
placed side-by-side with the renewed and prolonged lamentation for those who died in the first battle, and the sense
of confidence and well-being within the palace, epitomized
in the radiant appearance of Gyburc and her ladies (248,9-
249,15), is in ironic contrast to the forces assembling outside. Perhaps the most terrible contrast is in the reminder
that even the food which they are eating was provided by those
who died on the field of Alischanz (264,14-16). The setting
is vivid, then, in its impression, but it is created rather
by mood than by precise geographical description.

The next outstanding example of Wolfram's use of distinct
background comes in Book VII, when Willehalm speaks to his
men of the battle which they are facing. Willehalm climbs a
hill and surveys the assembled forces of Terramer. The geographical position is clear:

> zwischen dem gebirge und dem mer
> bî Larkant lac Terramêr.          (319,10-11)

The field of Alischanz, covered with the men and tents, is
shown as stretching out before him, and there is an echo of
the last time when Willehalm had seen the field of Alischanz
covered with the heathen army which has just inflicted such
losses on him (58,3-11). Then he had been making his way from
the battlefield: now he is heading towards it. The earlier
description was longer and fuller, stressing the power of the
heathens and implying, in the emphasis on their activity,
that here was a great force still undefeated. Now the description is briefer and more neutral. The battle is not yet
fought and the description is an objective one which speaks
only of the formidable sight of the amassed heathens and does
not in any way suggest the likely outcome. The effect is

repeated in the lines which follow:

> so beherberget was daz velt:
> niht wan mer und gezelt
> sâhen die des nâmen war.     (319,21-23)

It is an impressive sight, and aptly it leads to Willehalm's
exhortation that, in the face of such might, only those who
have the courage should remain, and to the ignominious flight
of the many Christians.

With these descriptions of the immense scope of the
field of Alischanz, which stretches out between the sea and
is covered with tents, Wolfram has said enough about the
place itself, and the awareness of the setting of the second
battle consists in these brief yet vivid impressions, in the
sense of the atmosphere of the first battle which lingers
throughout the second, and in his detailed descriptions of
the progress of the second battle itself.

b) Settings in time

Wolfram's strongly defined impressions of place and
movement are supported by the concept of time, which contributes to the vivid sense of background and furthers the
dominant sense of the reality of the work. Bumke[8] has drawn
attention to the time structure of the poem, showing that
Wolfram, who is in this respect quite independent of his source,
has created a temporal symmetry similar to the symmetry of
place already discussed.[9]

The first day is taken up with the first battle, until
the death of Vivianz. The second begins as Willehalm realizes
that he must leave the body of Vivianz and ride on; the day
is occupied by his ride to Orange, his arrival there, his
reunion with Gyburc, their decision that he should ride for
help; and as the day ends, Willehalm departs from Orange and
rides towards the French Court. Wolfram chooses not to define
the length of time between Willehalm's departure from Orange
and his arrival in Orleans:

> ich enhân der zal niht vernomn,
> wie maneges tages wære komn
> ze Orlens der marcrâve unverzagt.
> (112,3-5)

He is, however, specific when he says that Willehalm leaves
Orleans at daybreak (112,21) and that he comes to the monastery
at evening (125,5). The next day begins when Willehalm is
restless and eager to move on to Munleun (126,2-4) and it
ends when he lies awake in the house of Wimar (137,1).

The events at Munleun, we are told, occupy ten days
(186,2-4; 186,21-22), and at the end of that time, the forces
are assembled:

> der samnunge urhap
> sich huop nâch den zehen tagen.    (197,6-7)

After a further night in Munleun (198,16-17 ; 199,15-16), the
great army moves away at daybreak (200,4-5), and the whole
of that day is taken up with the second incident at the
monastery, close to which they spend the night. On the following morning, the army begins to move away (209,1ff), and until
the arrival in Orange, Wolfram gives no further indication of
time, although he does say that the fire which Willehalm sees
in the distance occurs at night (214,30). Which night this
is, in relation to the departure from the monastery, is not
said. The undefined length of time here balances that undefined period between the same two points on the outward
journey, supporting the parallels of specifically defined time.

This symmetry of time is broken only by the last period,
which embraces the arrival in Orange, the reception of the
royal visitors (1 day), the preparations for the battle (1 day),
the second battle (1 day) and the final day, which begins with
the lamentation of Willehalm for Rennewart, and the conversation with Matribleiz, and which does not end during the
course of the work as it stands. What Bumke calls the 'Stei-
gerung', of the second part of the work as against the first,
accounts for this imbalance, when the final four days correspond within this clear pattern to the first two. There is,
of course, nothing remarkable about this, for the principal
emphasis of the action lies in these last four days.[10]

This sense of an overall symmetry of time which corre-
sponds to that of place is interesting in the consideration
of the structure of the work, and it contributes to those

qualities of parallelism and compression which are so much
a part of the impact of the narrative. In the same way as
Wolfram creates a very coherent work by his insistence on
place and on movement away from one place and towards another, so too does his sense of the relationship of time
draw together incidents into close connection with one another. Together these two features of his style contribute
to the very marked concentration of the work, combining with -
and accentuating - the harmony of thought which has already
been considered.

Even apart from this significant effect for the work as
a whole, Wolfram's references to time are interesting, and
a close study of their occurrence contributes to the examination of his art as a narrator.

Early in the work he speaks of the day which separated
ladies from joy (15,12): the day is clearly the day of the
first battle of Alischanz. Later, as Willehalm realizes the
losses sustained, he weeps and Wolfram comments:

> bî liehter sunne gâben regen
> und âne wolkenlîchen wint
> sîn ougen, als ob sîniu kint
> wærn al die getouften,
> die sîn herze in jâmer souften.     (53,6-10)

This is the same day, then, and Wolfram is aware of the time
of day as the background to Willehalm's grief, the bright
sunshine contrasting with his tears.

Willehalm stays beside Vivianz for the whole night:

> Alsus rang er ob im die naht.          (71,1)

This single line sums up the nocturnal vigil and the mental
torment of the solitary man, as he thinks all the time of
the next day and the decision which he must make then:

> dicke wart von im gedâht
> des morgens, sô der tac erschin,
> ob er in möhte füeren hin,
> oder wie erz an gefienge,
> ob anderstunt ergienge
> daz er wurde an gerant.          (71,2-7)

While he is thinking, the day arrives:

> innen des gienc ûf der tac          (71,20)

and his decision is made:

> sîner neven kust er unde reit
> da er mit fünfzehen künegen streit.
> (71,21-22)

Wolfram passes on to the next action: night is for the
meditation which must be put into active terms at daybreak,
and so he mentions the time of day again, coupling it this
time with the activity of Willehalm:

> der marcrâve des morgens fruo
> reit den fünfzehen künegen zuo.     (72,17-18)

Two other references to the same period of time unite Willehalm with the heathens, when they, too, speak of the night
vigil just ended:

> die wârn ouch an der wache
> die naht mit ungemache          (71,23-24)

and
> ein ieslîch armer rîter truoc
> hêrrn od mâge ûz dem wal,
> dar umb die künege über al
> die naht der wache pflâgen          (72,4-8)

Different is Wolfram's reference to night and day at
Orange, where the day is seen to come to an end with the
decision of Willehalm and Gyburc that he must go for help.
Night represents the time for him to steal away, and Wolfram
indicates the change in a single line:

> der tac het ende und was nu naht.   (103,22)

The monastery represents, on the first occasion, a place
of rest during his ride, and, again, Wolfram indicates the
time clearly:

> gein dem âbende er ein klôster vant (125,5)

and again
> Grôz müede het in dar zuo brâht:
> den halben tac, die ganzen naht
> in dem klôster er beleip.          (126,1-3)

It is a period which is occupied, not by active events, but
by the description of the shield and the clothes which Willehalm is wearing and which bring with them a brief recapitulation of past events, in the reference to the killing of Arofel.
The period of rest is very brief, however, and the next lines
speak of the restlessness of Willehalm which urges him on,
as always on this journey:

> sîn unmuoze in fürbaz treip:
> des pîtens het in doch bevilt.     (126,4-5)

When, at the Court at Munleun, Willehalm remains un-
greeted and alone, until Wimar invites him to his home, Wolfram does not mention the time of day. It is on the following
day, however, when Willehalm returns to the same spot, that
a contrast is made which implies that the gloom of the visitor
on the previous day had been accompanied by oncoming darkness:

> ûf dez orz saz er dô
> und reit hin wider alze hant
> dâ in der wirt des âbents vant.
> nu het der tac sich hôhe erhabn.
>
> (138,20-23)

The impression of broad daylight coincides with that of renewed activity, both in the people of the town and in Willehalm himself:

> stapfen, zelten unde drabn
> ûf den hof begunde vil der diet.
> ungedult dem marcrâven riet
> daz er stricte des orses zoum
> vaste an ein ast von olboum.      (138,24-28)

Another example shows daytime linked with activity:

> Munlêûn ist der berc sô hôch:
> ê daz diu sunne im entflôch,
> er reit hin ûf, bî schœnem tage.
>
> (198,15-17)

Wolfram is often concerned, as here, with the idea of sunlight
and, as on this occasion, the light contributes to the general
impression of the background, though in other respects it may
be very little described. Similarly, Willehalm tells Rennewart that he should wake up early on the next day and set off:

> morgen vruo, so ez êrste tage ...(199,8)

On that next day, Wolfram again describes the morning in terms
of a change in colour and though little time is expended on
such description, Wolfram nevertheless supplies an additional impression of setting:

> diu naht ouch enden began,
> daz man den tac kôs al grâ.      (200,4-5)

A similar example occurs soon after this one, when, again,
daytime is linked with activity and when, even though Wolfram does not expand on the sense of time, the sense of time
is significant:

> Des morgens, do ez begunde tagen,
> hie die karrûne, dort der wagen,
> der hôrt man vil dâ krachen.      (209,1-3)

In the instance already treated,[11] when Wolfram speaks of
the fire by night, the time is important, in that it adds to
the dramatic effect:

> die nôt gap im bî naht ein fiur.    (214,30)

Similarly, he speaks later of the attack by night and the
fire in Orange, and the effect is vivid:

> slingære unt patelierre,
> sarjande und schützen,
> der stete die unnützen,
> unt über al diu rîterschaft,
> die erhuoben mit gemeiner kraft
> einen sturm bî der naht
> des wart Glorjet in angest brâht,
> ze Oransche der liehte palas.
> vor fiwer man noch wîp genas
> der getouften in der ûzern stat.
>
>    (223,10-19)

His subsequent description of the sea and the sky enflamed
increases in effect because he has laid stress here on the
fact that it is night:

> nu ersach die herzebæren nôt
> der marcrâve under sîme her,
> daz der himel unt daz mer
> beidiu wâren fiuric var.    (223,26-29)

The consciousness of the night pervades similarly two other
vivid descriptions of the fire:

> durh den rouch er innen wart
> daz dannoch stuont sîn palas,
> dâ von geflôriert was
> Oransche und al diu marke    (226,8-11)

and

> durh mangen rouch er kêren muoz,
> dâ die herberge wârn an gezunt.    (227,6-7)

Wolfram stresses on several occasions that day brings
with it a new stage of activity. At the end of Rennewart's
lament in Book VI Wolfram introduces the preparations of the
new day in these terms:

> do begundez alsô sêre tagn,
> daz de sunne durch die wolken brach.
>
>    (289,2-3)

The function of these lines is both the technical one of
indicating the passage from one subject to another, and that
of indicating, though without detail, the background of the
activity which follows. It is no chance that the majority

of Wolfram's references to time are to night and day, or to
the passage from the one to the other, for it is an essential
of his narrative that he juxtaposes contrasting periods and
incidents.

Such a contrast is evident in one of the last references to time at the end of the second battle:

> nu was diu sunne an dem tage
> harte sêr ze tal gesigen,
> manc getouftiu sêl hin ûf gestigen:
>
> (447,8-11)

The decline of day brings with it the thought of the many
Christians who have died on that day, and the two things are
brought together in the contrasting verbs. The contrast of that
day of tragic activity and the lavish feasting which now
follows with the night is made clear by Wolfram:

> geleschet nâch der hitze
> wart dâ maneger, daz sîn witze
> niht gein Salomône wac.
> dâ was ir naht unde ir tac
> unglîch an der arbeit.
> etslîcher tranc daz gar sîn leit
> mit liebe nam ein ende.          (448,11-17)

The new activity of the next day begins, on the other hand,
with another precise reference to time:

> Smorgens do ez begunde tagen ...     (451,1)

The lamentation of Willehalm and the grim surveyal of the
battlefield take place, one is justified in imagining, in
the grey light of dawn, and Wolfram gives no further indication of time.

c) The function of sound and colour within Wolfram's
   descriptions of setting

Though there are, in Willehalm, brief periods of quiet,
above all the gentle love scenes, the work is dominated by
the clamour of battle. Indeed, the harsh sounds which express
the conflict of opposing forces are brought into relief by,
and themselves stress, those periods of peace which represent
the gentler partner of conflict, the love which is shown to
be at the core of the conflict and the harmony of all creation
which is the unfulfilled ideal of the work. Between the two

things, the silence and the raucous sounds of battle, lie
also periods of verbal deliberation, when the prominent
characters in the work - Gyburc, Willehalm, Terramer and
Rennewart - break in on the action with speech.[12)

It is, however, in the two battles that one is most
aware of sounds, and these are, for the most part, the clash
of steel against steel, the noise of trumpets and drums, or
the human sounds of battle-cries, or the lamentation of a
man for his lost comrades. All these sounds Wolfram uses
in a way which, though there is repetition of substance, is
nevertheless varied, a significant factor in the narrative
texture.

A description early in the work combines the noise of
attack with the sound of the trumpets and drums, and the
shouts of the heathens as they launch into the fighting:

> Von manger hurte stôze
> und von busînen dôze,
> pûken, tambûren schal,
> und der heiden ruof sô lût erhal,
> es möhten lewen welf genesen,
> der geburt mit tôde ie muose wesen
> daz leben in gît ir vater galm.     (40,1-7)

Later it is specifically the spears which are mentioned:

> diu sper mit krache wâren hel
> ûf in, ze volge unde engegen.     (57,10-11)

It is this sound, the cracking of spears, which Wolfram
describes in the second battle:

> des wart ûf Alischanz vernomn
> von speren manec lûter krach     (351,22-23)

and

> man hôrt ûz manegen vorsten
> den walt dâ sêre krachen.     (370,16-17)

The noise is so great that the forest seems to resound with
the thunder of lances and spears:

> alrêrst nu donret der walt
> von lanzen krache und der sper.     (372,12-13)

The swords, too, resound, with a different noise:

> des wart erklenget manec swert
> von ir zweier massenîe.     (380,24-25)

> vil schilde der ganzen
> wurden dâ zerfüeret,
> manec helm alsô gerüeret
> daz diu swert derdurch klungen.     (383,6-9)

dâ wart grôz swerte klanc vernomn.   (407,30)
Bows clatter 'like storks in the nest' (375,10-11).  All
these sounds, individually described on occasions, are on
other occasions subsumed in a composite description of the
noise of battle:

> dâ wart gegeben und genomn
> donrs hurte als diu wolken rîz.   (389,18-19)

> von dem bibn und von dem schallen
> möht das tiefe mer erwallen.    (400,21-22)

At other times, the surge of battle, though not described in
terms of sound, contains all the sense of overwhelming noise
which is described in detail elsewhere:

> von rabînes poynderkeit
> durh den stoup inz gedrenge reit
> gein dem strîte ieslîchez her
> der künege von über mer.       (32,19-22)

> hurtâ, waz in nu strîtes kumt!
> wie ze bêder sît dâ wart gevrumt
> trunzûne sprîzen in den luft,
> durh wîbe lôn od sus durch guft! (379,11-14)

> da ergienc von in beiden
> hurteclîchez kriegen.
> si liezen gêre vliegen
> mit anderem ir geschôze.        (431,6-9)

Added to this sound of conflict is the sound of the trumpets
and the drums which characterizes the heathen fighting and
which continues, too, throughout the two battles.  Even before
the battle begins, this sound announces the arrival of Terramer's great army:

> dâ was von busînen krach
> und ouch von maneger tambûr.    (12,28-29)

Repeatedly it accompanies the description of the fighting on
the heathen side:

> der heiden rîterschaft ein wint
> was, wan die er fuorte.
> waz man tambûren ruorte
> und busîn erklancte!            (29,20-23)

> der heiden her dô grôzte
> von emerâln und amazsûren.
> vil pûken, vil tambûren,
> busînen und floytieren.         (34,4-7)

Like Wolfram's stress on the brilliantly coloured, exotic
clothing of the heathens, the repeated emphasis on these loud

and characteristic sounds contributes to his whole picture of
the extravagance and flamboyance of the heathen army, and,
as though to stress the relationship between the sounds and
the heathen knights, he reminds us at one point that the
trumpet was, after all, invented in heathendom (360,10-12).

Side-by-side with these tremendous noises of battle, it
is to be supposed, are the battle cries which recur throughout. These are mentioned very early in the first battle, the
cries of Mahmet! and Tervigant! (11,16-18; 18,28) juxtaposed
to those of Munschoy! (19,1). That these cries continue while
the battle continues to rage is obvious, though Wolfram does
not say so in so many words: what he does, however, is imply
the continuance of the battle cry by reference to its being
silenced on two occasions. The cry of Munschoy! gives way to
Willehalm's lament at one point:

> ... sît sus ist geswîget
> Monschoy unser crîe
> ey Gyburc, süeze âmîe,
> wie tiwer ich dich vergolten hân! ...
> (39,10-13)

A little later, the tragic depletion of Willehalm's army is
conveyed in terms of the silencing of the battle cry:

> Munschoy der crye was geswigen,
> sîniu zweinzec tûsent wârn gedigen
> unz an vierzehen der sîne.     (50,11-13)

It is, indeed, the cry of Munschoy! which occurs most frequently in this first battle, in which the Christians are defeated.[13]

In the second battle, in contrast, the battle cries become
more fragmented, the confusion of undistinguished cries corresponding at times to the chaos which Wolfram describes here.
Yet there is nothing orderly about this development, rather
as the strategy of the battle only gradually gives way to a
state of disarray. Sometimes the cries are distinctive (334,30,
374,18-19; 388,30; 401,28-29), but frequently they are undefined: at one point Wolfram speaks of the many and varied
cries of the heathens which he cannot name, and against these
the single, readily identifiable cry of Munschoy! surviving
still from the first battle:

> Ine mac niht wol benennen gar
> an den ruoft der heiden sunderschar,

          waz si kreiierten
          sô si pungierten.
          Munschoy wart ouch dâ niht verdagt.
                                                      (372,1-5)

Soon afterwards, however, he speaks of the six distinctive
cries of the Christians: the single cry of Munschoy! is used
now by Willehalm's division, while the other five divisions
shout the names of their leaders (397,6-23). Yet gradually
these six distinctive cries are forgotten, as the military
strategy and the need for each section to fulfil a particular
role are replaced by the urgent need for survival in the
general crush: now each man shouts the name of his place of
origin (437,1-9). Paradoxically, as Wolfram's narrative is
concerned increasingly with the mass of fighting men and
the total confusion of men and horses, the battle cries
reflect the individual clinging to his identity. In this
respect, too, Wolfram expresses simultaneously the sense of
the mass and the role within that mass of the individual.[14]

     A single line, characteristic of Wolfram's sense of the
effectiveness of economy at times of acute pressure,[15] expresses the totality of the sound of battle-cries, in which
he no longer attempts to distinguish Christian from heathen:

          Man hôrt dâ manege krîe.                   (420,1)

Yet, just as, in the work as a whole, activity and
moments of rest are set side-by-side, and peace is shown to
be a part of man's experience, though at times conflict may
seem to dominate, these harsh sounds of battle are just
occasionally, even in the course of the fighting, juxtaposed
to gentler ones. The sound of the battle-cry is replaced by
Willehalm's lament (39,9 - 20) and the reference to Halzebier's
lament for Pinel is contained within the account of bitter
fighting (45,23-30).

     Although, as has been seen, the awareness of noise in
the work is centred in the accounts of the two battles, the
absence of noise performs a function outside the accounts of
battle. That the tender meetings between Gyburc and Willehalm are periods of relative silence need not be said by
Wolfram. Instead he makes this clear by the quality of his

description of the interlude: the loving words, the sense of
the healing power of love and the gradual recovery of Willehalm from his state of exhaustion, all these things contribute
to an impression which need not be stated in any other way.

There are sounds, however, beyond the framework of the
two battles. In Orleans Willehalm fights off the rabble in
the streets and escapes, and Wolfram describes the shouts of
the people:

> Arnalt fîz cons de Narbôn
> erhôrt den jæmerlîchen dôn
> den man in al den gazzen rief.      (115,7-9)

In Munleun, Wolfram does not describe the sound of the celeb-
rations. Such descriptions, like the visual description which
he also declines to supply,[16] might prove stereotyped and
dull. Instead he implies it in a subtle way. The roses which
are strewn on the floor contain not only the quintessence of
the sight and fragrance of the scene, but, negatively, they
suggest the noise of the festivities:

> gein der hôhgezîte schalle
> Vil teppch übr al den palas
> lac, dar ûf geworfen was
> touwic rôsen hende dicke.      (143,30-144,4)

Wolfram has no need to speak further of the noise of the
Court, and his account can centre on the all-significant events
which take place, and not least on the many words which are
spoken there. Where sounds have expressed the conflict of
opposing forces, the absence of sound here expresses that
silence and peace which constitute the contrasting mood of
the work.

Just as Wolfram's narrative in telling of the two battles
at times describes and at other times suggests the clamour of
the fighting, the clash of steel and the cries of the men, so
too is the vivid impression of colour and brilliance which
pervades these parts of the work achieved by actual references
to colour and also by Wolfram's effective suggestions of the
brightness of the whole scene. We know from Parzival that
Wolfram loves colours, and in Willehalm too he is ungrudging
in his descriptions of the colourful scene. Yet where in
Parzival such descriptions had sometimes been more or less

gratuitous additions to his picture,[17] there is in <u>Wille-</u>
<u>halm</u> the further overlying factor, that the glamour and beauty
which_he describes with such delight are strangely allied to
the bitterness of the conflict and the appalling waste of
human life. There is, then, in Wolfram's use of colour another aspect of that irony which is basic to the work, although there is no denying that his references to colour contribute also to the picturesque, visual quality of the work.

It is above all with the heathens that Wolfram associ-
ates brilliant colours.[18] An early reference is one of the
simplest:

> von gesteine und von golde
> was rîchiu kost niht vermiten.     (24,2-3)

With the colours of the rich silks he links, too, the
brilliance of the armour:

> dem vanken in dem fiure
> sölher gelpfheit ie gebrast.
> dâ kom der sunnen widerglast
> an mangem wâppenrocke.     (33,20-23)

A little later he contrasts the black skin of the heathens
with their bright garments:

> manec swarzer Môr, doch lieht gevar,
> Die sich wol zimierten
> ê daz si pungierten.     (34,30-35,2)

These are basic ideas, which recur in different forms throughout the work. In his combat with Poufameiz, Willehalm is
dazzled by the brightness of the bejewelled armour (55,15-19),
and the same idea comes in the second battle, when the Christians are said to be much troubled by the dazzling brilliance of
the enemy (394,27-30; 398,10-13).

When Willehalm puts on the armour of Arofel, Wolfram
observes similarly:

> Diu zimierde gap kostbæren schîn     (82,3)

but here the statement is double-edged, no simple reference
to external appearance, but one which brings with it the
reminder of the association of this brightness with heathendom and, more than that, the irony that this gorgeous armour
has been linked with such a dreadful act. As so often, Wolfram achieves his effect by a very simple statement, and he

does so in this case because there are so many supporting
references to the brilliant garments and shining armour of
the heathens. The line anticipates, too, Willehalm's arrival at Munleun, when his exotic clothing surprises and puzzles
those who see him (128,12-13). Then, too, one will recall
the action which gained these rich possessions for Willehalm
and understand the perplexity of the onlookers. The way is
prepared, then, for the somewhat facetious comment of Loys
(203,14-17), who cannot understand why his brother-in-law
took such pains to equip himself on his desperate journey
and, from that, for the lengthy explanation of the shield.[19]
Wolfram's reference to the brilliance of the armour goes
beyond the external and takes on a deeper function within
the narrative.

　　Elsewhere, however, the descriptions are more generalized and often the brilliance of heathen clothing and equipment is implied rather then specifically described. Thus,
for example:

　　　　　　　　der starke junge Rennewart
　　　　　　　　ûf der heiden orsen sach
　　　　　　　　von pfellen manec tiwer dach　　(364,14-16)
and
　　　　　　　　die geflôrten künege viere,
　　　　　　　　iu enmöhte niemen schiere
　　　　　　　　ir zimierde benennen:
　　　　　　　　die muost man tiure erkennen.　　(372,27-30)

Of Poydjus he speaks at some length, but here, again, he
avoids specific description:

　　　　　　　　ob ers geruocht, ein rîcher munt
　　　　　　　　solt iu diz mære machen kunt,
　　　　　　　　wie sunder was gezieret,
　　　　　　　　mit kost al überwieret,
　　　　　　　　daz dach ob sîme harnasch.
　　　　　　　　ander kost dâ bî derlasch.　　(376,13-18)

Such descriptions make possible the brilliant comparisons at
other times of the men with the meadows of Maytime flowers:

　　　　　　　　bî Ehmereizes kursît
　　　　　　　　der heide glanz ins meien zît
　　　　　　　　mit touwe behenket
　　　　　　　　an prîse wære verkrenket:
　　　　　　　　sô clâr was er gemachet,
　　　　　　　　daz die bluomen wærn verswachet. (364,21-26)

There is something rather general and all-pervasive about
these descriptions, and it is such descriptions which make
one remember the two battles of Alischanz as tremendously
vivid in their narration.

In contrast, there are moments when individual colours
stand out: the fiery red of the silk which covers Terramer's
horse is mentioned (360,16-18). The skin of Gorhant's men
is specifically green (395,23). The buttons on the coat of
Heimrich are emeralds and rubies (406,15-16). Indeed, it is
red and green which dominate as colours, and with red is
linked the blood which flows, to epitomize the wastage of
human life, and which colours the beautiful heathen clothing
(381,12-17; 443,21-23). The blood stains the white flowers
and the green grass:

> blanke bluomen und daz grüene gras
> wurden rôt von sîner slâ.                     (384,8-9)

Wolfram is not subtle in his use of colours in the battle:
they are as bright as the glistening armour, contrasting in
a macabre fashion with the gloom of the battlefield and the
dire fate of so many brilliant, careless men.

The third specific colour which dominates is white.
Galafre is described as whiter than a swan (27,1), but more
effective still is the sudden whiteness of  Tybalt's dress:

> daz werc von salamander,
> ist iht wîzers danne der snê,
> het ich daz gehœret ê,
> sô möht ich wol gelîchen dar
> daz Tybalt an im hête gar.                     (366,4-8)

Like the sounds treated previously, these colours are
centred above all in the descriptions of battle, but the
Court of Munleun represents another place where, like the
sounds, colour is implied.[20] If Wolfram refrains from a
description of the beautiful colours of the French Court, he
does so, surely, to avoid the obvious. In the way he has,
however, of subsuming much description which is only implied
in a single brilliant stroke,[21] he concentrates his description of the colours of the Court in his description of
Alyze's dress:

dô zogt ouch dan diu künegîn
und ir tohter, diu sô liehten schîn
gap daz ich die heide
mit ir mangem underscheide,
des si noch phliget und ouch dô phlac,
gein ir niht gelîchen mac.          (200,11-16)

There is nothing extraordinary in the description - indeed
it echoes, in its comparison, those which he gives of the
heathens in battle - yet it is remarkably effective, concentrating all the attention on this single exquisite figure,
who is so much the focus of attention at this point.

Although Wolfram refers, with considerable dramatic
effect, to the fire in Orange, the red glow in the sky and
on the sea, he does not describe the colours, for example,
of the morning after the second battle, when Willehalm surveys the battlefield and gives expression to his immense
grief. Yet, because the battlefield has been so full of
colour, the absence of it is potent: the grey light of dawn
is as much present as the tremendous weight of silence which
must reign now that the sounds have ceased.

For any subtlety of shading one looks, as for subtlety
of thought, to that tender scene with Puzzat.[22] There the
colours are not the brilliant reds and greens and golds of
the battlefield, but the muted brown of the horse's coat
and the white of the foam on it which Willehalm wipes away
(59,9-10).

## 5. The Emergence of Individuals

The artistic compatibility of broad narrative and minute
detail is an essential feature of the work as a whole, and
it is clearly demonstrated in Wolfram's handling of individuals, above all in the battles, where he maintains a sense
of the scope and significance of the events, uncontradicted
by the way in which, again and again, he lingers on the details which make up the great conflict. Thus, though, for
example, one is always conscious of the two distinct armies
and of their distinct identity, one is made aware that these
two great forces are made up of individuals, and it is on the
individuals that Wolfram expends much of his descriptive power,
yet in a way which makes it clear that their individuality
achieves its greater significance in its relationship to the
whole.

An outstanding example occurs early in the work, in the
encounter between Vivianz and Nöupatris, where the latter is
described in detail comparable to that given here to Vivianz.
There is, in fact, a parallelism in what we learn of the two
knights, for here, as elsewhere, Wolfram is at pains to suggest the equality between the Christian and the heathen. In
the passage 22,14-23,14 both knights are named and the attributes of Nöupatris find an echo in those which Wolfram gives

to Vivianz. Thus he tells of the knightly prowess of Nöupatris and of his fame, and he stresses his youth and beauty:

> ... ein man den nie verdrôz
> strîts noch rîterlîcher tât.
> sîn werdekeit noch volge hât,
> daz er warp um rîterlîchen prîs:
> der hiez Nöupatrîs:
> er het ouch jugent und liehten schîn.
>
> (22,14-19)

Of Vivianz he speaks similarly:

> der kunde ouch werdekeit wol tuon.
> sus was bewart sîn clâriu jugent:
> dehein ort an sîner tugent
> was ninder mosec noch murc.      (23,2-5)

Both are of noble birth, the one a king, the other the nephew
of the Margrave, and both are pressed into battle by high
motives (22,22-23; 23,6-9). The balance of the descriptions
culminates in Wolfram's simple statement of the single aim:

> si wurben bêde umb den tôt,      (23,14)

a line which gains in irony when considered in the context
of events.

Thus for a time Nöupatris does come to the fore and in
his battle with Vivianz he receives due consideration as an
individual. Wolfram's description, though not unique in his
work, is vivid: Nöupatris fights with all his might, spurred
on by his desire for knightly fame, a colourful figure who
bears the emblem of love and fights for the sake of love. He
is remembered as the great knight in closely matched combat
with Vivianz and doomed, like Vivianz, to die for the sake of
the emblem he wears. As they engage in a fierce struggle,
attention is focused on these external things: the gold and
bejewelled banner of Nöupatris with the embossed figure of
Cupid with his arrow, and the splendid attire of Vivianz,
given to him durch sippe minne (24,13), by Gyburc. Already
the individuals have thereby been assigned a place in the
whole, and when Vivianz deals the fatal blow it is to the
king with the crown on his helmet (24,27) and it is the heathen
who dies (24,50): the brilliant, daring young Nöupatris has
returned to his place in the battle. The transition has been
a subtle one, but this is a work in which, though individuality

may be acknowledged, it may not for any length of time detract from the central themes or from the dominance of the two central figures.

Another character who comes to the forefront and receives distinctive, though very different, treatment from Wolfram is Halzebier. Like Nöupatris, he emerges from the mass of the battle into single combat with Vivianz. The first reference to him is early in the work, when his name is coupled with that of Arofel, two mighty kings who come with great force to the aid of Terramer. In the throng of battle, Halzebier is mentioned and described in conventional terms:

> zegegen, wider, her unt dar
> wart mit manlîchen siten
> Halzebiers der durhriten,
> des küenen und des starken.　　　　　(22,2-5)

Yet still he is known only really for the great army which he leads and which soon after faces a tremendous defeat (27,18-21; 28,2-5). With the defeat of his army, however, Halzebier seems to achieve a new individuality, hinted at already when Wolfram links him with the great King Synagun, his sister's son (27,14). It is in connection with another nephew, Pinel, that Wolfram gives to Halzebier the first real touch of individuality, when he tells of his great grief at the death of this man:

> man hôrt an Halzibiere,
> swaz iemen tet, er wold et klagen
> Pînel der dâ was erslagen.
> dem künge von Falfundê
> tet sînes neven sterben wê.　　　　　(45,26-30)

The excess of grief in a noble knight anticipates that of Willehalm for Vivianz but goes no deeper than in these five lines. However, they open the way for a description of Halzebier which, for all its conventional qualities, is relatively rare in this work which does not often linger on the physical appearance of individual characters:

> Halzibier der clâre
> mit reidbrûnem hâre
> und spanne breit zwischen brân,
> swaz sterke heten sehs man,
> die truoc von Falfundê der künec.
> der was al sîner lide frümec

                    und manlîches herzen,
                    zer zeswen und zer lerzen
                    gereht, ze bêden handen.
                    sîn hôher prîs vor schanden
                    was mit werdekeit behuot:
                    in wîbe dienste het er muot.          (46,1-12)

There is, moreover, in this description, the single feature
that Halzebier is equally adept with his left hand as with
his right: this is, it is true, a small point, but it provides
just that touch of individuality which distinguishes Halzebier from his fellow knights. It cannot be a shadowy figure
who deals the mortal blow to Vivianz, and it is characteristic of Wolfram that he should place the emphasis of his
description on a relatively small, though important, feature.

     Arofel for a time receives the full focus of attention.
He has, of course, a special function as the great antagonist
of Willehalm at a focal point of the first battle, and one
who dies explicitly in payment for the death of Vivianz, but
it is not in the nature of Wolfram to reduce a character to
an abstract value, and Arofel's ability to fulfil the role
assigned to him is increased by the vividness of his personality. This means that one experiences the account of his
death as of a very real character, and the memory of him
remains, balanced, for all its restraint, against the grief
at the memory of Vivianz.

     References to Arofel occur early in the work, and at
the first mention of him he is named as the brother of Terramer (9,22). In the next reference to him Wolfram adds to
the impression of the power of Arofel:

                    Arofel der Persân,
                    dem was in manegen landen lân
                    prîs ze muoten und zer tjost.
                    er het ouch dâ die hœhsten kost
                    von soldiern und von mâgen:
                    an sîme ringe lâgen
                    zehen künege, sînes bruoder kint.
                                                   (29,13-19)

This is a conventional description, but the reputation of
Arofel is established in anticipation of his death at the
hand of a great opponent. Again, too, the relationship with
Terramer is stressed, for his relationship will lead directly

to his death, when he reveals it to Willehalm, who might
still be expected to spare him as he lies wounded and offering so much in exchange for his life.[1]

As one of the many great heathens who perish in battle
and in particular because he is specifically selected to die
in revenge for Vivianz, Arofel clearly attains a certain
abstract quality, to which is added the distinctive feature
of his being recalled through his armour, his horse and his
shield. By means of these things, which save the life of
Willehalm, the death of Arofel is remembered. Seemingly
neutral references to Willehalm's apparel or his weapons
(137,3-4; 140,13-18) gain in depth with the memory of the
brave and mighty King of Persia pleading in vain for his life.
That Arofel is lamented is mentioned at 106,19ff, but with
him here are mentioned others who have perished in the battle,
and it is not until much later that those fighting in the
second battle of Alischanz lament the loss of their leader
<u>wand er ir ander vater was</u> (374,27). Here Wolfram adds this
personal note which recalls the warmth and vitality of the
great knight and ensures his individuality, despite the more
static roles which he must fulfil. Yet the most vivid reference  to the dead Arofel is a much earlier one, when Wolfram
is describing in some detail the richness of the armour which
Willehalm wears as he arrives at the monastery. The stress
is on the lavishness and fine workmanship:

> dâ ze Samargône
> in der houbetstat ze Persîâ,
> sîn schilt was geworht aldâ:
> des buckel was armüete vrî.
> Adramahût und Arâbî,
> die rîchen stet in Môrlant,
> sölhe pfelle sint in unbekant
> als sîn wâpenroc, mit steinen clâr,
> drûf verwieret her unt dar,
> daz man des tiwern pfelles mâl
> derdurch wol kôs al sunder twâl:
> als was ouch drob daz kursît          (125,8-19)

but Wolfram concludes with the reminder of the origin and
with a telling comparison:

> er nam dem Persâne
> Arofel, der vor im lac tôt,

> daz friwendîn friwende nie gebôt
> sô spæher zimierde vlîz;
> wan die der künec Feirafîz
> von Secundilln durch minne enpfienc:
> diu kost für alle kostegienc.  (125,24-30)

Indeed, the comparison leaves nothing to be said, but almost
more significant is the very mention of Feirefiz at this
stage. Inevitably, one recalls, as Wolfram surely intends,
the vigour and charm of Parzival's half-brother, and the
memory of his nobility and virtue colours, too, the memory
of Arofel, the noble heathen who is so close a match for Willehalm and who is fit to die in compensation for the saintly
Vivianz.

Comparison with Feirefiz serves to give individuality
to another heathen prince, Pinel, whose first appearance in
the work coincides with his death. This first reference is
an example of a different characteristic feature of Wolfram's
description of individuals in <u>Willehalm</u>, for into just ten
lines he compresses the introduction of Pinel, his courage in
battle and his bold activity in the forefront of the fighting,
his death at the hand of Willehalm and the lamentation of all
heathendom:

> Pynel fîz Kâtor,
> der ze allen zîten was dâ vor
> dâ man die poynder stôrte,
> von sîner hant man hôrte
> manegen ellenthaften slac,
> ê daz der helt tôt belac
> von des marcgrâven hant,
> des allez heidenische lant
> von freuden wart gescheiden.
> daz was ein werder heiden.  (21,1-10)

The force of this last line is considerable, for it sums up
the worth of Pinel, yet puts him firmly where he belongs, in
the past. It is now as a memory that Pinel will appear in
the work, yet the vividness of Wolfram's brief description
here ensures that even though he is dead, Pinel's name can
have a force and individuality of its own. Consequently he
is mentioned later, not in the groups of names of the heathen
slain, but in isolation; though he has not the distinctive
role of Arofel, Nöupatris or Halzebier, Pinel has a distinction of his own, as one great heathen soldier selected for

particular attention, fighting bravely and dying, like so
many, at the hand of Willehalm. Wolfram's technique, too,
is distinct: where these three characters emerged by means of
a gradual accumulation of details, Pinel appears suddenly and
vividly, to dominate the action for a few lines before sinking
back into a memory. Wolfram's technique, of allowing Pinel
to emerge into individuality from the mass of fighting men,
can best be demonstrated by two contrasting lines which are
juxtaposed, the first a line already mentioned which gives
to Pinel an individuality of his own and the second a swift
return to the battle and the suffering of men on both sides:

> daz was ein werder heiden.
> der strît wart bêdenthalben sûr.
>
> (21,10-11)

    A quite unique character who is also given by Wolfram a
unique role is King Purrel. He is introduced at 358,26, among
those men who will fight with great power on the side of Terramer. Wolfram lays stress on his physical appearance, for
it is this which distinguishes him. He is, we learn, an old
man whose beard is greyer than the mist (425,12-13). Soon
after this Wolfram speaks of the great King's strange, impenetrable armour, and of his helmet, both made from the skin
of a dragon (425,25-426,13). The skin is coloured like a
rainbow (426,16-28) and so Purrel is endowed with this further
distinguishing feature which will be used later in association
with him. More important, though, is the fact that, when
Purrel is wearing his armour, no blow can wound him (426,19-
25). In advance of the battle with Rennewart, then, this vital
fact is established, in order that it may be taken up in the
final picture of the mighty King, dreadfully crushed but im-
pervious to a mortal thrust. Wolfram's stress on the physical
thus both contributes to the quality of this unique figure
and anticipates the later course of events. At this point,
however, the suffering of Purrel is concentrated on the mental
anguish of the old father who sees his sons slain before his
eyes (427,23-25). It is characteristic of Wolfram that he
lingers on the human element here, showing this great King who
has grown old in the service of the sword, versed in the art

of battle and even now gaining for himself increase of fame
(427,26-428,12).

Though Wolfram speaks of the conquests of Purrel as he
defeats his opponents, he does so briefly, for these are
not what distinguishes Purrel from so many others. More important is the combat with Rennewart, when two picturesque
figures come together, and the visual impact is implied,
rather than described in explicit detail:

> Rennewart in werte
> noch mêr denn er im schuldic was.
> gein dem schilte grüener dann ein gras
> diu stange hôhe wart erzogn:
> der helm gelîchte dem regenbogn:
> dâ wart ungeschmeichet
> helm und schilt erreichet
> mit eime alsô starken swanc,
> daz diu stange gar zerspranc.    (429,14-22)

The unique weapon of Rennewart strikes at the impenetrable
armour of Purrel, but it is the rainbow-colours of the helmet
which are mentioned now, bringing with them the reminder of
what we have been told of the unique property of the material.
The pole of Rennewart, which has inflicted so much damage,
breaks as it comes up against the hard surface of his opponent's
helmet and shield, but if the blow has disarmed the hitherto
all-powerful Rennewart, it has crushed also the mighty Purrel:

> Purrelle erkracheten gar diu lit.    (429,27)

The horror of the dubious advantage which Purrel possesses is
summed up in this simple statement, where Wolfram relies on
the onomatopoeic effect of the verb to express the suffering
of the mighty King who falls unconscious to the ground.

In a relatively small space of time, Purrel has become
a very real figure, someone who has emerged with unusual
vividness from the conflict, and the sense which Wolfram thus
achieves of a great and human personality means that he cannot
be allowed to pass out of the work. Instead Wolfram relates
how his wounded knights drag him away from the battle, in
which Rennewart has once more become the focus of attention.
As they do so, the stress is still on his age and on his king-
ship (431,21) and as he is borne away across the sea, Wolfram
recalls again how, even in old age, he has brought renown upon

himself by his prowess in battle:

>Der rîche ellende
>hete dâ mit sîner hende
>sînem alter prîs errungen.          (432,1-3)

It is appropriate, too, that it is in this encounter with one
of the finest exponents of chivalry on the heathen side that
Rennewart's uncouth stange is rendered useless, to be replaced by the sword which is more fitting for one who is be-
having increasingly like the knight of the Princess Alyze.[2]

The figure of Purrel dominates the account for a brief
period, then, bringing warmth and individuality to it, yet,
like the others, destined to drift back into the broader context from which he has emerged. What happens to him subsequently is immaterial, for, though Wolfram is interested in
the individual, the individual may not be allowed to distort
the sense of the whole. When Wolfram permits his audience to
see that the mass of the two armies is made up of single men
who are capable of commanding interest and even, as is the
case with Purrel, affection, he underlines the belief of Gyburc
in the value of all men as the creatures of God. Yet the
battle is concerned, not with the individuals, but with the
cause for which they are fighting, and within this cause
their function is that of Christian and heathen. However, it
is an aspect of Wolfram's sense of the importance of the individual that in such instances, for a brief period, it is
the reality of the personality of the human being which is
stressed. Though at other times he is capable of speaking of
individuals in terms of Christian and heathen, on occasions
such as these the sheer humanity of the person transcends his
race and his religion.

That, in the last resort, an individual must resume his
place within the whole context of the battle is further stressed
by another feature of Wolfram's narrative. With the departure
of Purrel on his shield, the action is quickly taken up again:
Wolfram passes on to the next group of incidents, and in fact
a great deal is now compressed into relatively few lines
(432,4-28). Purrel must be allowed to merge with the context,
to be forgotten within the turmoil of activity, and to give

way to other individuals who are, however, treated more cur-
sorily. In this way Wolfram varies his narrative, quickening
the pace now and filling it once more with a great many people.
Other individuals are less rounded characters than Purrel.
Oukin, too, is an old man, who dies at the hand of Willehalm.
Here Wolfram describes the encounter at some length, from his
cry of grief when he recognizes the riderless horse of his son
Poydwiz, to the moment when his own body falls beheaded to the
ground (420,24-422,30). Wolfram's technique is different from
that which he uses in his treatment of Purrel, but it is equally vivid. Oukin's lament for his son occupies twenty lines of
the episode and culminates in his resolve:

> ich muoz ertœtet werden,
> ichn versuoche war du sîst getân.
> (421,16-17)

The concentration throughout on the relationship between Oukin
and Poydwiz recalls the first mention of Oukin at 411,11,
where he is specifically named as the father of Poydwiz. This
reference is not just a conventional one of kinship, for it
seems to anticipate the later, poignant episode, when the
father plunges into combat with Willehalm as though in search
of his dead son:

> sus kom der klagende grîse man
> ûf den marcrâven gevarn.        (421,18-19)

Like Purrel, Oukin is seen to some extent in relation to his
past, and this combat is the culmination of a lifetime of
courageous activity:

> er was ouch selbe ie unervorht
> In manegem sturme erkennet:
> sîn prîs was hôch genennet.
> ûz der jugent in sîns alters tage
> ranc sîn hant nâch dem bejage,
> mit milte, mit manlîcher tât,
> dâ von man lop ze reden hât:
> sîn lîp nie zageheit erschrac.     (422,2-9)

The death of Oukin is described with the economy of Wolfram
at times of great tension:

> rehte als ein swankel gerte
> wart ez hin ab gehouwen.
> den lîp man mohte schouwen
> âne houbt im satel sîn.
> dâ viel dem künege Oukîn

        dez houbet und der schilt ze tal,
        dar nâch der lîp über al
        underz ors ûf die molten.
        sus starp der unbescholten.          (422,22-30)

The last line sums up the incident and Wolfram passes quickly
to the next group of knights (423,1-5). Once more, then,
Wolfram has allowed a single figure to dominate the action
for a brief period, and Oukin does so in a distinctive manner,
above all through his lament for his dead son and the combat
motivated by revenge for him.

It is both Wolfram's interest in the individual and his
emphasis in <u>Willehalm</u> on the importance of the human being
in his own right which leads him to mention so many of the
protagonists by name. In this way, he contributes to the
sense of reality so dominant in the work. Some of the mentions are little more than passing references,[3] but others
are associated with a distinct visual impression which, again,
increases the sense that one is hearing of distinct personalities and not of undefined, shadowy figures. Thus, for
example, Josweiz, the half-caste, is associated with the two-
coloured swan, and his emblem is the swan (386,11-25). King
Gorhant, too, is described at some length, with the stress
on the strange properties of his army (35,12-28). The heathen
are often given a somewhat generalized individuality by their
association with rich clothing and brilliant jewels which is
a part of the sense of the exotic which pervades Wolfram's
impression of them.

Similarly, even where Wolfram does not isolate named
individuals, there is a strong sense that he is nevertheless
concerned with their fates, as, for example, when he says
that the Christians are risking their lives for the sake of
Christ and so will earn for themselves the music of the
angels (31,12-20). At other times simply by naming the men
he gives them a small measure of individuality, though the
speed of the narrative and the need to imply the vast numbers
make it impossible for him to linger on each of them. Thus,
for example, he speaks of four of them:

        der Burgunjoys Gwigrimanz
        und des marcgrâven swester kint

> Myle, die zwên fürsten sint
> ze Oransche komen în.
> der werden sol noch mêre sîn:
> ich meine den clâren Jozeranz
> und Hûwesen von Meilanz.
> die viere heten hie den prîs
> und sint nu dort en pardîs.          (14,20-28)

Immediately afterwards another four are singled out for a
brief mention:

> Gaudîns der brûne kom ouch dar,
> und Kyblîns mit dem blanken hâr,
> und ouch von Tolûs Gaudiers,
> Hûnas von Sanctes. ob ir miers
> geloubt, sô wil ich zieren
> diz mære mit den vieren.
> die heten ob dem wunsches zil
> der hôhen werdekeit sô vil:
> swer prîses dâ dez minre truoc
> under in, es hete iedoch genuoc
> von drîn landen al diu diet.         (15,1-11)

The epithets at this stage are conventional: later he will
speak of the individual deeds of some of them. Yet, even now,
Wolfram achieves a poignant effect, in that, although he
speaks of them as alive now, he nevertheless anticipates
their deaths.

Wolfram thus ensures simultaneously the awareness of
the mass and of the components of this mass, while something
like the reverse technique is used when he refrains from
naming one of the heathen slain by Willehalm and simply
comments:

> der was vil rîche.               (21,13)

Though the adjective is entirely conventional, the effect is
remarkable: once more Wolfram has isolated a single knight
while making it clear that the individual can remain anonymous
within the amorphous mass which dominates the scene.

From a description of the mass of the heathen forces in
terms of the waves of the sea (32,2-3), Wolfram can, on the
other hand, allow individuals to emerge when he names the ten
nephews of Arofel (32,8-17) and reminds us, for both relationships are important of course, that these men are also the
sons of Terramer. In this case the naming of the men is important, but equally significant is their emergence from the

mass to which they belong.

It is above all in Book IX, in the second stage of the
second battle, that Wolfram uses the technique of allowing
individuals to emerge from the mass. This technique is used
side-by-side with that of describing events simultaneously; [4]
indeed, it may be seen as an aspect of it, for while the
dominant impression is of confusion and activity, and while
the background of general fighting is to be seen as constant
throughout, a new order emerges from the disorder, not in the
encounters of pre-arranged groups of soldiers, but in chance
clashes between individuals.

Thus Wolfram focuses on the combat between Cernubile von
Ammirafel and Count Heimrich, whom he has previously isolated
by means of his stress on the Cross which adorns his cloak
(406,6-407,9). The King, mentioned hitherto only in passing
(360,6ff), comes to the fore now in this combat which brings
his death. In the brief picture of him fighting with the
old knight with the beard as white as snow, Cernubile emerges
too as an individual character; he has always before been
victorious, bringing death to many who, like the man with
whom he now fights, have borne the Cross on their clothes and
whose tongues have been rendered incapable of uttering their
battle cries:

> Cernubilê manc kriuce vant
> gesniten ûf ir wæte,
> die mit ritterlîcher tæte
> sînem puneiz vor gehielten
> und dâ manc houbet spielten,
> daz die zungen in den munden
> deheine krîe enkunden.          (408,8-14)

These few lines contribute briefly to the figure of Cernubile
and supply him with a past, which Wolfram links abruptly with
his present by means of his cry to Mahomet (408,15) as he
launches into combat with Heimrich. Here, too, there is a
sharp contrast, for on his cloak and helmet he wears the gifts
bestowed on him by his beloved, and, though Wolfram does not
mention the contrast, one must recall the previous description
of the Cross on the cloak of Heimrich. The combat is brief,
and the death of Cernubile again recalls the past victories

just mentioned, for Heimrich inflicts a blow on him which
strikes through his helmet <u>unz ûf die zene</u> (408,29): his cry,
too, is abruptly silenced. The notion of revenge thus implied in Wolfram's account is made explicit:

> sîner tohter sun dâ rach,
> den clâren Vivîanzen,
> Heimrîch an dem glanzen
> der sô manec zimierde truoc.      (408,24-27)

In turn, Cernubile's men desire revenge for their King, and
so, in a brief return to more general description of the
battle, Wolfram speaks of the death of many Christians at the
hands of the heathen (409,10-12), before again isolating a
single combat, that between Bernart, son of Heimrich, and
Cliboris, who, like Cernubile, has been mentioned hitherto
only as one of many engaged in the general fighting (358,29-
30) and who is distinguished now by the brilliance and vitality so soon to be extinguished. He comes into combat <u>flying
like a dragon</u> (409,18): on his helmet is a ship, and his
whole attire is brilliant and costly. There is nothing unique
in this, but Wolfram does make his description of Cliboris
distinctive, when he says that sparks seem to fly out of his
mouth when he moves his head (409,27-30). It is that same
head which receives the blow from Bernart, and at the death
of Cliboris Wolfram concentrates on the ship on his helmet:
that symbol of the vital young knight is isolated in his
death:

> des wart des Haropînes suon
> durch parken und durch helm erslagn.
>
> (411,2-3)

Wolfram passes at once to the third in this series of
encounters between brilliant heathen knights and the kinsmen
of Willehalm. This time it is Poydwiz, son of King Oukin,
who is shown first of all as the slayer of Kiun von Beaveis
and five other French knights, before he comes into combat
with Heimrich the younger. Wolfram spends little time on the
description of this battle before the death of Poydwiz, and
only afterwards does he speak of the reputation of the young
man who is mourned in many lands. The individuality of Poydwiz lies rather in Wolfram's explanation of his death, for he

gives him distinction by accounting for it afterwards and
in distinctive terms:

> waz half sîn grôziu hers kraft,
> die im sîn vater schuof ze wer,
> mange sunderrotte, über mer?
> ûz den het er sich erstriten,
> daz er in ze verre was entriten.
> swer die sînen ie verkôs,
> der wart ouch etswenn sigelôs.
> daz in der schêtîs eine sluoc,
> daz kom dâ von. daz ors in truoc
> durch den rinc des künec Grôhier.
> dâ was im durch daz tehtier
> dez houbetstiudel ab geslagn:
> ez mohte des zoumes niht getragn.
> des wart er umbe gewant
> von des schêtîses hant,
> daz er den rücke kêrte
> dem der in sterben lêrte.           (412,14-30)

The tragedy of the man who preferred to fight alone resumes
its place in the whole tragedy, for Wolfram never lingers on
the fates of individual men at this stage and here, too, he
suggests the conflict still raging by his reference immediately to the sounds of swords and to sparks flying from helmets:

> Lâzâ klingen! was dô swerte erklanc,
> und waz dâ fiwers ûz helmen spranc.
>                                     (413,1-2)

Yet out of this brief general description there emerge two
individual characters, Terramer and Rennewart, who in a new
stage of the narrative receive the focus of attention, moving
towards the moment when Wolfram deliberately evades the encounter between father and son which would seem to be the
inevitable culmination of so much tragic waste. The activity
of Terramer is described in very general terms:

> der getorste unde mohte.
> lützel iemen daz getohte,
> daz er im gæbe gegenstrît.       (413,5-7)

Wolfram thus implies that Terramer continues to fight bravely
throughout, though the limelight passes immediately to Rennewart and remains with him for a long time. Only Milon von
Nivers is singled out for personal mention as a victim of
Terramer, but his death provides Wolfram's impetus for bringing
Rennewart into the midst of the action, as he promptly slays
five noble kings in revenge for his comrade and thus begins

the defeat of the heathen when Halzebier's men, seeing this
slaughter, flee towards the sea.

To imply the force and scope of Rennewart's activity,
Wolfram uses two distinct techniques. He speaks in general
terms of the young man as he lays about him with his pole,
not isolating the individual victims.[5] On the other hand,
one single incident is made specific, that with Essere who
perishes at the hand of Rennewart:

> Esserê der emerâl
> mit zimierde lieht gemâl,
> Ein fürste ûz Halzebieres her,
> der hielt mit rotte aldâ ze wer
> dennoch unbetwungen.
> Rennewart kom gedrungen,
> daz er in möht erlangen.
> er stiez in mit der stangen
> durch den lîp der wâpen truoc.
> wol klâftern lanc: des was genuoc.
>
> (417,29-418,8)

The description is brief and to the point, but it serves, in
the midst of much generalization, to focus attention on an
individual among many who make up the whole.[6]

As Purrel is borne away on his shield and the heathen
are fleeing from the battlefield, Wolfram suddenly focuses
his attention on Terramer, significantly der rîche Terramêr
(432,13) who, it seems clear, has been watching the course
of events, Rennewart's victory over Purrel perhaps, the suffering of the old King and his men certainly, and the flight
which marks the final turning-point in his own fortunes. Now
a single line suggests the determination of Terramer, of the
great man so near to defeat. As he watches the suffering of
his kinsmen, he urges his people on:

> der begunde al die sîne manen.        (432,15)

He will not give in so easily, though he now has to hear of
the death of Halzebier and of the many other losses. The
great heathen King who has been seen in conversation with
his daughter, threatening her brutally and attacking the
cause of Christianity, is seen now in another role, as the
mighty ruler near to defeat, the man who has set his heart
on high achievement and who must now see the destruction of

his hopes. One is reminded of the much earlier description
of Terramer, when Wolfram had described the rich gifts which
were brought to him as he prepared for battle. He had stressed
the royal donors, the fine quality of the objects and their
distant origin, yet these factors had combined to contrast
with the picture of Terramer himself, grief-stricken by
events:              Sus der getriwe heiden saz
                  al klagende ûf sînem matraz.        (356,1-2)
The whole scene had contributed to a fuller picture of the
human being, complementing the picture which had seemed to
dominate, of the powerful ruler and the harsh father. The
memory of these other descriptions has contributed towards
a strange and complex picture and colours the greater moment
which now comes for Terramer as an individual, when Wolfram
chooses to give to him, not the encounter with Rennewart
which had at one point seemed inevitable, but the combat with
Willehalm himself.

    At the last, then, when so much of the description of
the second battle has been of the conflict of undefined masses,
or the emergence into combat of otherwise unknown figures,
Wolfram has the two great leaders stand physically opposed
to one another, as though to suggest in a final clash between
the two representative leaders the conflict between the two
forces described already at such length and in such detail.
Though the combat avoids its potentially tragic conclusion,
it represents a high point of drama in bringing together the
two men on whom so much responsibility rests.

    The aftermath of the battle and in particular the Matri-
bleiz-scene will focus attention on Willehalm, but before
that, to balance the picture of the victor, Wolfram turns to
Terramer who, in spite of everything, remains noble:

                daz klagete al sîne kumenden zît
                Terramêr der werde.
                sus schiet von rœmscher erde
                der dâ vor dicke ûf Rôme sprach
                ê daz diu schumpfentiure geschach.
                                        (443,26-30)
The full irony is contained in these last lines, of the dis-
crepancy between the ambitions of the man and his failure to

achieve them. More than that, Wolfram recalls, now that
victory is secured for the Christians, the significance of
their cause, which is in its widest terms the preservation
of Christendom. The sense of the scope of the battle is once
more combined with the awareness of the individual and of his
role within the wide, public issues. As he so often does,
and as he will do with Willehalm in the Matribleiz-scene and
before it, Wolfram sets the individual within his context,
but, by the vividness of his picture throughout of Terramer,
he ensures that the scope of this context does not in any way
detract from the fate of the individual man.[7]

At the Court of Loys in Munleun, Wolfram allows individuals to come forward and, for a brief period, to receive the
full concentration of the limelight. As in the battles, he
thereby achieves a sense of the mass of the people, and, side-
by-side with this, an awareness of the vivid personalities
which make up the mass. Loys and his Queen are already present
when Irmschart and Heimrich arrive, and Wolfram stresses the
great number of their retinue (142,24-28). It is against this
background of a very great many people and the noise of the
festivities (143,30ff) that Wolfram sets the momentous scenes
which ensue. One can justly speak of 'scenes' in this context, for though there is a continuity, of course, in the
events which follow, there is also in each case a concentration upon a single person or group of people. The entire
episode demonstrates again Wolfram's ability to create individualized characters, but to use them here in a different
manner, as the focal point of activity and advancing the chain
of events.[8]

Willehalm himself is the first to receive the focus of
attention, as he sits within the assembly, yet so completely
separated from it. In his soliloquy he contrasts the joy
which he sees about him with the losses which he has suffered
(144,15-30) and his action in striding before the King and
addressing him so angrily represents the culmination of these
thoughts and puts them into forthright terms. The immediate
effect of his speech is to arouse his brothers, who recognize

him and hasten to greet him, and thus the four brothers
hitherto unnamed are now identified by name:

> Bertram and Buov von Kumarzî,
> Schilbert und Bernart der flôrîs.
> (146,18-19)

The focus of attention shifts, then, with these lines, but it
soon returns to Willehalm, in the single statement which recalls the virtual challenge to the King:

> der marcrâve dennoch stuont.           (146,23)

It is now on Loys that attention rests, as he responds with
a brief, restrained speech which contrasts with that of Willehalm which preceded it and the unconsidered words of the Queen
which follow:

> dô sprach des rœmschen küneges muont
>  'hêr Willalm, sint irz sît,
> sô dunket mich des gein iu zît,
> daz ich bekenne iu fürsten reht:
> wan sît ich was ein swacher kneht,
> sô lebt ich iwers râtes ie,
> ouch liez mich iwer helfe nie.
> Iwer zorn ist ân nôt bekant
> gein mir. ir wizzet, al mîn lant,
> swes ir drinne gert, daz ist getân.
> ich mac gâbe und lêhen hân:
> daz kêrt mit fuoge an iwern  gewin.'
> sîn swester sprach, diu künegin,
> 'ouwê wie wênc uns denne belibe!
> sô wære ich d'erste dier vertribe.
> mir ist lieber daz er warte her,
> dan daz ich sînre genâde ger.'
> (146,24-147,10)

The verbal activity which has ensured that attention is
focused on each of the speakers in turn gives way to physical
activity, as Willehalm wrenches the crown from her head and
hurls it to the ground:

> vor al den fürsten daz geschach,
> die krône err von dem houbte brach
> und warf se daz diu gar zebrast. (147,15-17)

The first of these lines stresses the public nature of this
degrading scene, and it also recalls the background of the
royal festivities: one is made aware once more of the context,
just as in the battle scenes individual figures emerge from
the conflict, occupying the foreground for a time and then
returning to the broader setting.

As Willehalm seizes the Queen by her hair, it is Irmschart who steps forward, and this first physical intervention of the old woman anticipates her vital speech to the
assembled men.  This is not the moment for Wolfram to linger
on her, however, but he does remind his audience of the relationship of Irmschart to Willehalm and the Queen:

> wan derzwischen kom gedrungen
> ir beider muoter Irmenschart.     (147,22-23)

She stands now physically between them, but she is related
equally to each, and it is her metaphorical position between
the two of them which will be the basis of her later influence.[9)]

The Queen releases her hair from Willehalm's grasp and
flees to her room, bolting the door after her.  She is removed from the scene and it is the King who now occupies the
limelight, for all present must now be waiting to see his
reaction to this insulting behaviour towards his wife and,
through her, towards himself.  The expectation that Loys will
take some revenge on his subject for this action is not fulfilled, however, for Wolfram anticipates the later hesitation
of the King in giving aid to Willehalm in the somewhat luke-
warm reproach which he now utters (148,8-15).  Instead, Wolfram turns to Willehalm's father who steps forward to greet
his son.  In doing so, he evokes the central scene of this
early part of the period at Munleun, which contains Willehalm's
account of the first battle and the losses which he has sustained, until it culminates in the statement which strikes
at the hearts of all present:

> Myle and Vivîanz sint tôt.          (151,30)

A single line gives a weighty impression and is enough to
convey the reaction of all present, as Wolfram concentrates
on the old Count:

> Heimrîch stuont kûm daz er niht viel.
>                                      (152,4)

The idea that the great soldier should be overcome with grief
to the extent that he can hardly stand expresses the anguish
of the whole assembly.

Though this line focuses attention on Willehalm's father,

Wolfram passes in quick succession to Irmschart as she breaks
the silence with her scornful exhortation to courage:

> 'wie ist iwer ellen sus bewart?
> ir tragt doch manlîchen lîp:
> sult ir nu weinen sô diu wîp
> oder als ein kint nâch dem ei,
> waz touc helden sölh geschrei?
> welt ir manlîche lebn,
> sô müezt ir lîhen unde gebn,
> und helfet dem der zuns ist komn,
> des flust wir alle hân vernomn.
> dâ hab wir mit im an verlorn.
> die von Heimrîch sint erborn,
> ob sîn künne ir prîs wil tuon,
> sô wirt Willalm mîn suon
> ergetzet swaz im wirret.
> swen zageheit des irret,
> der möhte sanfter wesen tôt.'          (152,12-27)

Wolfram is building up his picture of the old mother in anticipation of her speech later, and so, again, he does not linger
on her, but remains with Willehalm, who passes to his verbal
attack on his sister.[10]  With the arrival of Alyze, Willehalm's anger fades and Wolfram comments:

> done mohter
> sîne zuht nimmêr zebrechen:
> swaz er zornes kunde sprechen,
> der wart vil gar durch si verswign.
> swes ir muoter was bezign
> von im, wærz dannoch ungetân,
> ez wære ouch dâ nâch fürbaz lân.     (154,2-8)

The lines are a subtle condemnation of Willehalm's behaviour
and seem to reflect the disapproval of the whole assembly of
actions and words which cannot continue in the presence of
the innocent young girl on whom all attention is now focused.

The tension of the scene is apparent.  Willehalm's angry
outburst has been interrupted, and no-one in the hall has
attempted a response to his outrageous accusation of the Queen.
Wolfram has described nothing of the festive apparel of those
present, though it may, of course, be assumed in the context
of this great royal occasion.  He does so now, and his technique in describing the radiant beauty and brilliant dress of
Alyze ensures that she is unique in this respect, as in the
remarkable effect which she achieves.  He describes in detail
her lovely hair and her crown, her slender figure and the

costly girdle (154,9-155,17), and his closely observed description of human beauty enhanced by riches reaches its peak
in the description of her superlative radiance:

> von der meide kom ein glast,
> daz der heimlîch und der gast
> mit gelîcher volge jâhen
> daz si nie gesâhen
> decheine magt sô wol gevar.     (155,13-27)[11]

Because the actual description is unique in <u>Willehalm</u>, Wolfram
achieves the effect intended, suggesting that all attention
is focused on Alyze as she makes her way in the stunned silence
into the hall, and embracing in the impression the wonder of
all present and the emotion of Willehalm himself. The impression is continued in her gesture of falling at his feet,
and in the silence which she maintains as Willehalm expresses
his emotion at her gesture and bids her rise from her knees,
and as he embraces her and tells her that he would kiss her
if it were not forbidden him. Only then does Alyze break her
silence with her tearful questioning about his behaviour towards her mother and the distortion of his normal disposition
which permitted it. Assuring him that his accusations bring
disgrace on her mother and on himself, she asks him to forgive
the Queen for what she has done to him. She asks this for
the sake of his mother, her own grandmother, and for the sake
of her lady Gyburc:

> durch dîne muoter (diust mîn an)
> und durch Gyburg die vrouwen mîn,
> diu mich als ir kindelîn
> hât dicke an ir arm genomn.
> diust mir leider nu ze verre komn.'
>
>                 (157,26-30)

Like everything in the appearance of Alyze, her final words
are perfectly timed, for, as she grieves that Gyburc is so
far away, she strikes at a chord in Willehalm which she knows
will bring a response from him.

The gentle scene of the encounter between Alyze and Willehalm is contrasted with the active intervention of Irmschart, who once more shows herself alert to the situation and
capable of contributing positively to it. She sends Alyze to
her mother, and herself embarks on the great speech in which

she declares herself ready to give material aid to her son
and, if necessary, to fight for him (160,20-161,10). The
speech is a culmination of the powerful though brief impressions which Wolfram has previously given of the old
woman. It is a magnificent one, too, beginning with her
declaration of her age and ending with the vision of her in
armour striking out with her swords. It has a brilliant
visual effect, coming so soon after the picture of Alyze,
innocent and radiant and with the healing power of youth and
purity. The near-juxtaposition of the two women shows again
Wolfram's acute sense of contrast and his sure sense of
dramatic effect.

When the Queen returns to the assembly, apprised now
of the events of Alischanz, she becomes the focus of attention, but Wolfram's technique is different again. There is
none of the previous visual effect, but he depends rather on
her speech of lamentation, in which she repeats, to some
extent, the account of the losses on the field of Alischanz
and reminds those present of their kinship with her and with
those slain (167,1-168,10). Her grief is perhaps excessive,
in view of her previous behaviour,[12] and the incongruity is
pointed out by her husband when she appeals to him for help
for her brother. When he rejects her appeal she turns instead to her other brothers and Wolfram anticipates, not only
their responses, but also the far-reaching consequences:

> dâ von was si bejagende
> daz si ir bruoder helfe erwarp;
> des sît ûf Alischans erstarp
> manec werder Sarrazîn.          (170,2-5)

Wolfram now concentrates in turn on all four of Willehalm's
brothers. The speeches are balanced, in alternating pairs.
Bernart von Brubant declares himself ready to fight for his
brother (170,23-30); Bertram follows immediately with a longer
speech in which he, too, offers his aid and the service of
his men, but in which he concentrates on the desire for revenge
and the grief at the losses of Alischanz (171,1-17); Gybert,
like Bernart, confines himself to the declaration of his
readiness to fight for Willehalm (171,21-30); Buov takes up

the lament of Bertram, speaking of the grief of the years to
come for the deaths of so many Christian knights but then rejecting passive grief in favour of activity and offering men
and horses to fight for Gyburc (172,1-30). Once more, then,
Wolfram allows individuals in turn to dominate the scene,
though for a very brief period.

When, on the order of the King, the feast continues,
Willehalm requests that Wimar, his host of the night before,
should sit with him at the King's table. The picture is a
very brief one, but it is a further example of Wolfram's
sense of detail and of his interest in the lesser characters:

> dô mohte Wîmâr gerne lebn,
> Wan er ans rîches tische saz
> und mit den hœhsten fürsten az,
>
> (175,30-176,3)

Side-by-side with the picture of Wimar enjoying this rare
experience is another of Willehalm himself, refusing the fine
food and accepting only black bread and water (176,10-15).
With the reference to his sacrifice comes the memory of Gyburc
and of the urgent need to act, and so Wolfram leads to the
next vivid scene, the clash between Willehalm and Loys, when
Willehalm leaps across the table at the King, recalling in
his lack of control his earlier ill-treatment of the Queen.
In this incident, and in the debate which ensues, Loys comes
to the fore, as everyone waits for his vital decision. Wolfram has concentrated on the two men, Willehalm, the active and
violent man, and Loys, the circumspect ruler, injured profoundly in his pride and slow to give in. During the course of the
discussion, other characters join in with their pleas - the
Queen, Heimrich and finally Irmschart - but it is on Loys himself that attention is focused, until the picture of power
and resolution culminates in Wolfram's assertion:

> der von Karle was erborn,
> der begienc dâ Karles tücke.
> daz was Gyburge gelücke.           (184,28-30)

The whole episode of the first day at Munleun is a vivid
composition of a distinctive, unchanging background and the
consistent sense of a large gathering, overlaid with a series
of incidents and individual characters, on whom attention is

focused in succession to one another.  As in the battles,
and indeed in the work as a whole, the sense of the whole
is in no way impaired by the force of individual events
and people.  Rather is the integrity of the whole conserved
by the consciousness of the background and the relationship
among the incidents, while the dramatic effect is enhanced
by the emergence of individuals and by the sense of individuals reacting to one another and to events.

6. <u>The Narrative Art of Wolfram in 'Willehalm'</u>
<u>and the end of the work</u>

Wolfram's <u>Willehalm</u> is a work of immense proportions,
presenting personal and public issues, in a thoroughly integrated whole. It is characterized, despite its scope, by a
unity of form and of thought, achieved by a variety of means
which serve to maintain the control over the substance so
evident in the work. Patterns of time and place, too, ensure
a framework for the action which moves between defined settings.

The distinctive settings contribute to the dramatic
qualities of the poem in which vivid activity and individualized characters are shown against real and significant
backgrounds. Yet, though the work is peopled with distinctive characters, most of these emerge from the mass which Wolfram describes so vividly and are then absorbed back into it.

Lasting dominance is given to only two, to Gyburc and
Willehalm, to whom Wolfram gives the task of expressing the
spiritual message of a work which, though it succeeds as a
tale of mediæval chivalry, has the more significant purpose
of conveying, by means of its impact as an exciting narrative, an abstract ideal.

The message of the work, the advocacy of a humane and
compassionate attitude towards all God's creatures, is

expressed above all in the words of Gyburc and the actions
of Willehalm.  Husband and wife are shown to join in the
expression of Wolfram's abstract theme.  Their individuality, and above all their mutual love, are shown in their
relationship to the broad picture of the conflict of great
forces and the immensity of the human dilemma.

The juxtaposition of the personal and the public, of
the individual and the mass, of love and hatred, light and
dark, echoes and re-echoes in Wolfram's narrative, in which
contrast is an important feature of his art.  His ability,
in a work which never loses its sense of the whole, to
concentrate on a small detail, to allow an apparently insignificant factor to assume significance, or, conversely,
to reduce an event of magnitude to a passing comment, contributes to the variety of the texture of the poem.

Although there are moments of light, of light-hearted-
ness even, the dominant mood of the work is of gloom.  Yet
this in no way contradicts its essential optimism, expressed
above all in the sense of the ultimate power of love for
good, the vision of the sanctity of Gyburc and the movement,
as the work ends, towards the reconciliation of opposing
forces in deference to their common source as the creation
of God.

Any consideration of Wolfram's _Willehalm_ must encounter
the problem of its ending, and the study of the narrative art
of the work can perhaps contribute to the discussion.  The
arguments are well known and have most recently been sum-
marized by Carl Lofmark, who himself takes the view that _Wil-
lehalm_ is not finished.[1]  It is difficult to conceive of a
mediæval narrator's leaving the fate of a major character
unknown, and Rennewart's disappearance means that many questions remain unanswered and a number of predictions unfulfilled.  Rennewart's love for Alyze has not yet led to his
baptism and his marriage with the young princess; he has not
received recognition of his innate nobility, nor has his role
in the battle been acknowledged formally.[2]  He has simply
vanished, without trace, and that, to most modern critics, as

perhaps to many of Wolfram's contemporaries, is a conclusion difficult to accept.[3] Lofmark observes emphatically: "The Rennewart action thus provides proof by itself that <u>Wille-halm</u> is a fragment: no complete court epic could leave such important motifs unresolved".[4] Against this view, Bumke declares: "In dem Augenblick, als Terramers Fahne niedersinkt, als der Sieg der Christen entschieden ist, in dem Augenblick ist Rennewarts Aufgabe erfüllt. Er könnte hier für immer abtreten, denn er wird fortan nicht mehr gebraucht."[5] These are, indeed, two irreconcilable opinions, from two scholars who know Wolfram well, and they draw attention to the almost certainly insoluble nature of this problem. Perhaps, however, there is a way in which they can be reconciled: perhaps, in this great work, Wolfram does something which seems impossible in the context of mediæval narrative, when he leaves the fate of Rennewart unknown and concludes the work in a way which seems to contradict his earlier intentions. This point of view seems to be contained in the more tentative suggestion by M. O'C. Walshe, who draws attention to the dangers of speculating on this question but goes on: "It seems not unlikely that Wolfram's lofty mind had inwardly transcended the theme".[6] This is not to say, however, that Wolfram was incapable of finishing the work satisfactorily: when Walshe says "It is conceivable that Wolfram found it impossible to discover a satisfying solution to the problems he posed, though he had been equal to the task of concluding <u>Parzival</u>", he does not say - though he certainly knows that this is so - that <u>Parzival</u> does not present problems as great as <u>Willehalm</u>. Moreover, we are not concerned with his capacity as a <u>narrator</u> to complete the work: here Lofmark is certainly right when, in rejecting the explanation of Bumke that Wolfram <u>suddenly</u> found the poem unfinishable, he says that Wolfram knew the end of <u>Aliscans</u> before he started his own work and that he "could scarcely fail to see a difficulty before reaching it".[7]

Wolfram could, of course, have told of the glorious return of Rennewart, his baptism and his marriage with Alyze,

but the point is: did he _want_ to? The answer to this would
seem to me to be a negative one: the work has, in the hands
of its great author, assumed immense proportions and the
somewhat facile conclusion of the source bears no relation
to these proportions.[8] Precisely here one may not, as
Maurer advocates, turn to _Parzival_ for the key to Willehalm:[9] to think of the problems of the reconciliation of
Christians and heathen in terms of the union of Repanse de
Schoye and Feirefiz is mistaken.[10] _Willehalm_ is quite
different in tone, and even during the course of it one feels
Wolfram maturing, just as his hero matures in the course of
his final speech.[11] It is quite possible, then, that his
attitude towards his own narrative changes and develops, and
that the conciliatory outcome which he seems to be anticipating, in accordance with his source, becomes unacceptable
to him as he perceives increasingly the complex situation
with which he is dealing. In such terms the ending of Wolfram's work and the incomplete Rennewart story can be reconciled, not quite in the negative way put forward by those who
support the 'Notdach' theory,[12] but as a further positive
and important example of Wolfram's originality and narrative
strength, which enable him to evade the conclusion to which
he may seem committed and to end the work, not in a hasty and
clumsy manner, but with perfect regard for what is fitting.[13]

In considering Wolfram's approach to the ending of his
poem, one may - and it seems indeed that one must - be guided
by what has emerged from the study of his narrative art. It
is clear that, although he is concerned to tell a good tale
and although one may not disregard his responsibility in this
respect towards his audience, the emphasis of his interest in
the work is on the religious message which it contains. That
this is so is apparent from the difference between _Willehalm_
and the French source. That which is new in Wolfram's work -
the stress on spiritual values, the great speeches of Gyburc,
the role of human love in leading to the love of God, the
humane and compassionate view of the Saracens - points to a
totally different interpretation of the old material. It is

these elements which give to <u>Willehalm</u> its quite distinctive
character, and one is surely justified in concluding that
Wolfram has wished to create an entirely new work. The objection will certainly be raised that Wolfram has, after all,
spoken of his source and that, since this source was presumably well known to his audience, he has an obligation to
follow it in telling of the mutual recognition of Gyburc and
Rennewart, the baptism of Rennewart, and his marriage with
Alyze. Yet the work as it stands does not contradict the
source: it simply does not follow it to its conclusion. The
emphasis of the whole of <u>Willehalm</u> is totally different from
that of <u>Aliscans</u>, and if, at the end, Wolfram chooses a different emphasis from his source, this can hardly be a surprise.

It has frequently been observed - and the comparative
accounts by Lofmark of the two works make this abundantly
clear - [14] that Wolfram diverges increasingly from his source
towards the end of his work. He is capable of making radical
changes to the material of his source, when, for example, he
describes the encounter between Terramer and, not Rennewart,
but Willehalm, or when he actually adds the Matribleiz-scene.
Yet these two instances point to significant qualities in
Wolfram's narrative, as has already emerged. The battle between the two great leaders is an æsthetic peak in the narrative, a moment of completely appropriate drama in what is a
very dramatic work. The incident in the source, when Rainouart encounters Desramé, tries to persuade him to become a
Christian by threatening to kill him if he refuses and subsequently wounds him and puts him to flight, [15] has nothing
to contribute to the direction of Wolfram's thought: indeed,
it contradicts it, for he has given no evidence of Rennewart's
advocacy of the Christian faith and the idea of forcing
Christianity on the infidel is alien to the spirit of Wolfram's work. The tragic conflict between father and son is
implied in the earlier moment of dramatic tension when Rennewart glimpses his father and Wolfram evades description of
the combat by his strange and seemingly wilful reference to
Frau Uote and Hildebrand (439,16). Wolfram declines to describe

the battle, which may, but need not, have taken place between father and son.[16] Instead he shifts the emphasis
from Rennewart to Willehalm[17] for, in what remains of his
poem, Willehalm is to be the central figure. When he
chooses to add the Matribleiz-scene and so to show the great
Christian leader expressing in tangible terms the abstract
thoughts of his wife, he reiterates and fulfils his purpose
of allowing Willehalm to assume the dominant role which, in
his source, was threatened by the figure of Rennewart.

Lofmark has shown that, although Rennewart is an important character in the work, Wolfram has made considerable
efforts to subordinate him to Willehalm.[18] Yet the major
part of his argument that _Willehalm_ is indeed a fragment
rests on the admittedly undeniable fact that the story of
Rennewart is not finished. For Lofmark, as for many of his
predecessors, this makes it inconceivable that _Willehalm_ is
a completed work. However, if one examines what is lacking
to complete the story of Rennewart one may well find that
the omissions are not, after all, so grave in the context of
Wolfram's new conception of his material which must, it seems
clear, place the demands of the character of Willehalm and
the progress towards a fulfilment of the spiritual ideals of
Gyburc above the claims of an interesting and attractive
character who is, however, a subsidiary one.

Poydjus, challenged by Rennewart, turns from the battle
and is not heard of again (444,28-30). This, for Lofmark,
is an impossible conclusion,[19] and Wolfram must have intended to follow his source and recount a battle between Rennewart and Poydjus. Lofmark observes "Wolfram's enthusiastic
portrait of Poydjus had led us to expect great things of him;
if he intended never to mention him again after his flight
from Rennewart, then his action would be as incomplete as
the Rennewart action and therefore unsatisfactory."[20] Here
he seems to have hit upon a significant point: the story of
Poydjus _is_ as incomplete as that of Rennewart, and that is
how Wolfram intends it to be. Both men are subordinated, in
the last resort, to the superior claims of the Willehalm

action. The study of Wolfram's treatment of his characters
has shown that he repeatedly allows individuals to emerge for
a brief period from the battle and then to be absorbed back
into the general fighting.[21] Rennewart, it is true, has
played a significant role but he, too, may not distort the
proportions of the work and the dominance of the two central
figures. The end of his story is left to the imagination,
giving way to a new emphasis which, though it has no correspondence in Wolfram's source, is entirely in accordance
with his interpretation of his material.

And although Wolfram does not relate the end of Rennewart's story, the imagination is aided by those predictions
which, because they are unfulfilled, constitute one of the
arguments of those who maintain that Willehalm is incomplete.
Wolfram has referred to a future improvement in the fortunes
of Rennewart, when his present smæhe will be replaced by
êre (285,11-22)[22] and Rennewart has spoken to Willehalm of
his hopes of a secret reward (331,13-20):[23] the two passages taken together justify an expectation that Rennewart
will indeed, as in the source, receive acknowledgement of his
innate qualities and his achievements in battle, in the form
of marriage with the Princess Alyze. Wolfram has spoken of
the intuition which Gyburc feels of something which she will
not know until much later (291,1-3). Her own revelation
to Rennewart that King Synagun was her nephew comes very soon
after (294,23) and this one-sided declaration of identity
finds no response in Rennewart: this certainly does not constitute the fulfilment of a prediction.

In telling the story of Rennewart, Wolfram, as has been
seen, is at pains to maintain suspense and to proceed by
means of hints and dramatic irony.[24] He has already gone a
long way: the audience, and those listening at the door, know
that he is the son of Terramer;[25] Gyburc has recognized him
as her brother and has all but told him so, but Rennewart
has declined to acknowledge their relationship. A mutual
recognition scene, though clearly signalled, has been postponed. Wolfram has quite deliberately built up the suspense

and then declined to bring it to its culmination. If one
seeks the reason for his failure to add what seems the fitting ending to his tale, then one finds it, surely, once more
in the nature of his work. The joyful recognition of brother
and sister, with Rennewart elevated by his achievements in
battle and about to accept baptism which will both represent
the formal acknowledgement of his role as the zeswe hant of
Willehalm and lead directly to his marriage with Alyze, would
represent a change in mood which would contradict Wolfram's
purpose. Although his work promises that joy will one day
come (12,2-3) this lies beyond the framework of his poem.
A work which has, as its prevailing mood, the darkness of the
human dilemma, the conflict between those who are bound by
love and by kinship, and only in periods of respite the awareness of the power of love to alleviate the gloom, can hardly
proceed to the undiluted joy which the unnarrated events must
contain.[26)]

Wolfram, it seems, allows these events to take place in
the imagination of his audience, supported by their knowledge
of his source and by his own predictions, and he himself ends
his narrative by taking a course which, though alien to his
source, is completely compatible with his own work. The objection that such a procedure goes against the custom of
mediæval writers is answered by pointing to the originality
of Wolfram. A poet who has interpreted his material as Wolfram has done and who has moulded it in accordance with this
entirely new interpretation, adding vital passages which have
no counterpart in the source and which are not even anticipated by it, can hardly be expected, in deference to his
source, to deviate from the course which he has taken.

From the opening of Willehalm, Wolfram has set the tone
of his poem and this tone is quite distinct from that of the
Aliscans. The prayer to the Trinity founds the work in the
spirituality which, sustained as it is by the person of Gyburc,
pervades the whole. Bumke, speaking of the two instances in
the second battle when Wolfram declines to follow his source,[27)]
observes "Von hier an bis zum Schluß ist Wolfram unabhängig

von seiner Quelle",[28] and this is true, as far as the substance is concerned. As far as the mood and emphasis of the
poem are concerned, however, Wolfram is always independent
of his source.

When he opens Book IX with that brief but powerful
address to Gyburc he is releasing himself from his source.
After this she cannot be brought back into the work, to take
part in the recognition scene which he has seemed to be
anticipating. Mergell is surely right when he declares:
"Der Dichter nimmt Abschied von Gyburg".[29] The final view
of Gyburc is this brief vision of her, raised above the human
activity in which, for much of the work, she has been engaged.
Already, then, Wolfram is moving towards the transcendance of
the events of his source, and it has been seen how the address
to Gyburc constitutes a vital factor in the harmony of the
spiritual thought, intimately related both aesthetically and
thematically to the words of Willehalm to Matribleiz which
end the work.[30]

Although Wolfram's account of the battle has been interrupted by this appeal to 'Saint' Gyburc, Wolfram has still to
tell of the remainder of that battle, and he turns at once to
resume his narrative. Yet the effect of those ten lines remains, as has been seen, to pervade the action with the awareness of the presence of Gyburc, not, as in the first battle,
with the physical sense of her existence but in a new and
heightened form, elevated as a saint and transported beyond
the present events. Though he has still to tell of those
events, Wolfram has in these lines moved beyond them in time
in his appeal to Gyburc and to those who <u>fought</u> in that battle.
Though much remains of his account of the fighting, of the
flight of the heathen and the aftermath of the battle, the
opening lines of this Book point towards the conversation
which closes it. The prayer is addressed to Gyburc, the loving
and suffering woman[31] who has advocated mercy and in deference to whose words Willehalm will spare Matribleiz and grant
honour to the heathen slain. The anticipated reunion with
Rennewart, when she will learn for sure what she has so

strongly suspected, is a matter quite unconnected with those
matters which now concern Wolfram. When he returns now to
his account of the most terrible stage of the battle, anticipated in the horror of his threefold lament,[32] the prevalent
mood of tragedy is established, and only partially alleviated
by the view of the future and Gyburc's power to intercede on behalf of the poet. When he relates the events which follow
the battle, that mood is sustained, with a dominant note of
irony which both reiterates the irony of so much of the work
and leads directly to the Matribleiz-scene.

Inevitably, the tempo of the narrative changes with the
departure of the heathen, and the excess of activity gives
way to passive grief, in which Wolfram stresses the mingling
of emotions and of fortunes. He begins with a clear statement of the ambiguity of Willehalm's situation:

> der marcrâve hete den sige
> mit grôzem schaden errungen
> und jâmers dâ betwungen
> manec getouftez herze.          (445,14-17)

The lines anticipate the clearer irony of Willehalm's own
statement:

> dirre sige mir schumpfentiure
> hât ervohten in dem herzen mîn ...
> (459,26-27)

That a victory won at such cost cannot bring much joy is made
clear, as Wolfram describes the survivors searching for their
comrades on the battlefield:

> Dâ was gewunnen und verlorn.          (446,1)
> ... ieslîcher sînen kunden
> suochte ûf dem wal und ûf der slâ.
> sô vant er sînen vater dâ,
> sô vant der sînen bruoder hie:
> des pflâgen dise unde die:
> sô vant der hêrre sînen man.          (446,10-15)

The grim drama of the scene increases with the awareness that
it takes place at dusk (447,8-11) and the celebration in food
and drink is overshadowed by the realization that the provi-
sions have been left behind by the heathen army, and that, if
they bring solace, then it is the solace of oblivion brought
about by drink:

> etslîcher tranc daz gar sîn leit
> mit liebe nam ein ende.              (448,16-17)

.... sîn selbes wunden smerze
> was im reht ein meien tou.
> weder der noch dirre in rou,
> ez wær sîn vater oder sîn mâc:
> ern ruochte wer dâ tôt belac,
> ern ruochte ouch wer dâ lebte.     (448,24-29)

In the majority of these examples, the irony of the situation
is reflected in the verbal irony which Wolfram uses. The
memory of the defeated heathen army lingers through the food
and drink which it left behind, and, negatively, in Wolfram's
words about the heathen gods who receive no devotions on the
battlefield that night (449,18-27). In contrast, Jesus has
restored to Willehalm the lovely Gyburc and the whole land
(450,1-3): this is the true victory of Willehalm:

> er brâht den prîs unz in sîn grap,
> daz er nimmer mêr wart sigelôs,
> sît er ûf Alitschanz verlôs
> Vivîanzen sîner swester kint,
> und der mêr die noch vor gote sint
> die endelôsen wîle.              (450,4-9)

This, too, is the permanent reminder of the battle which must
ultimately transcend the present grief, epitomized, in these
lines as so often, in the loss of Vivianz. Yet for the moment,
the mention of Vivianz recalls the revenge of the second battle
and the suffering inflicted on the heathens, and Wolfram himself enters with a cry of accusation which echoes Gyburc's
plea for mercy:

> die nie toufes künde
> enpfiengen, ist daz sünde,
> daz man die sluoc alsam ein vihe?
> grôzer sünde ich drumbe gihe:
> ez ist gar gotes hantgetât.       (450,15-19)

Already the verbal echo anticipates the role which will be
played by Gyburc in the gesture of Willehalm to Matribleiz,
but before Willehalm can perform this act of compassion and
respect he must pass through a new state of affliction.

Day brings with it, as before, the need for activity,
and activity consists in bringing together the Christian
slain for burial in the case of the common soldiers, and the
noblemen for embalming and transportation to their own lands.

The horror of death and the terrible wounds is alleviated,
yet, at the same time, brought into relief, by the sweetness
of the balm which is to conserve the bodies. This is a
gentle process, reflected in the slowness of Wolfram's narrative which contrasts so sharply with the speed of the battle:
he lingers on the embalming process, describing its effect
in terms which do nothing to soften the horror of the prospect
of so many recently slain (451,17-29). Nor does he shrink
from telling why the survivors are so slow in departing from
the battlefield which, strewn as it is with so many corpses,
is no place to linger:

> si zogten niht ze drâte:
> ir tagereise was niht lanc.
> etslîchen manec wunde twanc
> samfte dan ze rîten.           (452,4-7)

The appalling effects of the battle remain and accompany
Willehalm's lamentation now, as, with the full focus of attention on him, he speaks of the loss of Rennewart. The power
of his speech, with the excess of emotion in a man of supreme
military strength and valour, is increased by the setting of
prevailing gloom. It reaches its peak when Willehalm is overwhelmed with grief, so that his tears can no longer be counted.

What remains of this scene is concerned with Willehalm's
grief, expressed in his soliloquy and then in his lament to
Bernart. It is in the latter that the scope of his suffering
is expressed and Wolfram combines, as before, the personal
and the public in Willehalm's assessment of the two battles:

> ôwê tag, und ander tac!
> Ein tac, dô mir Vivîanz
> wart erslagen ûf Alischans
> selbe sibende fürste, und al mîn her,
> wan daz ich selbe entreit mit wer.
> mîn bestiu helfe aldâ beleip.
> diu grôze flust mich dar zuo treip
> daz ich dîne genâde suochte,
> und maneges der des ruochte
> daz er sîn triwe erkante
> und in mîn helfe ernante.
> gestern was mîn ander tac.
> Von den beiden ich wol sprechen mac.
> daz mîn vreude verzinset dran,
> swaz der mîn herze ie gewan.
>                    (459,30-460,14)[33)]

The affliction of the single human being is seen here in its
relationship to the immensity of the losses sustained: the
loving uncle suffers, and the leader of the great army suffers also. The lines compress, too, the events of the war,
the defeat at Alischanz, which left Willehalm defenceless,
his appeal to his kinsmen at Munleun, and the sufferings of
the second battle. Without necessarily accepting Mergell's
contention that this is the moment of Willehalm's 'Reifwerden zur höchsten Menschlichkeit',[34] it is possible to
agree with him when he says "Hier bereitet sich die Matri-
bleizszene vor". This is the lowest point of grief, when
Willehalm shows himself profoundly aware of the immensity
of affliction, and it is juxtaposed to his decision to act,
as he acknowledges his overriding duty as the leader of the
troops to console his men (460,15-20). The deepest point
of passive grief gives way, then, to what must be seen, in
Wolfram's view, as the highest point of Willehalm's action,
for the greatness of Willehalm's valour and military leadership throughout is subordinated to the magnificence of his
final gesture. The true victory of Willehalm is not the
military one on the battlefield, but lies in his ability now
to transcend his grief in order to make a gesture towards
those whom he has defeated in military terms.[35]

Yet within the Matribleiz-scene, Wolfram shows a development of Wolfram's intention. If, as may justly be
assumed, he begins with the relatively limited desire to
ensure burial according to heathen custom for the royal slain,
this, as he himself says, is for the sake of their kinship
with Gyburc. That this is indeed his intention is clear
from what he says to Matribleiz:

> mir ist ein dinc wol kunt
> an iu, künec Matribleiz,
> daz ich die wären sippe weiz
> zwischen iu und dem wîbe mîn.     (461,24-27)
>
> wir sulen si werdeclîcher habn
> durch die diu von in ist erborn:
> swaz Gyburg mâge ist hie verlorn,
> die sol man arômâten,
> mit balsem wol berâten,

> und bâren küneclîche,
> als ob in sîme rîche
> Dâ heime ieslîcher wære tôt.

(462,24-463,1)

One recalls the long account of the embalming of the Christian
slain and notes the equality of Willehalm's treatment of the
noblemen who have perished on both sides. What Willehalm
does is in itself the generous gesture of the victor, and it
is supported by his earnest wish to express his love for his
wife by his respect for her kin.

It would seem, then, that Willehalm develops in the
course of his conversation with Matribleiz, and that his intention changes. Though he begins by binding Matribleiz by
his word of honour (461,15), he later releases him (465,30).
Willehalm can hardly have forgotten that Matribleiz, künec
von Skandinâvîâ, is his most precious captive, that, as
Bernart has suggested, he can well be used to ransom Rennewart, if he, too, is found to be in captivity (458,26-459,3).
This possibility is sacrificed to an ideal which seems only
now to take form in Willehalm's mind. Though Gyburc is not
mentioned, it is surely in remembrance of her passionate plea
for mercy towards the defeated heathen that Willehalm grants
freedom to Matribleiz. It is not Gyburc who is mentioned,
but her God, who knows the number of the stars and has given
the light of the moon. In his closing lines of Willehalm's
speech to Matribleiz, Wolfram shows a man raised by love and
suffering to the ideal of humanity embodied hitherto in his
wife. The military victory which Willehalm has said has
wrought defeat in his heart is heightened in these moments
to a spiritual victory over hatred: St. Willehalm and 'Saint'
Gyburc are united in their reverence for the Creator of the
universe.

Although this ending has something of optimism about it,
the prevailing mood of sadness remains. The setting on the
battlefield, the sense of so many lost and the uncertainty
about Rennewart, and the memory of Vivianz, all contribute
to sustain the serious mood to the last. To break this mood
so consistently created would be æsthetically impossible.

Willehalm has moved from his passionate preoccupation with
his lost friend to a wider concern for those whom he has
defeated, and Wolfram himself has moved away from the story
of Rennewart to the issue which supersedes it; the fate of
Rennewart is left uncertain, while the fate of Matribleiz,
his release and Willehalm's commendation of him to the God
of Gyburc, bring the work to a conclusion which, though it
goes against all the conventions of mediæval narrative and
all the expectations for this particular work, is a thoroughly fitting conclusion in that it sustains the mood of the
whole work to the last.

Wolfram has raised questions in <u>Willehalm</u> which, as he
knows, are unanswerable: the reconciliation of Christians
and heathens is no more than a faint glimmer, and Willehalm's
treatment of Matribleiz and the other heathen is just one
step on a road which, as Wolfram knows, is a long one. If,
as the work ends, many problems remain unsolved, then this
surely is because Wolfram prefers to leave them unsolved, to
allow his audience to grope for their solutions, as he himself is groping. His story rarely speaks of joy, he has
told us (280,21), so how can its last word be one of reconciliation and happiness? And if, as he has said, human life
has sorrow as its beginning and its end (280,17-18), then he
cannot conclude on a note of joy. Joy, one feels, lies
beyond the framework of Wolfram's work.[36)]

Instead, as the work ends, one is left with Willehalm,
the solitary man who has just acted in remembrance of the
words of his wife. To her he will, no doubt, return; perhaps
Rennewart will be found and perhaps he will be baptized and
marry Alyze; in Willehalm's gesture towards Matribleiz the
way has been prepared for further negotiations between the
Christians and the heathen, although, as Wolfram well knows,
this is no easy matter.[37)] Yet these are issues which no
longer concern Wolfram, who concentrates as the work ends
on the confrontation between two men and the deference of
the one to the Creator to whom the work is addressed. The
scene arises from the description of the end of the battle

and the position of Willehalm, the victor whose heart is
filled with defeat; it is the culmination of the irony which
precedes it that this irony should be present as the defeated king leaves the land of Provence, granted his freedom
in the name of the God of whom he knows little and whom he
had come to overthrow.

    Line 467,8 -

              sus rûmt er Provenzâlen lant -

marks the end of one stage of activity and to that extent
it is a conclusive line. If it lacks the weight which one
has come to expect of the final line in a mediæval narrative poem, then this, I suggest, is because Wolfram looks
beyond it, to those events which must surely have followed
and of which his work will not tell. Although the work may
lack a formal epilogue to balance its prologue, artistic
balance is nevertheless present. The epilogue would inevitably have contained those statements of events and their
effects which, in my view, Wolfram deliberately declines to
make. Kienast's attempt to demonstrate the incompleteness
of Willehalm by comparison with Parzival is convincing only
if one assumes that Wolfram intended a similar construction
for his two poems,[38] and such an assumption disregards the
difference in mood and emphasis. The conciliatory ending
of Parzival, the tying-up of ends in the narrative, and the
concluding words of the narrator, are totally fitting to
that earlier work of optimism. The structural oneness of
Parzival accords with its theme of harmony achieved. The
harmony of Willehalm is more subtle, and its optimism beneath
the surface, and in my view Wolfram may deliberately have
refrained from a more obviously final ending, a formal conclusion,[39] in order to demonstrate the complexity of the
situation and his own unwillingness to trivialize his profound theme.[40] Although he may have surprised his mediæval audience by failing to tell of subsequent events, he
has surely been faithful to a higher intention in his ultimate stress on the abstract theme which transcends those
events.

Aesthetically, the work is beautifully balanced, with
the end coming full circle and reminding us, in the commendation by Willehalm of Matribleiz, of the schepfære über
alle geschaft of the opening lines. This is the God of the
Christians, of Willehalm and above all of Gyburc. She it
is who has spoken of Altissimus (100,28; 216,4-5) and of all
men as gotes hantgetât (306,28), terms which are taken up
now by Willehalm (454,22) and by Wolfram himself (450,19),
in these closing passages which call her so vividly to mind.
Her spirit has pervaded the second battle, from the address
to the assembled knights before it begins and with greater
intensity since Wolfram's prayer to her at the beginning of
Book IX. She is present, too, after the battle, but now in
the mind of Willehalm, as he remembers her kinship with
Matribleiz and the other heathen kings. His love for her
means that her love for all God's creatures acts now through
him, the active leader: this story of minne und ander klage[41]
has shown the love of Willehalm and Gyburc in its relationship
to the terrible war, and now at last to God's love of all
creatures. This is the ultimate theme of Wolfram's work, and
nothing remains to be said. Perhaps Wolfram has gradually
changed his mind about the events of which he will tell; certainly he has moved so far from his source that he cannot
follow it to its conclusion. Yet, great narrator that he is,
he supplies a conclusion which, with its lingering sadness,
is totally fitting to the mood of the whole work, and,
precisely because it leaves so many problems unsolved, is
completely commensurate with the work which precedes it.

N o t e s

## Preface

1) Heidelberg 1959 (=Bumke in subsequent references).

2) Ludwig Wolff: 'Der Willehalm Wolframs von Eschenbach',
   DVjs. 12, 1934, pp. 504-539 (=Wolff).

3) Bodo Mergell: Wolfram von Eschenbach und seine französischen Quellen, I. Teil: Wolframs Willehalm, Münster
   1936 (=Mergell).

4) J. Bumke: Wolfram von Eschenbach Forschung seit 1945.
   Bericht und Bibliographie, Munich 1970, p. 313.

5) W. Schröder und H. Schanze: 'Neues Gesamtverzeichnis
   der Handschriften von Wolframs Willehalm', ZfdA. 91,
   1961/2, pp. 201-226.

6) Wolfram-Studien II, ed. Werner Schröder, Berlin 1974.

7) F. P. Knapp: Rennewart. Studien zu Gehalt und Gestalt
   des Willehalm Wolframs von Eschenbach, Vienna 1970
   (=Knapp); C. J. Lofmark: Rennewart in Wolframs 'Willehalm'. A Study of Wolfram von Eschenbach and his
   Sources, Cambridge 1972 (=Lofmark).


## Introduction

1) Cf. Wolff p. 504: "Die Welten beider Werke scheinen
   völlig anders. Aus dem wunderdurchsetzten Lebensraum
   abenteuernder Artusritter, den das übernatürliche
   Phantasiebild der Gralsburg überhöht, führt uns der
   Willehalm mitten in die gewaltigen Heidenkämpfe, von
   denen die französische Geschichte der Karolingerzeit
   berichtet, und damit treten wir zugleich in einen
   Lebenskreis, in dem der einzelne mit seinen Taten in
   den Reihen und im Dienste der Gesamtheit steht; auch
   die Handlung ist hier von ganz anderer Art."

2) B. Mergell: Der Gral in Wolframs 'Parzival'. Entstehung
   und Ausbildung der Gralsage im Hochmittelalter, Halle
   1952, pp. 165-166.

3) Bumke p. 199.

4) Wolff p. 538.

5) Ibid. p. 539.

6) Mergell p. 177.

7) F. Martini: <u>Deutsche Literaturgeschichte von den An-<br>fängen bis zur Gegenwart</u>, 15. Auflage, Stuttgart 1968:<br>p. 48.

8) M. O'C. Walshe: <u>Mediæval German Literature. A Survey</u>,<br>London 1962 (=Walshe): p. 175.

9) For a discussion of the sources of <u>Willehalm</u>, see<br>Bumke, pp. 12-13, and Lofmark, pp. 50-59.

10) S. M. Johnson: 'A Commentary to Wolfram von Eschen-<br>bach's <u>Willehalm</u>' diss., Yale 1953 (=Johnson);<br>Lofmark; Mergell.

11) Johnson p. 201.

12) Bumke p. 201.

13) Lofmark (p. 135) summarizes the religious attitudes of<br>Wolfram, which he says are more complicated than those<br>of <u>Aliscans</u>.

14) Cf. Johnson p. LV.

15) Ibid. p. L.

16) Cf. Bumke p. 20 and p. 41ff.

17) Cf. Lofmark pp. 71-72.

18) Wolff pp. 538-539.

1. The Harmony of the Work

1) Bumke pp. 92-98.

2) All quotations from <u>Willehalm</u> are taken from the edition<br>of Wolfram's works by K. Lachmann, 6th edition, Berlin<br>and Leipzig 1926.

3) See pp. 27-28.

4) See p. 38.

5) On the question of Terramer's attitude to the mysteries<br>of Christianity, see Knapp p. 121.

6) See p. 232ff for a full discussion of this point.

7) See pp. 40-41.

8) Mergell p. 81.

9) I would not agree here with Wolff (p. 538) who speaks of Wolfram's growing tired of the work.

10) Cf. Werner Schröder: "Gyburc ist ... zunächst und vor allem ein liebender und leidender Mensch" ('Süeziu Gyburc', Euphorion 54, 1960, pp. 39-69: p. 69).

11) Bumke p. 66ff.

12) W. J. Schröder: Review of J. Bumke Wolframs 'Willehalm', PBB 82, 1960, pp. 411-421. Schröder continues: "Dieser Weg ist aber - und das ist von größter Wichtigkeit - nicht realistisch-biographisch der Weg einer ‚Karriere', auch nicht der Prozeß einer fortschreitenden Bewußtheit der Personen über Sinn und Zweck ihres Tuns, kein ‚Hineinwachsen' in höhere Aufgaben oder so etwas ähnliches. Der Dichter will vielmehr darstellen, wie Weltgeschichte, die ja immer unter Gottes Führung steht, sich menschlichem Verständnis nach und nach erschließt." (p. 415)

13) This is an idea which I treat at length elsewhere: Wîplîchez Wîbes Reht. A Study of the Women Characters in the Works of Wolfram von Eschenbach, Duquesne University Press, 1972.

14) Mergell p. 171.

15) For example: Schwietering: Die deutsche Dichtung des Mittelalters, Potsdam 1941, p. 173; W. Schröder: 'Zur Entwicklung des Helden in Wolframs Willehalm', Festschrift für Ludwig Wolff zum 70. Geburtstag, Neumünster 1962, pp. 265-276. Schröder has returned, not for the first time, to the question of Willehalm's 'development', in a recent article, in the second volume of Wolfram-Studien.

Mergell has stressed in particular the development of Willehalm, making it into the focal point of the work: it is, he maintains, "die Entwicklung Willehalms, die den eigentlichen Sinn und die geistige Einheit der deutschen Dichtung ausmacht" (Mergell, p. 128). Against this view, Bumke has taken an emphatic stand (Bumke, pp. 60-64).

16) Bumke p. 63.

17) Cf. 78,13-14; 78,16-18; 78,21; 78,19ff.

18) "Der Hergang gleicht einer Hinrichtung. Von Notwehr ist keine Rede, und es handelt sich auch nicht um eine Affekthandlung. Sie wird kaltblütig und mit Vorsatz ausgeführt." ('Die Hinrichtung Arofels', in Wolfram-Studien II, Berlin 1974: p. 222).

19) Ibid. p. 223.

20) Indeed, it is Arofel's kinship with Terramer which
finally urges him to act, in revenge for Vivianz,
though the notion of 'sippe' elsewhere plays a major
role in his actions, in his refusal to fight with
Ehmereiz, for example, and, most significantly, in his
treatment of Matribleiz.

21) Cf. Werner Schröder 'Hinrichtung...', p. 224.

22) Werner Schröder speaks of Wolfram's "kritische
Distanzierung von Willehalms Handlungsweise" ('Zur
Entwicklung des Helden...', pp. 270-271), referring
to his lament, not so much for the person of Arofel,
as for the loss inflicted upon heathen ladies and the
anguish of the day itself.

23) Ibid. p. 271.

24) 'Hinrichtung...', p. 226. Previously he had stated
emphatically: "Auch die Situation vermag ihn nicht zu
entschuldigen. Willehalm war mit ihm allein, er war
nicht bedroht (er konnte sich nachher in aller Ruhe
umkleiden) und hat durchaus nicht in Notwehr gehandelt."
('Zur Entwicklung des Helden...', p. 271).

25) W. Mersmann: Der Besitzwechsel und seine Bedeutung in
den Dichtungen Wolframs von Eschenbach und Gottfrieds
von Straßburg, Munich 1971 (=Mersmann): p. 164.

26) Cf. Mersmann p. 164, note 20: "Die Auskunft Willehalms,
der Schild sei ihm zu swære, mutet seltsam an ange-
sichts der Tatsache, daß er allein außer Rennewart dessen schwere Stange, die sieben Männer nicht tragen kön-
nen (196,21ff), die auf einem Wagen transportiert wird
(275,13ff; 315,29ff), heben kann (311,20ff). Ob hier
die Vorstellung von Leid, Sorge, Jammer, Sünde, Schuld
u.a. als einer Last im Hintergrund steht?" That Mersmann has no doubt that the answer to his question is in
the affirmative is clear, and upheld by the examples he
gives of similar usage elsewhere in Willehalm.

27) See p. 35.

28) Cf. in particular Bumke p. 62 who argues against Mergell's contention that the speech at the monastery
represents a declaration of guilt (Mergell p. 136):
"Selbst wenn man dem Wort (ie. schulde) hier eine
stärkere Bedeutung zutraut, ist dennoch von Willehalms
Erkenntnis „seiner tiefen Verschuldung" nichts zu
spüren: er rühmt sich seiner Tat und ist stolz darauf,
so viele Heiden erschlagen zu haben - und nicht nur
Arofel war Gyburgs Verwandter.... (206,19-23). So
spricht kein Verwandtenmörder, der seine Schuld er-
kennt. Von Schuldbekenntnis und Reue ist gar nicht
die Rede." Against this view, see Schröder ('Hinrichtung...', p. 228): "Ein Unterton des Bedauerns

ist in dem Tatenbericht nicht zu überhören. Und daß
die Selbstsicherheit des geschlagenen Markgrafen
nicht ganz so unerschütterlich ist, wie sie scheinen
möchte, verrät das Schuldbekenntnis gegenüber der
Minne." Again, Schröder seems to have moved slightly
from his earlier position, when he declared, speaking
of Willehalm at the monastery: "Das ist derselbe Mann,
der bei der Rast im abgebrannten Kloster wenig vornehm
mit seinen Heldentaten prahlt..." ('Zur Entwicklung
des Helden...', p. 270).

29) Mergell p. 136.

30) Mersmann p. 164.

31) Mergell p. 176. F. Maurer speaks similarly of 'das
Reifer- und Ruhigerwerden Willehalms' (Leid. Studien
zur Bedeutungs- und Problemgeschichte, besonders in
den großen Epen der staufischen Zeit, Bern and Munich
1951: p. 196).

32) Cf. Schröder ('Zur Entwicklung des Helden...', p. 273)
who speaks of "die sittigende Macht der Frau".

33) Cf. Bumke pp. 24ff. Bumke observes (p. 22): "Wolfram
schildert keinen Heldenkampf, sondern einen Todesweg.
Seine Vivianzdarstellung ist auf den Tod hingeordnet,
empfängt von dort ihren Sinn". W. J. Schröder (in his
review of Bumke) qualifies this view: "Richtig müßte
es heißen: Wolfram schildert einen Heldenkampf als
Todesweg! Denn es handelt sich hier doch um den Kampf
des Kreuzritters, der immer unter solchem Doppelaspekt
steht: der Kämpfer will den Sieg, da die Christenheit
dadurch Macht über die Heidenschaft gewinnt, er will
aber auch seinen eigenen Tod, da er damit zum Märtyrer
wird, der unmittelbar in die Seligkeit eingeht"
(p. 413).

34) See pp. 199-201.

35) Bumke pp. 32-33.

36) Ibid.

37) Cf. Bumke: "Vivianz' Tod steht als ein Mahnmal über der
Dichtung und prägt die düstere Stimmung des Ganzen"
(p. 31).

38) See p. 39ff and note 28 above.

39) Cf. 40,21-22; 53,11-12; 60,11-12; 151,11-12; 164,27-28;
171,13-14; 208,10; 214,19; 223,24; 253,25; 304,8; 306,22;
334,11-12; 363,11; 381,7-8; 396,26-27; 418,24; 443,1-2;
450,6-7; 454,12-14; 460,1-2.

40) See p. 49.

41) Cf. 40,21-23; 53,11-12; 60,11-12; 151,11-12; 164,27-28;
    171,13-14; 306,21-22; 334,11-12; 363,11-12; 396,25-26;
    443,1-2; 454,11-12; 460,1-2.

42) Bumke p. 31.

43) See p. 13ff.

44) Lofmark p. 99. Lofmark's unwillingness to see a sus-
    tained parallelism between Vivianz and Rennewart leads
    him to take what seems an extreme view. When he says
    that Wolfram devotes much time and attention to the
    beauty and virtues of Alyze and that there is no
    parallel to this in the Vivianz action, he overlooks
    the obvious fact that the love for a particular human
    being has no part in the depiction of Vivianz, who is
    specifically seen as the Christian martyr and the
    representative of many. It is, indeed, a case of a
    parallel with essential variations. Similarly, when
    he rejects the view of Bumke that the lament for Renne-
    wart is parallel to the lament for Vivianz, on the basis
    that they are different in content ("Willehalm's lament
    for Vivianz, expressed largely in religious terms, is
    concerned with Vivianz's death as a Christian martyr
    and with his own guilt at having raised him to knight-
    hood and led him to battle at such an early age. The
    lament for Rennewart is an expression of Willehalm's
    pain at being bereft and unable to reward the man to
    whom he owes victory...") he is again ignoring the
    essential differences in the depiction and function of
    the two figures who can nevertheless occupy parallel
    roles in two battles which, for all their parallelism,
    have undeniable essential differences. When he goes on
    to maintain that Wolfram "does not draw any parallels
    between them in relation to Gyburc" (p.98), he fails to
    take into consideration, not only the very tender re-
    lationship which exists between Gyburc and the young
    man in each case, but specifically the notion that
    Vivianz was sent into battle by Gyburc, and equipped
    for it by her, and that we actually see her arming
    Rennewart for the coming battle. One should not, it
    seems, deny the parallels which are clearly there.

45) Bumke p. 79.

46) See Bumke p. 174, note 95.

47) Ibid. p. 174.

48) See p. 126ff.

49) See pp. 39-40 and note 28 above.

50) This line is emended in accordance with the first
    edition of Lachmann. See p.261, note 33.

## 2. Compression of the Narrative

1) H.-H. Steinhoff: Die Darstellung gleichzeitiger Geschehnisse im mittelhochdeutschen Epos, (Medium Aevum 4), Munich 1964 (=Steinhoff): p. 19.

2) Cf. Steinhoff p. 24.

3) Mergell p. 81.

4) Cf. Steinhoff p. 39: "das Feuer ist Synkronisationspunkt".

5) Cf. Steinhoff p. 28.

6) Cf. Steinhoff pp. 31-32.

7) On Wolfram's use of the exchange of hearts, see Mersmann p. 171.

8) Steinhoff p. 37.

9) Bumke p. 96.

10) Steinhoff p. 41.

11) See pp. 114-115 and pp. 142-143.

12) See pp. 219-220.

13) See pp. 214-215.

14) Lofmark (p. 97) uses this as an example of Wolfram's actually declining to take up a parallel which existed in his source, where, as he says, it is Rainouart who had killed Haucebier, the slayer of Vivien. This, it seems to me, is not a case of Wolfram's dropping some of the parallelism of his source but of his using it in a subtle way, adapting it in accordance with his more subtle interpretation of the whole. See also Section 1, note 44.

15) The feelings of Aélis towards Rainouart are, in contrast, more explicit: the direct and ambiguous kiss in Willehalm replaces the passionate embrace with which she expressed her love for him in the source (1.3914). (References to Aliscans are to the edition by E. Wienbeck, W. Hartnacke and P. Rasch, Halle 1903.)

16) On Arofel's horse, see Mersmann p. 160ff., Mersmann himself rejects the notion of rêroup in this context: "Der Begriff rêroup erscheint im Willehalm nicht; die kriegerischen Ernstkämpfe schaffen nicht die Voraussetzungen für einen rêroup im engeren Sinne." In a wider sense, however, the term seems justified.

17) See pp. 230-231. On the significance of the conver-
    sation between Rennewart and Gyburc, see also Knapp
    pp. 104-111. Knapp concludes: "Wir werden nach dieser
    Szene ins Ungewisse entlassen. Daß Rennewart weit
    mehr ahnt, als er sagt und sagen will, erweist uns
    gerade sein absolutes Stillschweigen".

18) See also note 14 above.

19) See p. 39ff.

20) Cf. Mersmann p. 164: "Die Tötung Arofels, gleichsam
    verkörpert in seinem Schild, lastet auf Willehalm".
    See also p. 39.

21) See p. 39.

22) See pp. 21-22.

23) Cf. G. Rolin: <u>Aliscans, mit Berücksichtigung von Wolf-
    rams von Eschenbach Willehalm</u>, Leipzig 1897: p. XXVI.

24) Cf. Wolff p. 536, among others.

25) S. Singer (<u>Wolframs Willehalm</u>, Bern 1918) deduces from
    these lines that it was Wolfram's intention to tell
    the whole story of Rennewart (p. 91). F. Vogt, on the
    other hand, (<u>Geschichte der mittelhochdeutschen Litera-
    tur</u>, Berlin and Leipzig 1922) regards them as evidence
    that Wolfram did not propose to take the story further
    (p. 301).

26) Lofmark p. 215.

27) The verb <u>bewarn</u> does not necessarily suggest physical
    protection. Moreover, the line seems to be related
    closely to the preceding one and so to refer to the
    change in Rennewart's fortunes referred to also in the
    lines which follow: the love of Alyze will protect him
    from the <u>smæhe</u> to which he has been subjected. I would
    suggest, therefore, that this is not a promise on the
    part of Wolfram that the love of Alyze will 'bring him
    through' in the coming battle, but that her love will
    'sustain' him in a more abstract sense.

28) I would certainly reject, for example, Mergell's adamant
    assertion: "Diese Verse können eher mit Beziehung auf
    einen tragischen als auf einen freudigen Ausgang der
    Rennewarthandlung verstanden werden." (Mergell p. 56).
    It is difficult to see how he arrives at this conclusion
    on the basis of the passage.

29) See pp. 86-87.

30) See p. 215.

31) See pp. 86-87 and pp. 231-232.

32) See p. 237ff.


3. The Texture of the Narrative

1) This idea is clearly expressed in Parzival, in the words
of Sigune to Parzival (440,13-16) and in the marriage of
Repanse de Schoye and Feirefiz.

2) See pp. 27-32.

3) See p. 75.

4) Wîplîchez Wîbes Reht, p. 148.

5) See p. 199ff.

6) See p. 207.

7) Cf. L. Wolff ('Vom persönlichen Stil Wolframs in seiner
dichterischen Bedeutung. Ein Versuch', Ludwig Wolff.
Kleinere Schriften, ed. W. Schröder, Berlin 1967, pp.
262-293): "Man spürt die Freude, sich über die übliche,
ästhetisch verfeinerte höfische Art einmal heraus-
fordernd hinwegzusetzen und das Gleichmaß, nach dem
sie strebte, zu durchbrechen. Wie er so mit Ton und
Wirkung seiner Dichtung den Einschlag des Besonderen
liebt, so hat er eben auch - wo es Gehalt und Stimmung
nicht widerspricht - seine Freude an den ungewöhnlichen
und absonderlichen Vorstellungen und Bildern" (p. 269).

8) See p. 47.

9) See pp. 89-95.

10) Cf. Mersmann p. 163: "Neben die Bewunderung der Pracht
tritt die Betonung des vremeden (127,18; 128,14); die
phelle sind der kristenheite unbenennet, Volatin trägt
ein heidensch gereite (128,14ff). Der Reiter ist der
Franzoisære gast (129,4). Daß diese in der Beurteilung
des Äußeren sich kundtuende, auch in der Gestaltung des
Raumes sichtbare Distanz zwischen dem Ankömmling und der
festesfrohen Hofgesellschaft auch eine innerlich wesen-
hafte ist, wird sich im Verlauf der Szene immer mehr
offenbaren. Nach Meinung der Festgesellschaft gehört
er in den strît, nicht zum tanz (128,18ff)."

11) Cf. Mergell p. 135, but also Mersmann p. 160: "Parzivals
Ziel war der Gewinn der Rüstung, sein Tun gilt mehr der
Sache als der Person, bei Willehalm ist es umgekehrt."

12) See note 11 above. Cf. also Mersmann p. 164: "In der
    heidnischen Rüstung, Anlaß und Zeichen seiner Iso-
    lierung, ist Willehalm Fremdkörper in der Hofver-
    sammlung und unbequemer Mahner an die dem rîche zu-
    stehende Aufgabe des Heidenkampfes, zu dessen Anwalt
    er als ihr Träger wird.... Nach der Hoftagszene
    begegnet die Arofelrüstung nur noch in Willehalms
    Klage um Arofel (207,25ff.) und bei dem zweiten Ver-
    kennen Giburgs (228,10ff.). Danach wird ihre Herkunft
    von Arofel vom Dichter nicht mehr hervorgehoben. In
    dem Maße wie er von dem Rachehandeln an Arofel abrückt,
    verliert sie ihre Bedeutung als Arofels Rüstung."

13) See p. 117.

14) Lofmark p. 110.

15) See p. 76ff.

16) See p. 199ff.

17) See p. 26ff.

18) See pp. 47-48 and pp. 236-237.

19) See pp. 136-137.

20) See pp. 41-47.

21) See pp. 106-107 and p. 133.

22) Wolfram here differs from his source, where Guillaume
    replies to the accusations of Esmerés.

23) See pp. 24-35.

24) See pp. 35-38.

25) See pp. 129-130.

26) Wolfram here distorts the sequence of events related
    in the New Testament, where, of course, St. Peter
    drew his sword in Gethsemane *before* the arrest of
    Christ: John 18.10.

27) One has only to think of some of the complicated
    imagery in the prologue to *Parzival*.

28) For example, his description of the effect on Gawan of
    the sight of Orgeluse (593,14-18), or the comparison
    of the waist of Antikonie with that of an ant (409,26-
    410,4).

29) Cf. Wolff ('Vom persönlichen Stil Wolframs ...', p.269:
    "Unmöglich, innerlich und grundsätzlich unmöglich, ist
    es, die Grenze anzugeben, wo ein Bild nicht mehr ernst

genommen wird; es kann zugleich als gewichtig eine
ernste Aufgabe haben und braucht doch nicht buch-
stäblich ernst genommen zu werden. Ernst und Humor
sind keine Gegensätze."

30) Cf. Lofmark p. 143, particularly note 1, and Knapp
pp. 70-75.

31) Cf. Knapp p. 73: "Es dürfte hier eine nachträgliche
Änderung Wolframs vorliegen, der zuvor wohl eher seiner
Quelle folgen wollte, die des Knaben freiwillige
Flucht auf das Schiff der Kaufleute berichtet."

32) Parzival 57,10-14.

33) Cf. 190,1 and 270,19-22. Bumke (p. 44, note 94) draws
attention to the fact that, for Rennewart, Wolfram
uses images traditionally associated with the Virgin
Mary.

34) Cf. Parzival 228,4-6; 84,13-15.

35) Bumke p. 25.

36) For an interpretation of this image, see C. Gerhardt:
'Wolframs Adlerbild Willehalm 189,2-24', ZfdA. 99,
1970, pp. 213-222.


## 4. The Significance of the Setting

1) For the broad outline of his concept of geographical
location, Wolfram is, of course, indebted to his
source, but in comparison with Aliscans, Willehalm
shows a very much greater sense of background.

2) See p. 41ff.

3) Cf. Mersmann p. 171: "Die quantativ breitere Darstellung dieses Herzentausches gegenüber den Hartmann-
schen ist durch die Einbeziehung nicht unmittelbar
zugehöriger Einzelheiten begründet: Volatîn, Oransche,
wege, vriunde, vînde, vor untrôste nern. Der Herzen-
tausch steht unter den Bedingungen der schier auswegs-
losen Lage, die Willehalm ein blîben und zugleich ein
rîten gebietet. .... Der Herzenstausch grieft über das
Hier und Jetzt hinaus, er ist verankert in der Gesamt-
situation, besonders dem vorangehenden Rat Giburgs
(103,9ff) und dem nachfolgenden Ritt Willehalms um
Hilfe. Die Liebe Willehalms und Giburgs ist hier wie
überhaupt mit der äußeren Situation untrennbar verbunden, die Kriegsnot überschattet selbst die intimste
Begegnung."

4) See p. 39 and p. 90ff.

5) See p. 186.

6) Bumke p. 94.

7) See pp. 58-59.

8) Bumke pp. 92-95.

9) See p. 13ff.

10) Cf. Bumke p. 94.

11) See pp. 58-59.

12) See p. 140ff.

13) E.g. 41,27; 42,3; 53,30-54,1; 114,22.
    Arnalt is able to identify Willehalm by the report of
    his cry (116,10-12).

14) See Section 5.

15) See p. 121ff.

16) See pp. 177-178.

17) For example, <u>Parzival</u> 36,15-37,9; 260,24-261,30.

18) As he does, of course, in <u>Parzival</u>; cf., for example,
    his description of Feirefiz, 735,9-30.

19) See p. 39 and p. 90ff.

20) See p. 193.

21) See p. 121ff.

22) See pp. 114-115.


## 5. The Emergence of Individuals

1) See pp. 38-40 and pp. 89-92.

2) Cf. Lofmark (p. 163): "The sword is inappropriate for
   him as long as he does not behave like a knight. Gyburg
   knows that its time will come, and it is in this crisis
   of the battle that Rennewart reaches the maturity which
   makes his sword appropriate."

3) E.g. 33,13-15; 357,10; 358,14.

4) See p. 54 ff.

5) E.g. 416,28-417,1; 417,14-15; 417,19-21.

6) Wolfram has already, much earlier, given to Essere an individual feature, when he stated specifically that he was one of the former owners of the sword of Arofel: 77,24-29.

7) Johnson (p. XXI) speaks of Terramer similarly as a tragic figure. Cf. also F. Maurer: Leid, pp. 16-17.

8) Wolfram is, of course, indebted to his source, in which the events at Laon represent an important turning-point in the narrative. However, his treatment of them, and in particular the emergence of a series of scenes, distinctive yet related, with single individuals receiving the focus of attention, is his own development.

9) Although the source provides the inspiration for those vivid scenes, it is Wolfram who realizes their dramatic potential in these powerful encounters between clearly defined individuals.

10) Wolfram's deliberate omission of the insulting words used by Guillaume ('nu muoz ich si durh zuht verdagen': 153,6) does not, of course, detract from the violence of the uncourtly scene: rather does it intensify it. Cf. Lofmark p. 76: "The force of the episode is faithfully conveyed and Wolfram's reference to terms which zuht forbids him to translate only adds to the impression of Willehalm's violent and improper behaviour."

11) Something of this description exists already in Aliscans (2812-2815), but, again, Wolfram takes it up with full effect, as he endows Alyze here with an almost mystical radiance.

12) Indeed, her volte-face can only be explained in terms of the mystique of sippe, but her sense of kinship with those who have died, as well as with Heimrich, Irmschart and Willehalm, is convincingly emphasized by Wolfram in her speech.

6. The Narrative Art of Wolfram in 'Willehalm' and the end of the work

1) Lofmark pp. 210-243. Cf. in particular Wolff: "Man hätte es nie in Zweifel ziehen sollen, daß ein Schluß, der das Schicksal Rennewarts im Ungewissen ließ, - für das Mittelalter und also auch für die Gedanken Wolframs nicht in Frage kommen und er keinesfalls die Absicht haben konnte, die Dichtung so, wie sie mit dem 9. Buche (mitten in einem Dreißigzeiler) abbricht, endgültig als vollendet abzuschließen" (p. 519). In his Nachtrag of 1964, however, Wolff seems to retract slightly his adamant position: "Über den Ausgang, zu dem die Dichtung nach den Gedanken Wolframs hätte führen sollen, würde ich mich heute etwas zurückhaltender äußern."

2) See Section 5, note 2.

3) That Wolfram's contemporaries considered the work a fragment is perhaps most clearly testified by the fact that Ulrich von Türheim in his Rennewart undertook to complete it. For him the work was obviously as much in need of a conclusion as was Gottfried's Tristan.

4) Lofmark p. 218.

5) Bumke p. 45.

6) Walshe p. 174.

7) Lofmark pp. 225-226.

8) Cf. Walshe p. 174: "He may have felt that the conventional ending of Rennewart's return, conversion and marriage to the king's daughter Alyze would trivialize the metaphysical theme of God's children at war - for how was the theme of holy war to be reconciled finally with divine love?" Cf. also Knapp p. 344: "Somit stellt der 'Willehalm' den grandiosen Versuch des größten deutschen Dichters des Mittelalters dar, die ehrwürdige Gattung des Heldenepos und die neue aufstrebende des Höfischen Romans in einem zutiefst christlichen Werke zu verschmelzen. Daß dies letzlich scheitern mußte, war, wenn die hier herausgestellten Wesensunterschiede der Gattungen stimmen sollen, unvermeidlich. Wolfram wird dies wohl ebenso gefühlt haben, wie es ihm im Verlauf der Beschäftigung mit dem Stoff zusehends unmöglicher wurde, an einen endgültigen, bleibenden Sieg der Christen über die Heiden oder eine vollgütige Versöhnung zwischen beiden zu glauben. Der 'Willehalm' ist also kaum zufällig unvollendet geblieben".

9) Leid p. 197.

10) Cf. Bumke p. 39.

11) See p. 41.

12) See E. Bernhardt: "Zum Willehalm Wolframs von Eschenbach", ZfdPh. 32, 1900, pp. 36-57; A. Leitzmann:
'Untersuchungen über Wolframs Titurel', PBB, 26, 1901,
pp. 93-156 (p. 150ff. on Willehalm).

13) Cf. M. F. Richey: "Though more remained to tell, it may
well be that Wolfram himself recognized the poetic fitness of such an ending, and regardless of what posteri-
ty might think, chose to carry the tale no further"
('Wolfram von Eschenbach and the Paradox of the Chivalrous Life', German Studies Presented to Leonard Ashley
Willoughby, Oxford, 1952, pp. 159-170) p. 170.

Similarly Bumke p. 54: "Hier ist keine Bruchstelle,
sondern ein Schluß. Die Dichtung ist nicht abgebrochen,
sondern endet hier. Wenn man bereit ist, dem Dichter
bis hierher zu folgen, wenn man bereit ist, Rennewart
und die Gefangenen zu vergessen, dann gibt es keine
offenen Handlungsfäden mehr."

14) Lofmark pp. 60-71.

15) Aliscans 1.5970ff.

16) Lofmark (p. 95) observes: "Wolfram cannot deny that
Rennewart also fought with his father, since the source
is here quite explicit, but he prefers not to discuss
the matter and his brief reference to it (443,3-15) is
evasive and ambiguous." Bumke is more tentative in
interpreting these lines as a reference to such a combat
(p. 46, note 97): "Die abgebrochene Begegnung hat viel-
leicht ein Nachspiel in den Versen....443,3-5", while
Singer sees in 443,13-14 only the slightest suggestion
that Terramer's wounds were inflicted by his own son
(S. Singer: Wolframs 'Willehalm', Bern 1918: p. 125).
Indeed, they may well have been gained in the battle
which Wolfram has recounted between Terramer and Willehalm: cf. Bumke p. 46, note 97. Knapp (pp. 305-307) is
more positive in asserting that this is indeed the case.

17) Rennewart himself reappears considerably later, but
then only for a brief period, to accomplish the unfulfilled slaying of a kinsman in the form of his brother
Kanliun, a character unknown to the source (but see
Lofmark p. 93, note 1) and apparently introduced for
this purpose by Wolfram. On the battle with Kanliun,
see Knapp pp. 113-115: Knapp clearly sees this encounter
as a vital point in Rennewart's development. Later
(p. 134) he observes: "Rennewarts verhängnisvoller Irr-
tum erreicht sein vorläufiges grausames Ziel in der
Tötung des Bruders".

18) On Wolfram's reduction of the role of Rennewart see
Lofmark pp. 90-96.

19) Lofmark p. 234: "The career of a man like Poydjus
cannot end in flight".

20) Lofmark p. 236.

21) See pp. 199-223.

22) See pp. 98-99.

23) See p. 99.

24) See p. 98ff.

25) See pp. 85-86.

26) Wolfram's statement, early in the work, that he is going
to tell of mîne und ander klage (4,26) would seem to
offer unambiguous guidance in this matter. Thus Wolff
(p. 537): "Obwohl sie zur freudigen Lösung aller tragi-
schen Scheidungen aufstrebt, bleibt diese Heldendichtung
zugleich doch eine Klage, wie der Dichter es im Eingang
angedeutet hat" and Maurer (p. 168): "Nicht nur eine
'Klage' würde ich das Werk nennen; sein Thema ist das
Leid in der Welt, aber auch die Überwindung dieses Leids".
Even if one rejects the view that Wolfram is using the
word klage to denote a distinct literary genre (see
Kartschoke p. 271), his indication of the nature of the
material remains. Nor is this description of the substance of Willehalm removed if one accepts the recent
emendation by Werner Schröder ('Minne und ander klage.
(Zu Willehalm 4,26)', ZfdA. 96, 1964, pp. 300-313) who
has shown that the majority of manuscripts, including K,
usually favoured by Lachmann, have not mîne but minne,
that, moreover, the phrase minne und ander klage occurs
in Parzival (588,7), minne und ander nôt in Willehalm
(163,9). Such parallels, and indeed Schröder's whole
argument, are persuasive, though there remains the
legitimate objection that Wolfram nowhere else uses
minne as the direct object of sagen, the objection, no
doubt, which prompted Lachmann's decision (cf. Bumke
Bericht und Bibliographie, p. 332). On grounds of substance, too, the revision seems acceptable: Schröder
himself translates "von Liebesleid und anderem Leid".
Kartschoke goes further, though apparently accepting
Schröder's revision, when he translates, mistakenly
surely, "von dem Konflikt zwischen Liebe und Glaube":
this, it seems, is not what Wolfram is saying, though
it may constitute an aspect of what he means.

27) I.e. in the battle between Desramé and Rainouart, and
the encounter between Rainouart and Baudus.

28) Bumke p. 48.

29) Mergell p. 127.

30) See pp. 33-35.

31) See Section 1, note 10.

32) See p. 32ff.

33) I have here emended the text of the edition used, to correspond with the first edition by Lachmann and that by Leitzmann. 460,12 should read von den beiden and not, as in subsequent editions of Lachmann, von den heiden. Bumke comments (p. 61): "Gemeint sind die beiden Schlachttage, an denen Willehalm seine liebsten Freunde verlor."

34) Mergell p. 171. See also p. 37ff. above.

35) Cf. Mergell p. 171: "In diesem Augenblick aber erfolgt die große Entscheidung zur neuen Tat, die, in vollem Bewußtsein des unendlichen Verlustes, den Schmerz innerlich überwindet."

36) These quotations seem to be much more telling for the nature of the work than the lines quoted by Wolff, in support of his view that Wolfram intends the outcome of Willehalm to be happy:

ez muoz nu walzen als ez mac:
etswenne ouch hôhes muotes tac
mit freuden künfte sît erschein. (12,1-3)

Wolff comments: "..da weist er (unabhängig von der Quelle) schon darauf hin, daß künftig alles Leid noch wieder der Freude weichen werde" (Wolff p. 519). These lines would seem to refer rather to the instability of human fortune than to any permanent, or specific, state of joy. See also note 26 above.

37) Lofmark's statement that by this gesture Willehalm "makes possible a final settlement in mutual respect" (p. 243) seems to go rather far: though reconciliation is possible on personal terms, there are still immense obstacles to the reconciliation of whole races separated by their faiths.

38) R. Kienast: "Zur Tektonik von Wolframs Willehalm", Studien zur deutschen Philologie des Mittelalters. Friedrich Panzer zum 80. Geburtstag am 4. September 1950 dargebracht, Heidelberg 1950, pp. 96-115. Knapp (p.262) is similarly dubious about the validity of Kienast's argument.

39) 'das krönende Glied', as Kienast calls it (p. 114).

40) Kienast's analysis of the structure of the work according to arithmetical laws is ingenious, but it seems to lead him to disregard the particular genius of Wolfram. Indeed, his own conclusion begs an important question: "Die Frage nach den Gründen, die ein dichterisches Genie wie Wolfram zu einer derartigen Technik bestimmt haben, kann hier nicht mehr angeschnitten werden" (p. 115). Wolfram, the greatest poetic genius of the German Middle Ages, is quite capable of going against his own carefully created pattern in order to point to the proper emphasis of his own poem. Equally, he is capable of finishing it on a note of only partial finality, in order to draw attention to his own decision.

41) See note 26 above.

# Select Bibliography

## Editions of Texts, etc.

Aliscans, ed. E. Wienbeck, W. Hartnacke and P. Rasch, Halle 1903.

Aliscans, mit Berücksichtigung von Wolframs von Eschenbach Willehalm (Altfranzösische Bibliothek 15), ed. G. Rolin, Leipzig 1897.

Wolfram von Eschenbach, ed. K. Lachmann, 6th edition, Berlin and Leipzig 1926, reprint Berlin 1960.

Willehalm. Urtext und Übersetzung, Berlin 1968, by D. Kartschoke.

Willehalm (translated into modern German), F. Knorr and R. Fink, Jena 1944.

## Secondary Literature

Bernhardt, E.     'Zum Willehalm Wolframs von Eschenbach', ZfdPh. 32, 1900, pp. 36-57.

Bumke, J.     Wolframs 'Willehalm', Studien zur Epenstruktur und zum Heiligkeitsbegriff der ausgehenden Blütezeit, Heidelberg 1959.

Wolfram von Eschenbach (Sammlung Metzler 36), Stuttgart 1964.

Die Wolfram von Eschenbach Forschung seit 1945. Bericht und Bibliographie, Munich 1970.

Csendes, P.          'Zur Orlensepisode in Wolframs _Willehalm_',
                     _ZfdA_. 97, 1968, pp. 196-206.

Fischer, F.W.        'Der Stil des Aliscans-Epos', Inaugural-
                     Dissertation zur Erlangung der Doktorwürde,
                     Rostock 1930.

Gerhardt, C.         'Wolframs Adlerbild _Willehalm_ 189,2-24',
                     _ZfdA_. 99, 1970, pp. 213-222.

                     'Zur Überlieferungsgeschichte des _Willehalm_
                     Wolframs von Eschenbach', _Studi Medievali_, 3[a]
                     Serie, XI 1, 1970, pp. 369-380.

Happ, E.             'Kommentar zum zweiten Buch von Wolframs
                     _Willehalm_', Dissertation, Munich 1966.

Harms, W.            _Der Kampf mit dem Freund oder Verwandten in
                     der deutschen Literatur bis um 1300_, Munich
                     1963.

Johnson, S.M.        'A Commentary to Wolfram von Eschenbach's
                     Willehalm', diss. Yale, 1953.

                     'Wolfram's _Willehalm_: 1952-1962', _JEGP_ 63,
                     1964, pp. 72-75.

Kienast, R.          'Zur Tektonik von Wolframs _Willehalm_', _Studien
                     zur deutschen Philologie des Mittelalters.
                     Friedrich Panzer zum 80. Geburtstag am 4. Sep-
                     tember 1950 dargebracht_, Heidelberg 1950,
                     pp. 96-115.

Knapp, F.P.          _Rennewart. Studien zu Gehalt und Gestalt des
                     Willehalm Wolframs von Eschenbach_, Vienna 1970.

de Kok, B.           _Guibourc et quelques autres figures de femmes
                     dans les plus anciennes chansons de geste_,
                     Paris 1926.

Leitzmann, A.        'Untersuchungen über Wolframs _Titurel_', _PBB_ 26,
                     1901, pp. 93-156.

Lofmark, C.          _Rennewart in Wolfram's 'Willehalm'. A study
                     of Wolfram von Eschenbach and his sources_,
                     Cambridge, 1972.

                     'Zur Veröffentlichung des fünften Buches von
                     Wolframs _Willehalm_', _ZfdA_. 95, 1966, pp. 294-300.

Maurer, F.     Leid. Studien zur Bedeutungs- und Problemgeschichte, besonders in den großen Epen der
staufischen Zeit, (Bibliotheca Germanica 1),
Bern and Munich, 1951.

'Das Grundanliegen Wolframs von Eschenbach',
Deutschunterricht, VIII, 1, 1956, 46-61.

Meißburger, G.  'Willehalmprobleme', Archiv 198, 1962,
pp. 310-314.

'Gyburg', ZfdPh. 83, 1964, pp. 64-99.

'Zum Prolog von Wolframs Willehalm', GRM. 46,
1965, pp. 119-138.

Mergell, B.    Wolfram von Eschenbach und seine französischen
Quellen, 1. Teil: Wolframs Willehalm, Münster
1936.

Der Gral in Wolframs 'Parzival'. Entstehung
und Ausbildung der Gralsage im Hochmittelalter,
Halle 1952.

Mersmann, W.   Der Besitzwechsel und seine Bedeutung in den
Dichtungen Wolframs von Eschenbach und Gottfrieds von Straßburg, Munich 1971.

Ochs, I.      Wolframs 'Willehalm'-Eingang, (Medium Aevum 14),
Munich 1968.

Ohly, F.      'Wolframs Gebet an den Heiligen Geist im Eingang des Willehalm', ZfdA. 91, 1961/62,
pp. 1-37.

Poag, J.F.    'Wortstrukturen in Wolframs Willehalm', DVjs.
1972, 1, pp. 82-112.

Pretzel, U. and
  Bachofer, W.  Bibliographie zu Wolfram von Eschenbach,
Berlin 1968.

Richey, M.F.   'Wolfram von Eschenbach and the Paradox of the
Chivalrous Life', German Studies presented to
Leonard Ashley Willoughby, Oxford, 1952,
pp. 159-170.

Schanze, H.    Die Überlieferung von Wolframs 'Willehalm',
(Medium Aevum 7), Munich 1966.

Schröder, W.J.    Review of J. Bumke Wolframs 'Willehalm',
                  PBB, 82, 1960, pp. 411-421.

Schröder,W. and
  Schanze, H.    'Neues Gesamtverzeichnis der Handschriften
                  von Wolframs Willehalm', ZfdA. 91, 1961/62,
                  pp. 201-226.

Schröder, Werner.    'Armuot', DVjs. 34, 1960, pp. 501-526.

                  'Süeziu Gyburc', Euph. 54, 1960, pp. 39-69.

                  'Christliche Paradoxa in Wolframs Willehalm',
                  Euph. 55, 1961, pp. 85-90.

                  Review of J. Bumke Wolframs 'Willehalm',
                  Euph. 55, 1961, pp. 91-97.

                  'Zur Entwicklung des Helden in Wolframs
                  Willehalm', Festschrift für Ludwig Wolff
                  zum 70. Geburtstag, Neumünster 1962,
                  pp. 265-276.

                  'Minne und ander klage (Zu Willehalm 4,26)',
                  ZfdA 93, 1964, pp. 300-313.

                  'Zum gegenwärtigen Stande der Wolfram Kritik',
                  ZfdA. 96, 1967, pp. 1-28.

                  'Der Markgraf und die gefallenen Heidenkönige
                  in Wolframs Willehalm', in Festschrift für
                  Konstantin Reichardt, Bern and Munich 1969,
                  pp. 135-167.

                  'Die Hinrichtung Arofels', in Wolfram-Studien
                  II, Berlin 1974, pp. 219-240.

Schröder, Werner (editor):  Wolfram-Studien I, Berlin 1971

                            Wolfram-Studien II, Berlin 1974.

Singer, S.    Wolframs Stil und der Stoff des 'Parzival',
              (Sitzungsberichte der kaiserlichen Akademie
              der Wissenschaft in Wien, philosophisch-
              historische Klasse 180,4), Vienna 1916.

              Wolframs 'Willehalm', Bern 1918.

Steinhoff, H-H. Die Darstellung gleichzeitiger Geschehnisse im mittelhochdeutschen Epos (Medium Ævum 4), Munich 1964.

Walshe, M. O'C. Mediæval German Literature. A Survey, London 1962.

Weber, G. 'Die Grundidee in Wolframs Willehalm', Literaturwissenschaftliches Jahrbuch 6, 1965, pp. 1-21.

Wentzlaff-Eggebert, F.W.
Kreuzzugsdichtung des Mittelalters, Berlin 1960, ('Wolframs von Eschenbach Willehalm als Kreuzzugsdichtung', pp. 247-277).

Willson, B. 'Einheit in der Vielheit in Wolframs Willehalm', ZfdPh. 80, 1961, pp. 40-62.

Wolff, L. 'Der Willehalm Wolframs von Eschenbach', DVjs. 12, 1934, pp. 504-539.

'Vom persönlichen Stil Wolframs in seiner dichterischen Bedeutung. Ein Versuch', Ludwig Wolff. Kleinere Schriften, ed. W. Schröder, Berlin 1967, pp. 262-293.

Marion Gibbs was born in 1940 in Essex. She attended
St. Bernard's Convent High School, Westcliff-on-Sea, until
1958, when she became an undergraduate at Bedford College,
University of London; she was awarded First Class Honours
in German in 1961.

After a period of schoolteaching, she was appointed as
Assistant Lecturer in the German Department at the Royal
Holloway College, University of London, being promoted in
1967 to her present post of Lecturer.

In 1965, she gained the degree of MA of the University of
London for her thesis, which was published in 1972 under
the title Wîplîchez Wîbes Reht. A Study of the Women
Characters in the Works of Wolfram von Eschenbach by the
Duquesne University Press.

Narrative Art in Wolfram's 'Willehalm' represents, with
minor alterations and additions, the dissertation for which
she was awarded the PhD of the University of London in 1974.

Other published work includes reviews and articles in
German Life and Letters and The Modern Language Review.

## Zusammenfassung

In dieser Arbeit wird versucht, Aspekte der Erzählkunst Wolframs in seinem ‚Willehalm' darzulegen. Während sich die Forschung bis jetzt mit eingehenden Untersuchungen einzelner Stellen und mit verschiedenen Problemen der Interpretation beschäftigt hat, gilt hier das Interesse vor allem dem Zusammenhang zwischen der Kunst des Erzählers und dem Sinn des Werkes.

Es handelt sich in erster Linie um die Harmonie des Ganzen. Eine nähere Untersuchung der Erzähltechnik zeigt, wie eng die Einheit der Form mit Wolframs Ideal der universellen Liebe verbunden ist. Deutlicher noch als in seinem ‚Parzival' gibt er in diesem Spätwerk diesem Ideal Ausdruck, denn trotz des Konflikts, der zwei schrecklichen Kämpfe zwischen Christen und Heiden, zweifelt er nicht an der göttlichen Liebe, und die Auffassung des Menschen als gotes hantgetât durchdringt das Ganze. Durch die großen Reden, die religiösen Gespräche und die beiden Hauptcharaktere wird dieser Begriff zum Kern der Dichtung.

Die Einheit des Stoffes beruht auf verschiedenen Aspekten der Kunst Wolframs, z.B. auf der Reihenfolge und manchmal dem Nebeneinander der Episoden, dem Gebrauch der vielen Parallelen und der Kontraste, auf der Gleichzeitigkeit des Geschehens in vielen Fällen. Auch in der Wortwahl spürt man, wie behutsam der Erzähler vorgeht, indem er seine Begriffe wiederholt und zusammenstellt, und seine manchmal ganz überraschenden Bilder auf charakteristische Weise verwendet.

Auch die Darstellung der Charaktere gewinnt besondere Bedeutung: trotz der vielen bunten Gestalten ragen die beiden Hauptcharaktere hervor, um den Sinn des Werkes und dessen Botschaft zu betonen. Selbst Rennewart, der eine so wichtige Rolle in der Handlung spielt, nimmt letzten Endes eine untergeordnete Stellung ein.

Diese Untersuchung führt fast unvermeidlich zu neuen Erwägungen der Frage des umstrittenen Schlusses, und zwar zu der Meinung, daß Wolfram ganz absichtlich an der sinnvollsten Stelle endet und daß irgendeine Fortsetzung dem Sinn des Werkes, den er so sorgfältig herausgearbeitet hat, zuwider laufen müßte.

## GÖPPINGER ARBEITEN ZUR GERMANISTIK
herausgegeben von
ULRICH MÜLLER, FRANZ HUNDSNURSCHER und CORNELIUS SOMMER

GAG 1: U. Müller, „Dichtung" und „Wahrheit" in den Liedern Oswalds von Wolkenstein: Die autobiographischen Lieder von den Reisen. (1968)

GAG 2: F. Hundsnurscher, Das System der Partikelverben mit „aus" in der Gegenwartssprache. (1968)

GAG 3: J. Möckelmann, Deutsch-Schwedische Sprachbeziehungen. Untersuchung der Vorlagen der schwedischen Bibelübersetzung von 1536 und des Lehngutes in den Übersetzungen aus dem Deutschen. (1968)

GAG 4: E. Menz, Die Schrift Karl Philipp Moritzens „Über die bildende Nachahmung des Schönen". (1968)

GAG 5: H. Engelhardt, Realisiertes und Nicht-Realisiertes im System des deutschen Verbs. Das syntaktische Verhalten des zweiten Partizips. (1969)

GAG 6: A. Kathan, Herders Literaturkritik. Untersuchungen zu Methodik und Struktur am Beispiel der frühen Werke. (2. Aufl. 1970)

GAG 7: A. Weise, Untersuchungen zur Thematik und Struktur der Dramen von Max Frisch. (3. Aufl. 1972)

GAG 8: H.-J. Schröpfer, „Heinrich und Kunigunde". Untersuchungen zur Verslegende des Ebernand von Erfurt und zur Geschichte ihres Stoffs. (1969)

GAG 9: R. Schmitt, Das Gefüge des Unausweichlichen in Hans Henny Jahnns Romantrilogie „Fluß ohne Ufer". (1969)

GAG 10: W. E. Spengler, Johann Fischart, genannt Mentzer. Studie zur Sprache und Literatur des ausgehenden 16. Jahrhunderts. (1969)

GAG 11: G. Graf, Studien zur Funktion des ersten Kapitels von Robert Musils Roman „Der Mann ohne Eigenschaften". Ein Beitrag zur Unwahrhaftigkeitstypik der Gestalten. (1969)

GAG 12: G. Fritz, Sprache und Überlieferung der Neidhart-Lieder in der Berliner Handschrift germ. fol. 779 (c). (1969)

GAG 13: L.-W. Wolff, Wiedereroberte Außenwelt. Studien zur Erzählweise Heimito von Doderers am Beispiel des „Romans No 7". (1969)

GAG 14: W. Freese, Mystischer Moment und reflektierte Dauer. Zur epischen Funktion der Liebe im modernen deutschen Roman. (1969)

GAG 15: U. Späth, Gebrochene Identität. Stilistische Untersuchungen zum Parallelismus in E. T. A. Hoffmanns ‚Lebensansichten des Kater Murr'. (1970)

GAG 16: U. Reiter, Jakob van Hoddis. Leben und lyrisches Werk. (1970)

GAG 17: W. E. Spengler, Der Begriff des Schönen bei Winckelmann. Ein Beitrag zur deutschen Klassik. (1970)

GAG 18: F. K. R. v. Stockert, Zur Anatomie des Realismus: Ferdinand von Saars Entwicklung als Novellendichter. (1970)

GAG 19: St. R. Miller, Die Figur des Erzählers in Wielands Romanen. (1970)

GAG 20: A. Holtorf, Neujahrswünsche im Liebeslied des ausgehenden Mittelalters. Zugleich ein Beitrag zum mittelalterlichen Neujahrsbrauchtum in Deutschland. (1970)

GAG 21: K. Hotz, Bedeutung und Funktion des Raumes im Werk Wilhelm Raabes. (1970)

GAG 22/23: R. B. Schäfer-Maulbetsch, Studien zur Entwicklung des mittelhochdeutschen Epos. Die Kampfschilderungen in „Kaiserchronik", „Rolandslied", „Alexanderlied", „Eneide", „Liet von Troye" und „Willehalm". (2 Bde. 1972)

GAG 24: H. Müller-Solger, Der Dichtertraum. Studien zur Entwicklung der dichterischen Phantasie im Werk Christoph Martin Wielands. (1970)

GAG 25: Formen mittelalterlicher Literatur. Siegfried Beyschlag zu seinem 65. Geburtstag von Kollegen, Freunden und Schülern. Herausgegeben von O. Werner und B. Naumann. (1970)

GAG 26: J. Möckelmann / S. Zander, Form und Funktion des Werbeslogans. Untersuchung der Sprache und werbepsychologischen Methoden der Slogans. (1970) (2. Aufl. 1972)

GAG 27: W.-D. Kühnel, Ferdinand Kürnberger als Literaturtheoretiker im Zeitalter des Realismus. (1970)

GAG 28: O. Olzien, Wirken. Aktionsform und Verbalmetapher bei Goethe. (1971)

GAG 29: H. Schlemmer, Semantische Untersuchungen zur verbalen Lexik. Verbale Einheiten und Konstruktionen für den Vorgang des Kartoffelerntens. (1971)

GAG 30: L. Mygdales, F. W. Waiblingers „Phaethon". Entstehungsgeschichte und Erläuterungen. (1971)

GAG 31: L. Peiffer, Zur Funktion der Exkurse in „Tristan" Gottfrieds von Straßburg. (1971)

GAG 32: S. Mannesmann, Thomas Manns Roman-Tetralogie „Joseph und seine Brüder" als Geschichtsdichtung. (1971)

GAG 33: B. Wackernagel-Jolles, Untersuchungen zur gesprochenen Sprache. Beobachtungen zur Verknüpfung spontanen Sprechens. (1971)

GAG 34: G. Dittrich-Orlovius, Zum Verhältnis von Erzählung und Reflexion im „Reinfried von Braunschweig". (1971)

GAG 35: H.-P. Kramer, Erzählerbemerkungen und Erzählerkommentar in Chrestiens und Hartmanns „Erec" und „Iwein". (1971)

GAG 36: H.-G. Dewitz, „Dante Deutsch". Studien zu Rudolf Borchardts Übertragung der ‚Divina Comedia'. (1971)

GAG 37: P. Haberland, The Development of Comic Theory in Germany during the Eighteenth Century. (1971)

GAG 38/39: E. Dvoretzky, G. E. Lessing. Dokumente zur Wirkungsgeschichte (1755 bis 1968). (2 Bde. 1971/72)

GAG 40/41: G. F. Jones / H. D. Mück / U. Müller, Vollständige Verskonkordanz zu den Liedern Oswald von Wolkenstein. (Hss. B und A) (2 Bde. 1973)

GAG 42: R. Pelka, Werkstückbenennungen in der Metallverarbeitung. Beobachtungen zum Wortschatz und zur Wortbildung der technischen Sprache im Bereich der metallverarbeitenden Fertigungstechnik. (1971)

GAG 43: L. Schädle, Der frühe deutsche Blankvers unter besonderer Berücksichtigung seiner Verwendung durch Chr. M. Wieland. (1971)

GAG 44: U. Wirtz, Die Sprachstruktur Gottfried Benns. Ein Vergleich mit Nietzsche. (1971)

GAG 45: E. Knobloch, Die Wortwahl in der archaisierenden chronikalischen Erzählung: Meinhold, Raabe, Storm, Wille, Kolbenheyer. (1971)

GAG 46: U. Peters, Frauendienst. Untersuchungen zu Ulrich von Lichtenstein und zum Wirklichkeitsgehalt der Minnedichtung. (1971)

GAG 47: M. Endres, Word Field and Word Content in Middle High German. The Applicability of Word Field Theory to the Intellectual Vocabulary in Gottfried von Strassburg's „Tristan". (1971)

GAG 48: G. M. Schäfer, Untersuchungen zur deutschsprachigen Marienlyrik des 12. und 13. Jahrhunderts. (1971)

GAG 49: F. Frosch-Freiburg, Schwankmären und Fabliaux. Ein Stoff- und Motivvergleich. (1971)

GAG 50/51: G. Steinberg, Erlebte Rede. Ihre Eigenart und ihre Formen in neuerer deutscher, französischer und englischer Erzählliteratur. (1971)

GAG 52: O. Boeck, Heines Nachwirkung und Heine-Parallelen in der französischen Dichtung. (1971)

GAG 53: F. Dietrich-Bader, Wandlungen der dramatischen Bauform vom 16. Jahrhundert bis zur Frühaufklärung. Untersuchungen zur Lehrhaftigkeit des Theaters. (1972)

GAG 54: H. Hoefer, Typologie im Mittelalter. Zur Übertragbarkeit typologischer Interpretation auf weltliche Dichtung. (1971)

GAG 55/56: U. Müller, Politische Lyrik des deutschen Mittelalters. I Einleitung, tabellarische Übersicht mit Einzelkommentaren von den Anfängen bis Michel Beheim. II Untersuchungen.

GAG 57: R. Jahović, Wilhelm Gerhard aus Weimar, ein Zeitgenosse Goethes. (1972)

GAG 58: B. Murdoch, The Fall of Man in the Early Middle High German Biblical Epic: the „Wiener Genesis", the „Vorauer Genesis" and the „Anegenge". (1972)

GAG 59: H. Hecker, Die deutsche Sprachlandschaft in den Kantonen Malmedy und St. Vith. Untersuchungen zur Lautgeschichte und Lautstruktur ostbelgischer Mundarten. (1972)

GAG 60: Wahrheit und Sprache. Festschrift für Bert Nagel zum 65. Geburtstag am 27. August 1972. Unter Mitwirkung v. K. Menges hsg. von W. Petters und P. Schimmelpfennig. (1972)

GAG 61: J. Schröder, Zu Darstellung und Funktion der Schauplätze in den Artusromanen Hartmanns von Aue. (1972)

GAG 62: D. Walch, Caritas. Zur Rezeption des ‚mandatum novum' in altdeutschen Texten. (1973)

GAG 63: H. Mundschau, Sprecher als Träger der ‚tradition vivante' in der Gattung ‚Märe'. (1972)

GAG 64: D. Strauss, Redegattungen und Redearten im „Rolandslied" sowie in der „Chanson de Roland" und in Strickers „Karl". (1972)

GAG 65: ‚Getempert und gemischet' für Wolfgang Mohr zum 65. Geburtstag von seinen Tübinger Schülern. Hsg. von F. Hundsnurscher und U. Müller. (1972)

GAG 66: H. Fröschle, Justinus Kerner und Ludwig Uhland. Geschichte einer Dichterfreundschaft. (1973)

GAG 67: U. Zimmer, Studien zu ‚Alpharts Tod' nebst einem verbesserten Abdruck der Handschrift. (1972)

GAG 68: U. Müller (Hsg.), Politische Lyrik des deutschen Mittelalters. Texte I. (1972)

GAG 69: Y. Pazarkaya, Die Dramaturgie des Einakters. Der Einakter als eine besondere Erscheinungsform im deutschen Drama des 18. Jahrhunderts. (1973)

GAG 70: Festschrift für Kurt Herbert Halbach. Hsg. von R. B. Schäfer-Maulbetsch, M. G. Scholz und G. Schweikle. (1972)

GAG 71: G. Mahal, Mephistos Metamorphosen. Fausts Partner als Repräsentant literarischer Teufelsgestaltung. (1972)

GAG 72: A. Kappeler, Ein Fall der „Pseudologia phantastica" in der deutschen Literatur: Fritz Reck-Malleczewen. (1972)

GAG 73: J. Rabe, Die Sprache der Berliner Nibelungenlied-Handschrift J (Ms. germ. Fol. 474). (1972)

GAG 74: A. Goetze, Pression und Deformation. Zehn Thesen zum Roman „Hundejahre" von Günter Graß. (1972)

GAG 75: K. Radwan, Die Sprache Lavaters im Spiegel der Geistesgeschichte. (1972)

GAG 76: H. Eilers, Untersuchungen zum frühmittelhochdeutschen Sprachstil am Beispiel der Kaiserchronik. (1972)

GAG 77: P. Schwarz, Die neue Eva. Der Sündenfall in Volksglauben und Volkserzählung. (1972)

GAG 78: G. Trendelenburg, Studien zum Gralraum im „Jüngeren Titurel". (1973)

GAG 79: J. Gorman, The Reception of Federico Garcia Lorca in Germany.

GAG 80: M. A. Coppola, Il rimario di bispel spirituali dello Stricker.

GAG 81: P. Neesen, Vom Louvrezirkel zum Prozeß. Franz Kafka unter dem Eindruck der Psychologie Franz Brentanos. (1972)

GAG 82: U. H. Gerlach, Hebbel as a Critic of His Own Works: „Judith", „Herodes und Mariamne" and „Gyges und sein Ring". (1972)

GAG 83: P. Sandrock, The Art of Ludwig Thoma.

GAG 84: U. Müller (Hsg.), Politische Lyrik des deutschen Mittelalters. Texte II: Von 1350 bis 1466.

GAG 85: M. Wacker, Schillers „Räuber" und der Sturm und Drang. Stilkritische und typologische Überprüfung eines Epochenbegriffes. (1973)

GAG 86: L. Reichardt, Die Siedlungsnamen der Kreise Giessen, Alsfeld und Lauterbach in Hessen. Namenbuch. (1973)

GAG 87: S. Gierlich, Jean Paul „Der Komet oder Nikolaus Marggraf. Eine komische Geschichte." (1972)

GAG 88: B. D. Haage (Hsg.), Das Arzneibuch des Erhart Hesel. (1973)

GAG 89: R. Roßkopf, Der Traum Herzeloydes und der Rote Ritter. Erwägungen über die Bedeutung des staufisch-welfischen Thronstreites für Wolframs „Parzival". (1972)

GAG 90: B. Webb, The Demise of the „New Man" An Analysis of Late German Expressionism. (1973)

GAG 91: I. Karger, Heinrich Heine. Literarische Aufklärung und wirkbetonte Textstruktur. Untersuchungen zum Tierbild.

GAG 92: B. S. Wackernagel-Jolles (Hsg.), Aspekte der gesprochenen Sprache. Deskriptions- und Quantifizierungsprobleme. Eingeleitet von S. Grosse.

GAG 93: A. Harding, An Investigation into the Use and Meaning of Medieval German Dancing Terms. (1973)

GAG 94: D. Rosenband, Das Liebesmotiv in Gottfrieds „Tristan" und Wagners „Tristan und Isolde". (1973)

GAG 95: H.-F. Reske, Jerusalem Caelestis. Bildformeln und Gestaltungsmuster. Darbietungsformen eines christlichen Zentralgedankens in der deutschen geistlichen Dichtung des 11. u. 12. Jhds. Mit besonderer Berücksichtigung des „Himmlischen Jerusalem" und der „Hochzeit" (V. 379–508). (1973)

GAG 96: D. Ohlenroth, Sprechsituation und Sprecheridentität. Untersuchungen zum Verhältnis von Sprache und Realität im frühen deutschen Minnesang.

GAG 97: U. Gerdes, Bruder Wernher. Beiträge zur Deutung seiner Sprüche. (1973)

GAG 98: N. Heinze, Zur Gliederungstechnik Hartmanns von Aue. Stilistische Untersuchungen als Beiträge zu einer strukturkritischen Methode. (1973)

GAG 99: E. Uthleb, Zeilen und Strophen in der Jenaer Liederhandschrift.

GAG 100: Wolfram von Eschenbach. Willehalm, Übersetzt von O. Unger. Mit einem Geleitwort von Ch. Gerhardt.

GAG 101: H. Kalmbach, Bildung und Dramatik in Goethes „Faust".

GAG 102: B. Thole, Die „Gesänge" in den Stücken Berthold Brechts. Zur Geschichte und Ästhetik des Liedes im Drama. (1973)

GAG 103: J.-H. Dreger, Wielands „Geschichte der Abderiten". Eine historisch-kritische Untersuchung. (1973)

GAG 104: B. Haustein, Achim von Arnims dichterische Auseinandersetzung mit dem romantischen Idealismus.

GAG 105: F. B. Parkes, Epische Elemente in Jakob Michael Reinhold Lenzens Drama „Der Hofmeister". (1973)

GAG 106: K. O. Seidel, „Wandel" als Welterfahrung des Spätmittelalters im didaktischen Werk Heinrichs des Teichners. (1973)

GAG 107: I–V DIE KLEINDICHTUNG DES STRICKERS. In Zusammenarbeit mit G. Agler und R. E. Lewis hsg. von W. W. Moelleken

GAG 108: G. Datz, Die Gestalt Hiobs in der kirchlichen Exegese und der „Arme Heinrich" Hartmanns von Aue. (1973)

GAG 109: J. Scheibe, Der „Patriot" (1724–1726) und sein Publikum. Untersuchungen über die Verfassergesellschaft und die Leserschaft einer Zeitschrift der frühen Aufklärung. (1973)

GAG 110: E. Wenzel-Herrmann, Zur Textkritik und Überlieferungsgeschichte einiger Sommerlieder Neidharts. (1973)

GAG 111: K. Franz, Studien zur Soziologie des Spruchdichters in Deutschland im späten 13. Jahrhundert. (1974)

GAG 112: P. Jentzmik, Zu Möglichkeiten und Grenzen typologischer Exegese in mittelalterlicher Predigt und Dichtung. (1973)

GAG 113: G. Inacker, Antinomische Strukturen im Werk Hugo von Hofmannsthals. (1973)

GAG 114: R. S. Geehr, Adam Müller-Gutenbrunn and the Aryan Theater of Vienna 1898–1903. The Approach of Cultural Fascism. (1973)

GAG 115: R. M. Runge, Proto-Germanic /r/. (1973)

GAG 116: L. Schuldes, Die Teufelsszenen im deutschen geistlichen Drama. (1974)

GAG 117: Christa Krüger, Georg Forsters und Friedrich Schlegels Beurteilung der Französischen Revolution als Ausdruck des Problems einer Einheit von Theorie und Praxis.

GAG 118: G. Vogt, Studien zur Verseingangsgestaltung in der deutschen Lyrik des Hochmittelalters. (1974)

GAG 119: B. C. Bushey, „Tristan als Mönch". Untersuchungen und kritische Edition. (1974)

GAG 120: St. C. Haroff, Wolfram: And His Audience: A Study of the Theme of Quest and of Recognition of Kinship Identity. (1974)

GAG 121: S. Schumm, Einsicht und Darstellung. Untersuchung zum Kunstverständnis E. T. A. Hoffmanns. (1974)

GAG 122: O. Holzapfel, Die Dänischen Nibelungenballaden. Texte und Kommentare. (1974)

GAG 123: Rosemarie Hellge, geb. Keller, Motive und Motivstrukturen bei Ludwig Tieck. (1974)

GAG 124/125: Hans-Friedrich Rosenfeld, Ausgewählte Schriften. Festschrift herausgegeben von Hugo Kuhn, Hellmut Rosenfeld, Hans-Jürgen Schubert. (1974)

GAG 126: Beatrice Wehrli, Imitatio und Mimesis in der Geschichte der deutschen Erzähltheorie unter besonderer Berücksichtigung des 19. Jahrhunderts.

GAG 127: Jürgen Vorderstemann, Die Fremdwörter im „Willehalm" Wolframs von Eschenbach. (1974)

GAG 128: Eckhardt Meyer-Krentler, Der andere Roman. Gellerts „Schwedische Gräfin". (1974)

GAG 129: Roy F. Allen, Literary Life in German Expressionism and the Berlin Circles. (1974)

GAG 130: Hella Kloocke, Der Gebrauch des substantivierten Infinitivs im Mittelhochdeutschen. (1974)

GAG 131: Udo von der Burg, Strickers „Karl der Große" als Bearbeitung des „Rolandsliedes". Studien zu Form und Inhalt. (1974)

GAG 132: Rodney Winstone Fisher, Studies in the Demonic in Selected Middle High German Epics.

GAG 133: Gisela Zimmermann, Kommentar zum VII. Buch von Wolfram von Eschenbachs „Parzival". (1974)

GAG 134: Eberhard Ockel, Rhetorik im Deutschunterricht. Untersuchungen zur didaktischen und methodischen Entwicklung mündlicher Kommunikation. (1974)

GAG 135: Dietmar Wenzelburger, Motivation und Menschenbild der Eneide Heinrichs von Veldeke als Ausdruck der geschichtlichen Kräfte ihrer Zeit. (1974)

GAG 136: R. Dietz, Der „Tristan" Gottfrieds von Straßburg. Probleme der Forschung 1902–1970. (1974)

GAG 137: F. Heinzle, „Der Württemberger". Untersuchung, Texte, Kommentar (1974)

GAG 138: H. Rowland, Musarion and Wieland's Concept of Genre. (1975)

GAG 139: D. Hirschberg, Untersuchungen zur Erzählstruktur von Wolframs „Parzival". (1974)

GAG 140: G. Mauch, Theatermetapher und -motiv bei Jean Paul. (1975)

GAG 141: G. Holbeche, Optical Motifs in the Works of E. T. A. Hoffmann. (1975)

GAG 142: W. Baur, Sprache und Existenz. Studien zum Spätwerk Robert Walsers. (1974)

GAG 143: U. v. d. Burg, Indizes zu Strickers Karl der Große: Wortindex, Reimpaarindex. Statistisches Material. (1974)

GAG 144: M. Rheinheimer, Rheinische Minnereden Untersuchungen und Edition. (1975)

GAG 145: H. Fleig, Sich versagendes Erzählen (Fontane). (1974)

GAG 146: W. Valynseele-Große, Deutschlehrbücher im Ausland. (1974)

GAG 147: J. Sieß, Zitat und Kontext bei Georg Büchner. (1975)

GAG 148: W. H. Wilkening, Otto Julius Bierbaum's Relationship with his Publishers. (1974)

GAG 149: P. Lucke, Gewalt und Gegengewalt in den Flugschriften der Reformationszeit. (1975)

GAG 150: K. Fuchs, Bürgerliches Raisonnement und Staatsräson. Zensur als Instrument des Despotismus. (1975)

GAG 151: R. Zobel, Der Dramentext- ein kommunikatives Handlungsspiel. (1975)

GAG 152: J. Kunhel, Grundkurs HISTORISCHE LINGUISTIK. Materialien zur Einführung in die germanisch-deutsche Sprachgeschichte. (1975)

GAG 153: Ch. Lehfeldt, Der Dramatiker Ferdinand Bruckner. (1975)

GAG 154: R. E. Lewis. Symbolism in Hartmann's „Iwein". (1975)

GAG 155: K. Brandes, Heinrich von Morungen: Zyklische Liedgruppen. – Rekonstruktion, Forminterpretation, kritische Ausgabe. (1975)

GAG 156: G. Lotzmann, Zur Aspiration der Explosivae im Deutschen

GAG 157: E. Schutz/K. Kunze/K.E. Geith, Altgermanistische Grundkurse. Modelle und Erfahrungen. (1975)

GAG 158: H. Dewald, Minne und „gräles äventiur". Äußerungen der Subjektivität und ihre sprachliche Vergegenwärtigung in Wolframs „Parzival". (1975)

GAG 159: M.E. Gibbs, Narrative Art in Wolfram's „Willehalm".

GAG 160: D. A. Krooks, The Semantic Derivation of the Modal Verb in the Old High German „Williram".

GAG 161: W. Kersken, Untersuchungen zu den Kalendergedichten Oswalds v- Wolkenstein.

GAG 162: H. Grundmann, Untersuchungen zur mündlichen Rede der Schüler an Wirtschaftsoberschulen. (1975)

GAG 163: H. Laubner, Studien zum geistlichen Sinngehalt des Adjektivs im Werk Mechthilds von Magdeburg. (1975)

GAB 164: E. Haymes, Mündliches Epos in mittelhochdeutscher Zeit.

GAG 165: P. Schefe, Statistische syntaktische Analyse von Fachsprachen mit Hilfe elektronischer Rechenanlagen am Beispiel der medizinischen, betriebswirtschaftlichen und literaturwissenschaftlichen Fachsprache im Deutschen

GAG 166: C. D. M. Cossar, The German Translation of the Pseudo-Bernhardine „Epistola de cura rei familiaris".

GAG 167: W. Gewehr, Hartmanns „Klage-Büchlein" im Lichte der Frühscholastik (1975)

GAG 168: U. Meves, Ludwig Tiecks „König-Rother"-Übersetzung.

GAG 169: W. Schmaltz, Reimar der Alte. Beiträge zur poetischen Technik. (1975)

GAG 170: R. Firestone, Elements of Traditional Structure in the Couplet Epics of the Late Middle High German Dietrich Cycle. (1975)

In der Reihe „GÖPPINGER ARBEITEN ZUR GERMANISTIK" erscheinen ab Bd 160 ausschließlich Bände zur Älteren Literaturwissenschaft und zur Sprachwissenschaft. Veröffentlichungen zur Neueren Literaturwissenschaft erscheinen unter dem Titel „STUTTGARTER ARBEITEN ZUR GERMANISTIK" im Verlag H. D. Heinz, Stuttgart

# LITTERAE
## GÖPPINGER BEITRÄGE ZUR TEXTGESCHICHTE
### hsg. v. U. MÜLLER, F. HUNDSNURSCHER, C. SOMMER

LIT 17 Ulrich von Lichtenstein, Frauendienst (Ausschnitte). In Abb. aus dem Münchner Cod. germ. 44 und der Großen Heidelberger Liederhandschrift hsg. v. Ursula Peters. (1973)

LIT 18 Die sogenannte „Mainauer Naturlehre" der Basler Hs. B VIII 27. Abbildung, Transkription, Kommentar. Hsg. von Helmut R. Plant, Marie Rowlands und Rolf Burkhart. (1972)

LIT 19 Gottfried von Straßburg, Tristan. Ausgewählte Abbildungen z. Überlieferung. Hsg. von Hans-Hugo Steinhoff. (1974)

LIT 20 Abbildungen zur deutschen Sprachgeschichte. I Bildband. Hsg. von Helmut R. Plant.

LIT 21 Hans Sachs, Fastnachtspiele und Schwänke. In Abbildungen aus der Sachs-Hs. Amb. 2° 784 der Stadtbibliothek Nürnberg hsg. von Walter Eckehart Spengler. (1974)

LIT 22 Heinrich Haller, Übersetzungen im „gemeinen Deutsch" (1464). Aus den Hieronymus-Briefen: Abbildungen von Übersetzungskonzept, Reinschrift, Abschrift und Materialien zur Überlieferung. Hsg. von Erika Bauer. (1972)

LIT 23 Das Nibelungenlied. Abbildungen und Materialien zur gesamten handschriftlichen Überlieferung der Aventiuren I und XXX. Hsg. von Otfrid Ehrismann. (1973)

LIT 24 Hartmann von Aue, Iwein. Ausgewählte Abbildungen zur handschriftlichen Überlieferung. Hsg. von Lambertus Okken. (1974)

LIT 25 Christoph Martin Wieland, Das Sommermärchen und andere Schriften. Abbildungen zur Handschriften- und Druckgeschichte. (1974)

LIT 26 Wolfram von Eschenbach, Titurel. Abbildungen sämtlicher Handschriften mit einem Anhang zur Überlieferung des Textes im „Jüngeren Titurel". Hsg. von Joachim Heinzle. (1973)

LIT 27 Bruder Wernher. Abbildungen und Materialien zur gesamten handschriftlichen Überlieferung. Hsg. von Udo Gerdes.

LIT 28 Hartmann von Aue, Gregorius. Ausgewählte Abbildungen zur handschriftlichen Überlieferung. Hsg. von Norbert Heinze. (1974)

LIT 29 Die Bruchstücke der Altsächsischen Genesis. In Abbildung hsg. von Ute Schwab.

LIT 30 Hartmann von Aue, Der arme Heinrich. Fassung Bb. In Abbildung aus dem „Kalocsaer Kodex" hsg. von Cornelius Sommer. (1973)

LIT 31 Hartmann von Aue, Erec. Abbildungen der gesamten handschriftlichen Überlieferung. Hsg. von Franz Hundsnurscher und Ulrich Müller.

LIT 32 Kudrun. Abbildungen der gesamten handschriftlichen Überlieferung. Hsg. von Johannes Janota.

LIT 33 Der „Moriz von Craûn" und die Erzählungen Herrands von Wildonje. Aus dem ‚Ambraser Heldenbuch' hsg. von Franz Hundsnurscher.

LIT 34 Wolfram von Eschenbach, Parzival. Abbildungen und Transkriptionen zur gesamten handschriftlichen Überlieferung des Prologs. Hsg. von Uta Ulzen. (1974)

LIT 35 Die Kolmarer Liederhandschrift. In Abbildung hsg. von Horst Brunner, Ulrich Müller und Franz V. Spechtler (zur Subskr.).